TENNYSON'S FIXATIONS
Psychoanalysis and the Topics of the Early Poetry

Victorian Literature and Culture Series

Karen Chase, Jerome J. McGann, *and* Herbert Tucker, *General Editors*

———••⧓••———

TENNYSON'S FIXATIONS

Psychoanalysis
and the
Topics of the Early Poetry

———❦———

Matthew Rowlinson

UNIVERSITY PRESS OF VIRGINIA
Charlottesville and London

THE UNIVERSITY PRESS OF VIRGINIA
Copyright © 1994 by the Rector and Visitors
of the University of Virginia

First published 1994

Library of Congress Cataloging-in-Publication Data

Rowlinson, Matthew Charles, 1956–
    Tennyson's fixations : psychoanalysis and the topics of the early
poetry / Matthew Rowlinson.
        p.   cm. — (Victorian literature and culture series)
    Includes bibliographical references and index.
    ISBN 0-8139-1478-7
    1. Tennyson, Alfred Tennyson, Baron, 1809–1892—Knowledge—
Psychology.   2. Psychoanalysis and literature.   I. Title.
II. Series.
PR5592.P74R68   1994
821'.8—dc20   93-35019
                                                                 CIP

Printed in the United States of America

Contents

Preface

In the course of its readings of Tennyson, this book aims to develop procedures of hermeneutic and formal analysis that can account for some of the most salient features of lyric poetry in English, especially during the period extending from Wordsworth to Hardy. The materiality of language, as manifested most notably in its rhythmic articulations and in its iterability, haunts this poetry. Its own discourse acquires the status of an object with the power to arouse desire and to cause pleasure and pain. *Tennyson's Fixations* analyzes the way Tennyson's early poems represent these properties of language in allegories organized by the insistent topics of gender and topography.

Inasmuch as its primary concern is with ways in which Tennyson's poems refer to their own conditions of existence, this book's critical practice can appropriately be described as formalist. The central problem of any formalism that does not view language theologically will always be its incapacity to distinguish between its own ontological ground and that of its object. Language about language cannot claim to know more than language itself—even supposing that there was such a thing as language itself and that all language was not already language about language. I have not sought to mitigate this problem or the consequent tendency of my readings to repeat the structures they describe.

The inability of formalist criticism to make a critical break with its object need not preclude it, however, from undertaking the critical articulation of one text or set of texts with another. The central theoretical claim of this book is that the materiality of language—or, more generally, of the signifier—is always produced within allegory. Tennyson's poetry provides one set of instances of this claim. The other is provided by Freud, a choice which reflects my view that psychoanalytic theory offers for the bourgeois cultures of the West in our era the most compelling account of the allegorical structures within which objects—bodies, language, artifacts—bear meaning.

Freud and Tennyson do not function here, however, merely as distinct instances of a single generalization. As a trope, allegory transforms whatever enters its field. To read Tennyson with Freud, and to take up the challenge of what I understand as the allegorical force of their texts, must thus be to recognize the meanings that these texts produce in each other. That, at any rate, is the primary, interpretive, task of this book. And although I have also undertaken the secondary, antithetical, task of locating certain points of opacity in the recognitions thus produced, it is nonetheless the moment of recognition that fixes the area of the work's concern and the direction of its argument.

Tennyson's Fixations opens with an introduction in which I expand on the theoretical questions touched on above; then follow four chapters that read the major poems of Tennyson's early canon. The poems are treated roughly in the chronological order of their composition, though I have not hesitated to deviate from chronology when it served the clarity of my argument to do so. The value of chronology as an explanatory device is in fact at issue throughout the book. I have not in general sought to relate the structural changes I see in Tennyson's poetry to the events of his life; chapter four briefly considers some of the problems that would be involved in doing so.

A chronology of my own work on this book would be long and involved; its recurrent theme would be the generosity of the friends and colleagues who have read the manuscript and discussed it with me. In its earliest form, *Tennyson's Fixations* was a dissertation at Cornell, where I was advised by Dorothy Mermin, Paul Sawyer, Stephen Parrish, and Cynthia Chase. Their teaching has continued to affect the book at every stage of its writing, as has that of Neil Hertz, both in his seminar on Freud and in his published work on the sublime. More recently I have been enabled to write by the responses and by the affection of my friends, here at Dartmouth and elsewhere. This book is really addressed to Adela Pinch, Louise Fradenburg,

Peter Stallybrass, Juliet Fleming, and Jonathan Crewe. Finally, in the last stages of composition, I have greatly benefited from extraordinarily scrupulous and helpful readings by Marjorie Levinson and Herbert Tucker. To all of those I have named, my deepest thanks.

A partial version of chapter 2 appeared in *Victorian Poetry* 22 (1984):349–63 as "The Skipping Muse: Repetition and Difference in Two Early Poems of Tennyson." As I write, a version of chapter 3 is scheduled to appear in *Boundary 2* 20 (1993) as "Mourning and Metaphor: On the Literality of Tennyson's 'Ulysses.'" The copyright to *Boundary 2* is held by Duke University Press, and I am grateful to the press and to the Editor of *Victorian Poetry* for permission to reprint.

A Note on Citations

I cite Tennyson's poetry in the text of Christopher Ricks's second edition of *The Poems of Tennyson*. I have referred to the poems by title; where necessary, I have cited Ricks's apparatus as *Poems*. The writings of Freud are cited as they appear in *The Standard Edition of the Complete Psychological Works of Sigmund Freud*. I refer to this edition as *SE*. Finally, quotations from the Bible refer to the King James Version. Each of these general rules has occasional exceptions; these are explained in notes as they occur.

TENNYSON'S FIXATIONS
Psychoanalysis and the Topics of the Early Poetry

Introduction: On Fixation in Tennyson, Freud, and Elsewhere

This is what determines the character of allegory as a form of writing. It is a schema; and as a schema it is an object of knowledge, but it is not securely possessed until it becomes a fixed schema: at one and the same time a fixed image and a fixing sign.

(Walter Benjamin, *The Origin of German Tragic Drama*)

The Winds come to me from the fields of sleep.

(Wordsworth, "Ode: Intimations of Immortality")

I

THIS BOOK IS centrally concerned with various forms of topographical allegory and with the ways in which their deployment in Tennyson's early poems and in psychoanalytic theory generates incoherencies in the narrative or diegetic order of exposition. Its project is therefore a deconstructive one; it follows Paul de Man in seeking to show that allegory comes into being only within a structure of repetition. Unlike de Man, I have not sought on the basis of this account of allegory to propose a general critique of hermeneutics or even to pursue systematically the specific ways in which this book reproduces the allegorical structures it sets out to describe. I will say at the outset, however, that one of the ways it does so is by its organization as a sequence of readings of particular poems. To consider the poem as delimiting the principal site within which the work of reading takes place is to leave unanalyzed the allegoresis that makes such a delimitation possible. Do the boundaries of the poem allegorize its production as a single event determined by a single context or its multiple formal and historical overdeterminations? I have not sought to answer this kind of question; in consequence the organization of my book and the topics of its readings should be regarded as motivated by pragmatism rather than theory.

We might understand allegory by thinking of it as figurality raised to the second power;[1] that is to say, it designates the moment when a figure appears not only to convey meaning but also to describe its own mode of operation. The allegorical gesture will on this understanding always impose a certain resistance to a reading of the figure in its primary sense because its effect is to denaturalize that sense, to render it visible precisely as figural and hence as an effect of rhetorical technique rather than of a prior truth. Allegory, we may say, gives to figural language an embodied or material form and hence endows it with a particular kind of opacity. We may also suggest the converse—stronger—proposition, that figural language acquires material form only within allegory.

The readings that follow will primarily be concerned with formal and thematic structures in Tennyson's early poetry that in this sense materialize the figural operations of language. The readings will demonstrate how these structures render opaque or arrest the movement of the figures they make visible in moments of what I call fixation. Before passing to the main work of reading, we must first attend to certain complications or limitations that arise from the theoretical paradigm within which we will proceed. I have represented allegory as a specific figural gesture of which particularly rich instances are to be found in Tennyson's early poems. Now it may well be that any utterance can be interpreted allegorically and thus that allegorization refers not to a poetic but to a critical moment, one that can in theory occur in the reading of any text. Allegory will then be a phenomenon whose point of origin in the history of a text's production and reception is peculiarly difficult to specify. Indeed, we could say that the moment of allegorization will prove asynchronous with respect to any historical event. As Walter Benjamin wrote, allegory "expresses everything about history that, from the very beginning, has been untimely" and consequently calls into question, among other things, "the biographical historicity of the individual" (*Origin of German Tragic Drama,* 166).

In our reading of Tennyson's poems we shall have repeated occasion to discuss their registration of the always untimely moment in which allegory has its being. The poems we shall be concerned with typically represent their meaning either as predetermined, so that the poem itself appears only as the reiteration of a structure already in place, or as suspended, pending an outcome that may never arise. Sometimes both conditions obtain, as in "Tithonus," which we will read as in this regard Tennyson's most characteristic poem. But to trace these registrations of allegory's untimeliness in the poems is not to exhaust its effects. On the contrary, any rigorous reading of these poems will tend either to achieve only a repetition of their structure or to allegorize them after the fact, according to a rule that they have not suggested. These two tendencies are the forms taken by fixation in the work of reading, and for better or worse they recur throughout this book.

So far, I have named allegory as the figure in which language is materialized and I have described the problematic nature of the time in which it operates. I have further claimed that the problematic temporality of allegory is not only a formal effect of the poems in which it appears but also bears upon and reproduces itself in the time of reading. We shall return to the issue of the time of reading; more needs to be said here about the issues of materiality and language and the ways they will be theorized in this study. In the chapters that follow we shall not be primarily concerned with allegory as such but rather with constructions of gender and topography that function in Tennyson's poetry as the specific instances of allegory within which language—or more generally the linguistic signifier—assumes material properties. In theorizing these constructions, we shall have primary recourse to the work of Freud, and more especially to the structuralist reading of Freud whose advent Lacan may be said to have announced with the Discourse of Rome in 1953 and ratified with the publication of his *Ecrits* in 1966. In making the turn to theory, however, we shall not be able to set ourselves outside the structures of allegory. On the contrary, I shall argue that within psychoanalytic theory, no less than within Tennyson's poetry, the materiality of language—more generally, of the signifier—is constituted by allegory. This argument will primarily be concerned with the topics of the castration complex and of the paternal metaphor. Since in the body of the book the theoretical argument will appear only somewhat elliptically, frequently lodged in the interstices of an explication of Tennyson, it may be as well to rehearse it here in a relatively stripped-down form. Readers whose primary interest is in explication may wish to omit the following section on repetition, allegory, and the materiality of the signifier, and rejoin us on our return to Tennyson and the domain of poetics.

In Lacan's writings, the subject of psychoanalysis is represented above all as a subject that comes into being in relation to the material signifier.[2] To say so much is in part only to say that for Lacan the analytic subject is a linguistic subject—one that can only think, feel, or even have a body insofar as its thought, its feeling, and its body belong to language. In this understanding of human subjectivity every aspect of being is determined by the structures and contingencies of language; Lacan's term for the field of linguistic structures and contingencies into which the subject is born is the *Symbolic order.*

In the context of such an understanding of subjectivity Lacan reads Freud as showing that, for all the diversity of human signifying practices, there is only one way into the Symbolic. That way is through the castration complex. The castration complex establishes the phallus for all subjects as the paradigmatic instance of the material signifier and determines the nature of their relation to it. In so doing it positions gendered subjects in the Symbolic and decides how the Symbolic will be articulated through them.

It cannot be doubted that the phallus and the castration complex play a more central role in Lacan's thought than they do in Freud's—or, to put the point otherwise, that one of Lacan's achievements is to show how the castration complex structures psychic effects that Freud theorizes without appearing to recognize their relation to it. For instance, in the seminar of 1964, published as *Four Fundamental Concepts of Psycho-Analysis,* Lacan devotes sessions two through five to the compulsion to repeat and to the genesis of the unconscious in what he terms a *gap.* This gap founds the signifier for the subject as a mediation—not as representing what has never been present for the subject but as taking the place of representation (60). The signifier takes the place of representation and constitutes that place along with the possibility of presence itself within a dialectical opposition of presence to absence. But that dialectic is established across the gap, or bar, whose status is irreducible to either of its terms. The interplay of the signifier's presence and absence constantly restages for the subject a missed encounter with what, although it is constitutive of this interplay, remains foreign both to it and to the network of signification it produces. For Lacan this insistently reiterated gap in the Symbolic order is the ground of the compulsion to repeat.

The references to the castration complex in this part of the 1964 seminar are characteristically elliptical. They include the reference to a poem of Louis Aragon with which the second session opens (17–18) and a brief discussion of the status of the primal scene in Freud's case history of the Wolf-Man (54). Perhaps the most important of these references itself has the status of a gap in Lacan's text: at the opening of the third session

Lacan refers to an intervention into the previous meeting by Jacques-Alain Miller, in which Miller had articulated Lacan's discussion of the gap with the structuring function of lack in his earlier writings (29). This intervention is not reproduced in the published text of the seminar. Nonetheless, I suggest that Lacan's argument that the ontology of the signifier is founded on a "pre-ontological" gap (29) entails a drastic critique and revision of the Freudian conceptualization of the castration complex. According to Freud's narrative of the male child's development, the discovery that the maternal phallus does not exist and that the phallus belongs exclusively to men marks a moment of closure, inducing the boy's decisive turning away from his mother and his subjection to the paternal Law against incest. Lacan's argument suggests not only that the phallus is constituted as a signifier at the moment the child recognizes its lack in the mother but also that this moment must be theorized precisely as a re-cognition, as occurring within a logic of repetition. It might seem that the experience of recognizing that a thing one had expected to see is lacking entails some prior knowledge of what that thing is. For Lacan, however, this presumption is not possible because the phallus's significance as an object derives from the castration complex. The institution of the castration complex is thus not determined in Lacanian theory by the subject's recognition of an object as missing but as the iteration of a structure. This structure, which is logically prior to any signification or to any predication whatsoever, is that of the encounter with the gap in the Real.

Such an understanding of the castration complex as iteration is certainly legible in Freud, as we shall see in more detail in later chapters. Nonetheless, it goes distinctly against the grain of Freud's writing on the subject, in much of which he treats the institution of the castration complex, especially for boys, as a unique event belonging to a specific stage of development. Lacan rejects much of the Freudian narrative according to which children pass through a series of distinct stages in a predetermined order; in his work, the castration complex acquires explanatory force, not because its institution is a critical event in such a narrative, but because it is the determining instance of an iterated structure.[3] It is not too much to say that for Lacan the castration complex reinstitutes itself in every signifying relationship.

The theoretical problem of the relation between repetition and the castration complex largely defines the field of the first two chapters of this book. At the level of theory, the fundamental claim of these chapters is that the castration complex functions in psychoanalytic theory as an allegory whose effect is to institute the phallus as a material signifier. In chapters 3 and 4 the focus shifts to the distinct but related topics of the trope of metaphor and its functions in the institutions of paternity and of the effect of signature. I will not expand on those functions here. However, my argument will again be that the psychoanalytic theory of metaphor relies upon a topographical allegory.

In his discussion of metaphor Lacan defines it as the trope that substitutes one signifier for another (see for instance the account in "The Agency of the Letter in the Unconscious," *Ecrits: A Selection,* 157). This definition is unusual only in that it makes metaphor the master trope of substitution rather than one such trope among others. At least since Aristotle, the substitution of one signifier for another in metaphor has been figured as a transference by which a term is displaced from the site of its literal or proper reference and made to convey its freight of meaning elsewhere, to the site of its figural reference. The effect of this allegory—a metaphor of metaphor—is to represent metaphor at the level of the signifier as a reinscription of the same. That is to say, this allegory of the displaced signifier underwrites the claim that the signifier is the same when it signifies metaphorically as when it signifies literally. It underwrites this claim above all by representing the signifier as material in nature—as an object, transportable from one place to another.

At the level of theory, then, my claim will be that Lacanian psychoanalysis, together with certain long-standing rhetorical traditions it incorporates, constitutes the signifier as a material object within the structures of allegory. As is well known, Lacan's understanding of the signifier is adapted from Saussurean linguistics, which, however, Lacan appropriates under a fundamental reversal. For Saussure, because only differences carry signification, language must be understood as "a form and not a substance" (122). In his work the signifier's existence is theorized as radically distinct from the material that supports it in any given instance of its use: "It is impossible for sound alone, a material element, to belong to language. It is only a secondary thing, substance to be put to use. All our conventional values have the characteristic of not being confused with the tangible element which supports them. For instance, it is not the metal in a piece of money that fixes its value. . . . This is even more true of the linguistic signifier, which is not phonic but incorporeal—constituted not by its material substance but by the differences that separate its sound-image from all others" (118–19).

Saussure's analogy between language and money only underscores the difficulty of the problem it is designed to solve. We may accept that the value of a piece of money, like the significance of a word, is not determined by its material form. Just as significance is a function of the relations between signifiers, so value is a function of the relations between objects—in a money economy these relations will be relations of exchange. A coin has value as the embodiment of a given relation of exchange. That said, however, it must be recognized that without the mediation of money, the relations among objects that constitute their exchange value cannot be theorized or properly said to exist. Money may be only the material support for the relations that constitute exchange value in the abstract, but its existence is a necessary precondition for the institution and systematizing of these relations. We thus arrive at a paradox: the material object—the piece of money—that symbolizes an abstract relationship is a necessary precondition for that relationship's existence.[4]

This paradox returns us in another register to the problematic temporality it has been my central task thus far to identify with allegory. And, since we shall have occasion to touch on the topic of money again in chapters 2 and 4, it is not wholly beside the point to suggest here that money, as the materialization of relations of combination and substitution, operates to allegorize value. Still, our primary concern is not with the question of value but with signification. If Lacan's appropriation of Saussure rejects his distinction between the signifier and its material support, it is not because Lacan rejects Saussure's fundamental claims regarding the differential constitution of the signifier. On the contrary, Lacan follows Saussure quite precisely in the view that the signifier's existence—its signifying function for the individual—is constituted differentially, by the relations of contiguity and substitution in which it stands with respect to other signifiers. But Lacan's work also shows at every turn that these relations could not come into being without a material prototype whose circulation gives to all subsequent relations between signifiers their schema or their law. For Lacan, the function of this prototypical signifier-before-the-signifier belongs to the phallus.[5]

To the proposition that the signifier as such must be distinguished from the material object that, in Saussure's term, supports it we must therefore add the claim that the signifier's existence nonetheless entails the necessity of an instance of this distinction's failure. It is the recognition, or misrecognition, of a material object as a signifier that determines the schema within which every signifying relation comes into being. Within psychoanalysis this instance of misrecognition is theorized as the institution of the castration complex. In the terms of our own argument thus far, as an instance of the material embodiment of a relation between signifiers, it may also be theorized as the moment of the institution of allegory. In neither frame of reference, as I have already argued, can this moment be understood as synchronous with any specifiable event, because its appearance in each occurs within a structure of repetition—a fact to whose consequences we now turn.

Tennyson's poetry holds exceptional rewards for readers who pay attention to the materiality of its language. One thinks in this regard of Eric Griffiths' work on moments in which the poems play off the graphic and phonetic materials of language against each other (97–170), and of Garrett Stewart's on the semantic consequences of their encoding of vocal effects like assonance and elision (6–7, 173–75), as well as of the more eclectic and wide-ranging work of Christopher Ricks. Effects such as those traced by these critics are in one sense produced by a poem; in another sense they are given to it by the language in which it is composed—as a rhyme, for instance, belongs in one sense to a language and in another to the utterance in which it is formed. The production of effects of materiality within a poem thus provides a general paradigm of linguistic performance. The evidence of Tennyson's poems and of his methods of composition suggests that this paradigm was for him the determining one.[6]

Tennyson's poetry, then, works to materialize its own language. This work cannot be understood as simply an accumulation of local effects; on the contrary, its local effects must of necessity be produced within a general structure systematically elaborated throughout the poem. Rhythm, for example, as a property of particular words or verbal sequences, can be recognized only when it appears in the context of a general metrical structure. The broad claim of this book is that the poetic structures within which language acquires material properties are always allegorical in nature. We normally designate such structures in their totality as a poem's form, a term that itself figures the poem under a spatial allegory.

In the readings of Tennyson that follow, my concern will not be so much with the general nature of form as a category in poetics as with the specific allegories within which language assumes material properties in Tennyson's poetry. In chapter 1, we shall examine a group of related poems that figure the signifier as a visible object, in chapter 2 a group in which it is figured as audible. In chapters 3 and 4 we shall be concerned with the signifier as subject to displacement and iteration and with its capacity to function as a gift.

Nonetheless, as the general type of the spatial allegory by which a poem represents and delimits its own operations, the notion of form remains an implicit topic in this book. In this respect, my concerns are at odds with some of the most productive recent tendencies in poetics, which in different ways take the rejection of formalism as their point of departure. Exemplary instances are the work of Jerome McGann and Stanley Fish. In a series of essays published in the early 1980s, McGann drew attention to the separation of textual and editorial scholarship from critical and pedagogical practice that marked much of the formalist criticism of poetry in the preceding forty years. Working within a wide range of formalist disciplines, criticism in those years evolved a highly productive array of strategies for the reading of poetic texts under the condition of a systematic disregard for the conditions of those texts' production, reproduction, and circulation as material objects. For McGann, this blindness to the historicity of texts imposed a double burden: it condemned criticism to ignore both the historical conditions in which poems originate and the historicity of its own work. To restore texts in their materiality to visibility within critical discourse, McGann has argued that we must distinguish between poems and the texts that are their material form and recognize the multiple moments of the poem's writing and publication, of its various editions, and of its encounters with different readers as events, each textually productive in different ways and each embedded in a distinct social matrix. For McGann, the task of a historical criticism is to describe the dialectical relation between these events and so to give what he calls, in his theses on the philosophy of criticism, "the meanings of the meanings" that the poem has historically produced (343).

The years when McGann laid out his program—which he continues, with growing effect, to pursue—also saw the publication and widespread discussion of Stanley Fish's *Is There a Text in This Class?* In this book, Fish collected a series of essays laying out his own critique of formalism. This critique derived from his work in affective stylistics during the 1970s, in which he rejected the view that poems could be understood as objects and came instead to view them as constituted only within the temporality of their readers' experience, theorized as an event or a series of events: "A criticism that regards 'the poem itself as an object of specifically critical judgment' . . . transforms a temporal experience into a spatial one; it steps back and in a singe glance takes in a whole (sentence, page, work) which the reader knows (if at all) only bit by bit, moment by moment" (44–45). As Fish's views evolved, he modified and generalized his argument that a poem consists only of the series of affective and interpretative positions taken up by its readers, adapting it so as to contain and account for the notion of poetry that he had previously simply rejected. By the time of the later essays in *Is There a Text in This Class?* Fish had arrived at the view that all interpretative strategies, his own as much as those of formalism, will inevitably make of reading the occasion to produce a poem that they can recognize as such and that will yield the kind of reading the reader has already determined to find.

For both McGann and Fish the poem may be said to exist uniquely as an event. Working within different philosophical traditions, they naturally theorize the event in different ways. For McGann, the poetic event is above all a form of work whose historical meaning is determined by the social relations within which it is performed. For Fish, writing under the influence of American pragmatism, the event that constitutes the poem is understood as the effect of an intention (readerly or authorial—for Fish the two are indistinguishable) operating within a social context capable of making the intention recognizable as such. It could be said that McGann's dialectical model offers a more adaptable instrument for historical analysis than pragmatism's totalizing fiction of intention; nonetheless, both para-digms continue to prove highly productive in a wide range of fields.

Within both paradigms formalism's encounter with the poem as an object constitutes an error, whose effect they dissipate by theorizing it as an event that takes place within a matrix of social relations or intentions. Nothing in this book will dispute the view that the encounter with the poem as an object is an instance of error or misrecognition. But I will argue that this misrecognition is a necessary one and that its recurrence as an effect of reading poses a set of problems that no theory of reading as an event can resolve.

In the context of my argument, these problems can be described as the bequest of Freud. The event has been a problematic concept for psycho-analysis from the moment in 1897 when Freud abandoned his belief in the reality of the scenes of sexual abuse his hysterical patients described to him and was in consequence forced to abandon his theory that such abuse was the cause of hysteria. The problem is not simply one of telling the differ-ence between real and fantasized events. This difference can be called into question without risk to the category of the event itself. Moreover, the abandonment of the seduction theory by no means meant for Freud the abandonment of his belief in the diagnostic and curative value of bringing to light the traumatic events in which his patients' illness originated. This task remained to the end of Freud's life, and indeed remains to this day, central to most psychoanalytic practice. Still, in our own time, as in Freud's, questions regarding the ontological status of events that are recollected or reconstructed in the course of analysis have proved extraor-

dinarily persistent, and their ramifications have extended beyond the scene
of analysis proper and into, for instance, the court of law. I will contend
that psychoanalysis cannot offer final answers to questions of this kind,
because the structures it postulates for human subjectivity are ultimately
not such as can be accounted for on the hypothesis of any originary event.

In the late essay "Analysis Terminable and Interminable" (1937),
Freud took up the question of whether the task of analysis can ever be
wholly completed. He concluded that in a certain sense it cannot; in every
instance it appears to meet insuperable resistance when it attempts to
resolve the effects of the castration complex: "At no other point in one's
analytic work does one suffer more from an oppressive feeling that all
one's repeated efforts have been in vain, and from a suspicion that one has
been 'preaching to the winds,' than when one is trying to persuade a
woman to abandon her wish for a penis on the ground of its being
unrealizable or when one is seeking to convince a man that a passive
attitude to men does not always signify castration and that it is indispens-
able in many relationships in life" (*SE* 23:252). Freud here describes the
castration complex in terms of its differential effects on men and women;
his description suggests, however, that it has two fundamental implications common to subjects of both genders. First, it implies a belief in the
penis as a material object alienable from the subject who possesses it,
which can thus be lost, can circulate, and can be recovered.[7] Second,
it implies a belief that this object so invariably mediates certain social
relations—such as between activity and passivity—that it determines their
significance.

These beliefs, to which Freud refers as founded on biological fact, are
surely most remarkable for their divergence from the reality of life in the
body. Indeed, this is actually the point of Freud's argument. As he asserts,
passivity does not necessarily denote castration. Nor, more basically, is the
penis an object that might have been lost or could be regained. As I shall
document in more detail in later chapters, there is no event that determines
the beliefs Freud describes here. The scandal of Freud's account of the
castration complex is that it theorizes the engendering of the human
subject, not as an event or as the consequence of an event, but as the effect
of its structural relation to an object whose objective nature and functions
it fundamentally—constitutively—misrecognizes.

In Lacan's reading of Freud, this misrecognition of the object in its
reality constitutes the object as signifier. We may stipulate that on this
point Lacan does not read against the grain. On the contrary, from as early
as the section "Secondary Revision" in *The Interpretation of Dreams* to as

late as the guide to the analysis of the defenses in "Analysis Terminable and Interminable," Freud demonstrates repeatedly that in the setting of analysis itself the signifying function in the patient's discourse depends upon a prior misrecognition. By a dialectical necessity, this misrecognition constitutes the object in which analysis finds its truth.

On this basis one might claim that the reason analysis reaches its limit when it discovers the castration complex is that, in doing so, it discovers the structure in the subject that determines the nature of the analytic relationship. But one might also argue that it discovers the structure that it has itself imposed on its own data. The impossibility of adjudicating between these incompatible claims underscores the fundamental point. The castration complex in psychoanalysis names a relation to the material signifier that is instituted in a misrecognition whose moment is impossible to specify as an event.[8] This misrecognition of what Lacan calls the Real recurs throughout Freud's writing as a point of resistance to the totalizing work of representing events as scenes.

If the misrecognition of the Real resists the specification of its time within the logic of the event, it nonetheless bears or institutes a time signature. In the third section of the Discourse of Rome, Lacan discussed the function and significance of the rhythmic articulation of the time of analysis (*Ecrits: A Selection*, 77–107); later, in the section of *Four Fundamental Concepts of Psycho-Analysis* to which I have already referred, he spoke to the rhythm of the subject's fundamental relations with objects. In "Freud and the Scene of Writing," a reading of Freud whose orientation is very different from that of Lacan, Derrida too has stressed the necessarily rhythmic operation of memory as it records the time of the subject's perceptions (*Writing and Difference*, 225–27).[9]

This book begins with the premise that Tennyson encounters language as an object and that in all such encounters it bears for him a certain rhythm. As we shall see, especially in chapter 1, Tennyson was preoccupied with other rhythms besides those of language narrowly defined. Nonetheless, his attention to the rhythms generated in language by patterns of stress and quantity and by patterns of phonic variation and recurrence remains the single most distinctive characteristic of his poems. These patterns, together with the larger-scale structures of iteration by which the poems are organized, will define one axis of our argument.

Besides the evidence of the poems, a wealth of anecdotal evidence documents Tennyson's responsiveness to rhythm. From this body of material we may select a single item. In 1890, over eighty years old and in the course of preparing his legend, Tennyson wrote a note on his childhood for his son Hallam. Hallam in due course published this note in his *Memoir* of his father; it includes a text that it would not be completely whimsical to call Tennyson's earliest poem: "Before I could read, I was in the habit on a stormy day of spreading my arms to the wind, and crying out 'I hear a voice that's speaking in the wind' " (1:11). This story describes an encounter with a language borne on the wind, whose origin profoundly resists recognition. The encounter is moreover a "habit," not a singular event; iterative in its essence, it simultaneously obeys and encodes a rhythm. It seems partly appropriate to assert that the voice Tennyson hears is his own, misrecognized, and audible only in its dispersal. But the anecdote does not entirely yield to this reduction; commenting on it, Herbert Tucker observes that Tennyson's cry takes the form of a perfect line of iambic pentameter (*Tennyson and the Doom of Romanticism*, 40). What would be the source of the rhythm that speaks in the voice of the preliterate boy? Perhaps chance, perhaps the adult's revision, perhaps the recollection of some other, parental voice, reading aloud. The metricality of the child's cry is the formal marker in this story of the unanswerability of such questions—as rhythm is in Tennyson's poems the material quality of language in which his voice is at once most clearly recorded and most dispersed.

II

I have named allegory as the structure that fixes the material properties of the signifier, and I have argued that the time in which it does so resists specification as a historical or narratable event. Our work will nonetheless concern texts written and published at given historical moments and will cite authors, notably Tennyson and Freud, who were themselves historical agents. I do not mean to be quixotic but rather to designate as rigorously as possible the limits of my project when I remark that the authors cited as such in this book appear, in the last analysis, exclusively as figures in an allegory. The institution or authorship is itself best understood as an allegorical or fixative one; in later parts of this book we shall turn explicitly to a deconstructive reading of certain of its supporting structures, notably those of citation and signature.

For the moment, to pursue the question of the relation of allegory to the time of the historical or narratable event, I propose to examine another text that reads Tennyson allegorically—though it might be said to render allegory visible in his poems only to relegate it to the margin of its own narrative and historical project. The text is the novel *Wives and Daughters* by Elizabeth Gaskell, a writer who admired Tennyson's poetry and referred to it often in the course of her work.[10] *Wives and Daughters* was serialized in the *Cornhill* from August 1864 to January 1866; it belongs to that group of novels of the 1860s that turned back from the high point of Victorian prosperity to take as their topic the first three decades of the century. In so doing, these novels reflect self-consciously on the prehistory of the political, technological, scientific, and cultural innovations that for them constituted their modernity.

Wives and Daughters announces in its opening pages and repeatedly at critical points in its narrative that its stance is a retrospective one. Within the first few paragraphs, for instance, we learn that the period when the novel opens predates both the Reform Bill and the building of the railways (36, 37). These two events, among others, appear in the text as markers of the difference between the historical moment of the novel's writing and the historical moment it represents.

Wives and Daughters opens around 1820, and it is set in a provincial England that at first sight seems frozen in a Tory idyll. Gaskell imagines a social order centered upon a large landowner, who is also the sole holder of political power. That the landowner in question, Lord Cumnor, is a Whig aristocrat does not modify the essential conservatism of the political structure: " 'The earl' was the lord of the manor, and owner of much of the land on which Hollingford was built; he and his household were fed, and doctored, and, to a certain measure, clothed by the good people of the town; their fathers' grandfathers had always voted for the eldest son of Cumnor Towers, and following in the ancestral track, every man-jack in the place gave his vote to the liege lord, totally irrespective of such chimeras as political opinion" (36–37). Outside the town of Hollingford, however, and in contrast to the Whig grandees of Cumnor Towers, the novel sets the figure of Squire Hamley of Hamley Hall, who personifies reactionary Toryism in its fullest bloom.

Although the novel stresses the stability and long endurance of this political culture, which remains in place at its close, its narrative is nonetheless designed to open up a space of cultural authority for a new class whose power is not based on the tenure of land. In fact, we may anticipate by saying that it opens a space for those whose status derives from their possession of knowledge and from their function of producing and using it. If we contrast the families at Hamley and Cumnor, we see that the former is characterized by an ideal self-sufficiency. The Hamleys "never traded, or speculated, or tried agricultural improvements of any kind. They had no capital in any bank; nor, what would perhaps have been more in character, hoards of gold in any stocking" (72). These facts are connected; the Hamleys lack the finance capital to pay for agricultural improvements because their wealth is tied up in their land—a fact that becomes of consequence as the novel unfolds. Moreover, just as the squire's wealth remains at home, so too does he; he doesn't go to university, and as an adult rarely leaves the property on which he grew up. The consequence, the novel implies, is that it is not only lack of money but also lack of knowledge that has prevented him from bringing his farming techniques up to date.

The much wealthier family of Lord Cumnor, in contrast, is away from their property more often than not. The earl himself has cronies in London; his eldest son is the local M.P. and also has scientific interests that keep him away from Cumnor Towers and often take him to the continent. The Cumnor family lacks neither money nor technical knowledge; consequently the earl's land is run according to the most profitable and modern methods. But in consequence of the frequent absence of the landlords, its actual supervision is entrusted to land agents. Of these, only one is characterized in any depth; his name is Robert Preston, and he is a principal locus of the novel's anxieties about class and sexuality. Neither fully dependent upon nor wholly independent of the landed aristocracy he serves, he is represented as a rootless, hypermasculinized figure who is both socially ambitious and unscrupulous—a critical episode turns on his attempt to blackmail a woman into marriage.

The ground of the novel's critique of a social order where status is based on the tenure of land is therefore the argument that the value of land cannot reproduce itself; its preservation depends upon the supplements of money and technical knowledge. In a social order where these supplements are not themselves sources of status, they will necessarily appear as disruptive forces. The logic of this argument determines the novel's preoccupation with the professional classes. Its protagonist, Molly Gibson, is the daughter of Hollingford's doctor, whose gradual rise in prestige is part of its background. Much of the narrative unfolds in his household. The man Molly will marry at the novel's close is Roger Hamley, the second son of Squire Hamley. Roger's career, more than any other element of the novel, foreshadows the achievements of the coming Victorian era. In particular it foreshadows the period's embrace of both scientific research and imperialism, for by the close of the narrative Roger has embarked on a life's work of scientific research and exploration in Africa. Gaskell's intent that Roger should appear as the novel's man of destiny is underscored by a letter she wrote to her publisher at the outset asserting that she modeled his career on that of the young Charles Darwin (Chapple and Pollard, 731).

For most of the novel, however, Roger's promise remains unrecognized. His parents and much of the society of Hollingford view him as far less gifted than his elder brother, Osborne, who is of course the squire's heir. But Osborne proves a disappointment. Unlike his hardworking brother, he runs up bills at Cambridge and fails to take his degree. Eventually he dies, suggestively enough of a weak heart, whereupon his father learns that he has been secretly married to a French servant, who appears on the scene after Osborne's death to present the grieving squire with their son, who will survive to inherit the Hall.

Osborne is a poet—it is almost the first thing we learn about him—and it is to the significance of his foreshortened career that I now wish to turn. I have argued that one of the novel's projects is to trace the prehistory of the Victorian era. This project is evident both in the way the novel maps a particular fault line in the social order of the 1820s and early 1830s that will open to make room for specifically Victorian sociopolitical formations and in the way it refers to historical events in such a way as to mark the difference between the period it represents and the period when it was written. Now, one might have expected the novel's plentiful literary allusions to function in the same way. More specifically, one might have expected it, if it referred to Tennyson, to refer to him in the same way it refers to the Reform Bill or to the railways, as a phenomenon of the future. Or it might have referred to Tennyson's early publications—say the Cambridge prize poem of 1829 or the *Poems* of 1830—as events marking the actual period of the action.

It does not quite do either of these things. The first explicit reference to Tennyson comes when Molly Gibson is visiting Hamley Hall and Mrs. Hamley begins to speak of her favorite son: " 'Ah! I think I must read you some of Osborne's poetry some day; under seal of secrecy remember; but I really fancy they are almost as good as Mrs. Hemans'.' To be nearly as good as Mrs. Hemans was saying as much to the young ladies of that day, as saying that poetry is nearly as good as Tennyson's would be in this. Molly looked up with eager interest" (97). This moment, like others I have mentioned, certainly marks the difference between the period the novel represents and that in which it was written. But those other moments marked that distance by registering a historical break; the mentions of the railways and the Reform Bill, for instance, represent them as bringing to an end practices and institutions of the period in which the narrative is set and thus tend to introduce into it a note of nostalgia. The allusion to Tennyson, on the contrary, establishes in the field of poetry a logic of historical recurrence according to which the supersession of the poetry of one period by the poetry of another makes, at least for young ladies, no difference at all.

The scene of a young woman reading poetry thus seems to repeat itself across the forty-odd years that separate the writing of *Wives and Daughters* from the events it represents, instantiating a certain resistance to the historical change that otherwise frames Gaskell's narrative. If this seems to make too much of what is after all only an illustrative analogy, we may turn to another passage on reading in which the topic of repetition is much more insistent. It occurs somewhat later in the narrative of Molly Gibson's visit to Hamley Hall; she has by this time not only heard Osborne's poetry but has obtained from Mrs. Hamley some of his manuscripts:

(116)

> *Molly had asked permission to copy one or two of those which were her greatest favorites; and this quiet summer afternoon she took this copying for her employment, sitting at the pleasant open window, and losing herself in dreamy outlooks into the gardens and woods, quivering in the noon-tide heat. The house was so still, in its silence it might have been the "moated grange"; the bomming buzz of the blue flies, in the great staircase window, seemed the loudest noise indoors. And there was scarcely a sound out-of-doors but the humming of the bees, in the flower-beds below the window. Distant voices from the far-away fields where they were making hay—the scent of which came in sudden wafts distinct from that of the nearer roses and honeysuckles—these merry piping voices just made Molly feel the depth of the present silence. She had left off copying, her hand weary from the unusual exertion of so much writing, and she was lazily trying to learn one or two of the poems off by heart.*
>
> > *I asked of the wind, but answer made it none,*
> > *Save its accustomed sad and solitary moan—*
>
> *she kept saying to herself, losing her sense of whatever meaning the words had ever had, in the repetition which had become mechanical. Suddenly there was the snap of a shutting gate; wheels crackling on the dry gravel, horses' feet on the drive; a loud cheerful voice in the house, coming up through the open windows, the hall, the passages, the staircase, with unwonted fulness and roundness of tone.*

The insistent allusions to Tennyson constitute, in one sense, a snare for the reader. The relevant texts are "Mariana," to which Gaskell explicitly alludes by quoting its epigraph (a quotation, then, of a quotation); "The Lady of Shalott," from which derives the contrast between the midsummer landscape, where reapers are making hay, and the solitary woman indoors engaged in a mechanical repetition; and more generally the poems of rural and domestic life that Tennyson grouped in his 1842 volumes under the heading "English Idylls." Throughout these texts are woven the motifs of marriage hindered or thwarted by class barriers and of women in love with men who are inaccessible to them. The snare, then, is to suppose that the stories of these poems adumbrate what will be Molly's story—that is to say, that she will fall in love with Osborne, the author of the poem she is reading and the heir to Hamley Hall. This supposition is strengthened by Molly's daydreams about Osborne before she meets him, in which she imagines him as very much like the Lancelot of "The Lady of Shalott": "Molly's little wavering maiden fancy dwelt on the unseen Osborne, who was now a troubadour, and now a knight, such as he wrote about in one of his own poems" (182). And it is further reinforced by its apparent plausibility for other characters in the novel. Both Molly's father and Squire Hamley worry that she may fall in love with Osborne—an eventuality that the squire sets out to forestall by trying to prevent her from meeting him.

In these circumstances it seems naive of Mrs. Hamley to press Osborne's poetry on Molly, but in the event none of the possibilities apparently foreshadowed by the allusions to Tennyson arise. Molly's fantasies about Osborne barely survive her first meeting with him; and when she eventually discovers the secret of his marriage, the novel does not suggest that she feels any sense of loss on her own account. Its allusions to Tennyson thus seem inconsequential to its narrative. Moreover, we can say that they are inconsequential in the same way as Molly's reading of Osborne's poems. If Molly's reading seems briefly to suggest a false analogy between characters in Osborne's poetry and Osborne's own character, so our reading—or misreading—relied on the possibility of an analogy between the characters in Tennyson's poetry and that of Molly herself.

Gaskell's allusions to Tennyson, like the story of Molly's relations with Osborne, imply an argument for the inconsequentiality of poetry to her narrative. Such an argument is also implied by Osborne's own oddly inconsequential life. To determine what is at issue in this argument, we may return to the passage quoted above. The passage juxtaposes three different kinds of text or textual effect. First, there is the effect by which the passage itself represents Molly reading Osborne's poems and the setting in which she does so. Second, there is the effect by which the text of this representation alludes to poems of Tennyson's; and third, there is the effect by which it incorporates a passage supposedly quoted from the poetry Molly is reading.

We may skirt the complex topic of the distinctions between these three instances of textuality; my concern here is rather with their similarity. In particular, I want to draw attention to the recurrence in each of the texts of the twin motifs of repetition and silence, or of a certain failure to answer. Molly's attempt to learn Osborne's poem by heart eventually leads her to dreamily repeat one couplet over and over, "losing her sense of whatever meaning the words had ever had, in the repetition which had become mechanical"—just as, to mention only the Tennyson poem to which Gaskell explicitly alludes, Mariana in her moated grange is reduced to repeating over and over her refrain of

> My life is dreary,
> He cometh not. . . .
> . . . I am aweary, aweary,
> I would that I were dead.

And in the fragment that we are given of Osborne's poem, the wind answers the speaker by repeating the sound that it has always made, "its *accustomed* sad and solitary moan" (my italics). But this answer, of course, is in effect no answer at all—no more than the repeated daily round of sounds and sights described in "Mariana" offers an answer to her complaint. Finally, the passage represents Molly as repeating Osborne's lines in a silence that the distant sounds drifting in from the fields outside serve only to deepen. As she repeats her couplet, she seems to hear only herself; and by dint of repetition the words she speaks lose their meaning and cease to say anything to her.

The scene is interrupted by the sounds of Roger Hamley's arrival at the gate and his "loud cheerful voice" in the hall, which break into Molly's reading. She soon returns to it; but the break makes it all the clearer that reading is the central topic of this scene, which we can now see to be organized by the opposition between the sound of the speaking voice and the silence of the written text. The motifs I have traced in this passage have recurred in polemics against writing since Plato's *Phaedrus,* where Socrates argues for an analogy between writing and painting: "The painter's products stand before us as though they were alive, but if you question them, they maintain a most majestic silence. It is the same with written words; they seem to talk to you as though they were intelligent, but if you ask them anything about what they say, from a desire to be instructed, they go on telling you just the same thing forever" (*Phaedrus,* 275 d). This passage from *Wives and Daughters* is not simply an instance or set of instances of textuality; the recurrence in it of the motifs of repetition and silence enable us to recognize it as an allegory of the text in general and of the general structure of the scene of reading.

Gaskell's novel thus refers to poetry in general, and to Tennyson's early poetry in particular, as the paradigmatic instance, not simply of textuality, but of the text that allegorizes its own reading. In this account, writing's insistence on repeating itself and its incapacity to answer the demand of its readers are themselves the topics of Tennyson's poems: they proleptically tell the story of their own reading so as to situate all subsequent readings within a logic of repetition already established by the text itself.

Now, however, we must recall that the staging of this scene of reading as a repetition does not define a general law of reading for the novel as whole; on the contrary, its aim is to contain and mark as inconsequential the effects it describes. The need for such containment is suggested by the extent to which the narrative is determined by a very different model of reading, one in which reading, far from being a repetition of the text, is imagined as misappropriating or transforming it.

To a striking extent, the erotic transactions of *Wives and Daughters* are conducted by letter. Even more striking is the frequency with which these letters go astray. In fact, the inability of the written letter to control the context in which it will be read determines virtually every major crisis in the novel's sexual plot. The visit of Molly Gibson to Hamley Hall initially comes about because Molly's father has intercepted a love letter addressed to her by one of his apprentices. Mr. Gibson doesn't allow this letter to reach its addressee, but it does prompt him to rebuke its writer and to send his daughter away from home on an extended visit. At a later point in the novel, Roger Hamley becomes engaged to Molly's stepsister Cynthia Kirkpatrick and then leaves England on an expedition into Africa. But when he writes to Cynthia, she will not read his letters through; Molly, however, reads all the parts that Cynthia finds dull and gradually falls in love with Roger herself.

Cynthia's engagement to Roger is eventually broken off as a result of some love letters she had written some years earlier to Robert Preston, the land agent. Preston saved these letters and now threatens to hand them over to any subsequent lover she may have, or to her stepfather, in hopes of blackmailing her into marrying him. He is defeated in this plan, and Molly persuades him to return the letters; nonetheless, their contents become known and consequently Cynthia breaks off her engagement. Finally, in a last instance of letters going astray, the letters of Osborne Hamley's wife, Aimée, to her husband turn up among his papers after he dies. The result is that Molly reads them aloud to the squire, translating from the French as she goes, and so begins the long process of reconciling him to his unknown daughter-in-law.

Both the narrative and the historical projects of *Wives and Daughters* thus rely on the way the contextualized event of reading produces meaning, desire, and narrative. As we have just seen, in the novel's marriage plot the transformations of desire are determined by the unpredictable circulation of letters. And as I argued earlier, the novel's historical argument interprets a prior era in a context marked as that of the 1860s. It is this context that produces the historicity of the era the novel describes and determines its appearance as fissured and open to change in ways that it cannot represent to itself. The method of historical fiction in this respect depends upon the constitutive power of the event in the determination and redetermination of meaning.

Moreover, the narrative and historical projects of *Wives and Daughters* are themselves historical events. They function, at any rate, as techniques of textual production that were made available to Gaskell by the disciplinary history of the realistic novel and are the marks of the novel's affiliation with that history. Yet even as it deploys these techniques the novel stages a scene of reading that is in a double sense anomalous. With respect to the novel's historical project, it is anomalous as an instance of repetition. And with respect to its narrative project, it is anomalous as an instance of fixation—as a momentary halt in the circulation of desire, resulting from a seduction that is unlike any other in the novel because it has no consequences, as if it obeyed a logic incompatible with narration.

Even if we read this scene as locating a point of resistance to history and narrative and as identifying this resistance with the poetry of Tennyson, we may doubt whether it performs a *reading* of Tennyson, as I claimed above. It is certainly true that the passage in which Molly reads the poems of Osborne Hamley alludes to Tennyson with some explicitness and sets Molly in an allegorical setting that repeats some of the most characteristic topoi of his early poems. But the possibility of such a repetition should underscore the doubt: when we read a passage in a novel by Elizabeth Gaskell in which one fictitious character reads the poems of another, and when the passage more or less repeats passages more or less by Tennyson, then we can only wonder who might answer for what we are reading. The question is one to which we will return.

Still, the allusions to Tennyson's poetry suggest that if he is not the author of the effects with which the scene is concerned, his poetry can nonetheless be involved in them. In any case, these effects—of repetition, of the fixation of desire, and of spatial allegory—are my principal topics in this book. I have perhaps made too free with Tennyson's name in frequently assigning their authorship to him—and I would not much resist the argument that this book is less about Tennyson than about Keats; or about Felicia Hemans, or Swinburne, or Poe.

III

The finding of an object is in fact a re-finding of it.

The poets and philosophers before me discovered the   (Freud)
unconscious. . . . What I discovered was the scientific
method by which the unconscious can be studied.

Or, indeed, Freud. Nothing I have written should imply that the effects I am setting out to describe in Tennyson's poetry are in any sense naturally or self-evidently visible. On the contrary, in explicating the poems I have made use of theoretical constructions deriving from a number of authors and fields, but most systematically from Freud and his subsequent exegetes, notably Jacques Lacan, Jacques Derrida, and Harold Bloom. But the phrase "deriving from" here designates a relation that will remain extremely vexed throughout this study. Within psychoanalytic theory the notions of authority and originality are themselves rendered extraordinarily problematic by the recurrent issue of repetition. Although Freud did not turn to an explicit discussion of this topic until relatively late in his work, it is nonetheless from the beginning an implicit problem in many of his major theoretical contributions. Dreams, jokes, repression, object relations, the transference, the castration complex—none of these can be interpreted or can properly be said to exist as objects of interpretation except under repetition.[11] And this is to say nothing of Freud's writings on the uncanny and on the death drive, in which he explicitly attempts to theorize a compulsion to repeat.

The insistence of the topic of repetition in Freud's work would be less consequential if that work was not itself centrally concerned with human cognitive processes and with the conditions and constitutive limits of knowledge. Samuel Weber has posed the necessary questions: "Can psychoanalytic theory itself escape the effects of what it endeavors to think? Can the disruptive distortions of unconscious processes be simply recognized, theoretically, as an object, or must they not leave their imprint on the process of theoretical objectification itself? Must not psychoanalytic thinking itself partake of—repeat—the dislocations it seeks to describe?" (xvi). Weber's suggestion that psychoanalytic theory may be constrained to repeat the processes it describes opens to question the distinction Freud makes in the second of the passages quoted as epigraph between the unconscious and the method by which it can be studied, and so also his distinction between the work of poetry and that of psychoanalysis. Indeed, such a suggestion implies that the unconscious might be most visible in Freud's method at the points where the method collapses into its object or itself repeats the dislocations it sets out to interpret.

It is in any case such points that have most interested me in the Freudian readings of Tennyson that follow. The production of a Tennysonian Freud is almost as much a part of my enterprise as the production of a Freudian Tennyson; that such an enterprise has seemed to me possible, indeed necessary, is not in my view the result of some master discourse of history or theory that would encompass and authorize the conjunctions I have made. It is rather, I think, the result of the reading effect by which one all at once begins to see the same thing everywhere one looks. Even as my book stages this effect, I hope it also does something to analyze the textual structures that are its cause.

I

———————••❦••———————

Memory and the Place of the Eye

The dark and vicious place where thee he got
Cost him his eyes.

(King Lear)

I

IN ABOUT 1824, the year he turned fifteen, Tennyson wrote the earliest surviving version of a poem on the battle of Armageddon.[1] At the age of nineteen, in his third month at Cambridge, he remained sufficiently impressed with his four-year-old poem to revise it extensively and then to use large parts of this revised version the following year in his successful entry for the Chancellor's Gold Medal in poetry, on the assigned topic of "Timbuctoo."[2] This story testifies to a certain continuity of interest, though the shift in the text's ostensible subject in its final revision does entitle one to ask what, exactly, that interest might be said to be engaged in.

Both poems take their titles from places and they are places whose significance and status depend on their temporality. I shall argue that the time in which these places are constituted is the time of the look, a time that makes a difference while remaining irreducible to the before-and-after logic of narrative. This is particularly true of "Armageddon," a poem that begins by promising a vision of the "Latter Times" ([1824] 1.13) but ends by seeming to have been a little too early, or not quite latter enough, so that it remains profoundly unclear what the poem is actually just in time to see. In its later presentation as "Timbuctoo," which we shall examine in more detail below, the poem ends with a proleptic invocation of the spirit of Discovery and of the narrative that it implies—here given from the imagined perspective of the spirit of Fable occupying the mythological city soon to be supplanted:

Oh City! oh latest Throne! where I was raised
To be a mystery of loveliness
(ll. 236–44)   Unto all eyes, the time is well-nigh come
When I must render up this glorious home
To keen *Discovery:* soon yon brilliant towers

> Shall darken with the waving of her wand;
> Darken, and shrink and shiver into huts,
> Black specks amid a waste of dreary sand,
> Low-built, mud-walled, Barbarian settlements.

This narrative can be differently understood in terms of its several different elements. In the register of the agent, it is a story of displacement in which the spirit is thrown out of the palace it had created and animated. Read in this way, it is the story of "The Palace of Art" or "The Lady of Shalott." In the register of setting it is the story of a place that is darkened and ruined by the departure of its (male) genius—the story of "Mariana" and "Œnone." And in the register of the phenomenology of an implied author it is the story of a shift in perception from seeing to a mode of knowing figured as imperial dominance—the story of the "Ode to Memory" and *The Lover's Tale,* to say nothing of the principal texts of High Romanticism.

Whatever one takes the story introduced in "Timbuctoo" to be, it was for Tennyson clearly one that demanded repetition. That is one of the points of the poem, which begins with a conspectus of other places, inhabited like Timbuctoo by fable, that have suffered its same fate. So, as a way of leading to a reading of this story as a repetition, I return to the material to which Tennyson added it, in "Armageddon."

If the name Armageddon denotes the site of an event that is in its very nature unrepeatable, the poem that Tennyson wrote under that name nonetheless displays a marked pattern of repeated contraction and dilation—or what the text itself calls "an indefinable pulsation" ([1824] 4.29). Here is a cento of such dilations and contractions:

>   throughout the lurid waste
>   Of air, a breathless stillness reigned, so deep,
>   So deathlike, so appalling, that I shrunk
>   Into myself again, and almost wished
>   For a recurrence of those deadly sounds,
>   Which fixed my senses into stone, and drove
>   The buoyant life-drops back into my heart. . . .
>   In the East
>   Broad rose the moon . . .
>   . . . with dilated orb and marked with lines
>   Of mazy red athwart her shadowy face,
>   Sickly, as though her secret eyes beheld
>   Witchcraft's abominations. . . .

([1824]
1.64–70,
96–104,
111–13;
2.21–23;
3.26–29)

There was a windless calm, a dismal pause,
A dreary interval, wherein I held
My breath[3] and heard the beatings of my heart.

. . . . .

I felt my soul grow godlike, and my spirit
With supernatural excitation bound
Within me, and my mental eye grow large. . . .

. . . . .

. . . his ambrosial lip
Was beautifully curved, as in the pride
And power of his mid Prophecy: his nostril
Dilated with Expression.

Together, these passages manifest this poem's preoccupation with the involuntary contractions and dilations of the body's orifices and surfaces—including the diaphragm as an interior surface—that mediate its most elementary relations with the Other. These movements establish the split between the subject and the objects that constitute for it the signifiers of its desire—in Freud, the mother's breast, the feces, and the phallus, a list to which Lacan has added what he calls the gaze, whose split from the subject takes place at the eye.[4]

For Lacan, the gaze is that function of *being seen* that belongs in the field of the Other. One cannot see oneself being seen; the desire to do so constitutes the gaze as always hidden. This structure Lacan reads as a splitting at the eye of the gaze from the function of seeing, a splitting that establishes the subject as such in the scopic relation. This relation is thus with the signifier of the gaze which the subject has been brought into being as lacking—and thus, one would have thought, with any signifier at all; for what signifier cannot signify the hidden gaze of another? This signifier Lacan calls the *objet petit a* in the register of the scopic, and so aligns it with the other objects I have listed above, to which in their respective registers he assigns the same name and status.[5]

Tennyson's text frequently combines imagery deriving from several of the different part-objects, as in the following passage, in which the sun's rays are figured in successive lines as glaring on the earth, as nourishing it, and as begetting children on it:

([1824]
1.32–34)

Never set sun with such portentous glare
Since he arose on that gay morn, when Earth
First drunk the light of his prolific ray.

Nonetheless, the object with which "Armageddon" is most concerned is the gaze; as Daniel Albright has shown, the poem's visionary project repeatedly resolves itself into "an elaboration of the minutest processes of vision itself" (16).

The poem opens with an address to the Spirit of Prophecy, thanking it for the vision the poem goes on to record:

> Spirit of Prophecy whose mighty grasp
> Enfoldeth all things, whose capacious soul
> Can people the illimitable abyss
> Of vast and bottomless futurity
> With all the Giant Figures that shall pace
> The dimness of its stage,—whose subtle ken
> Can throng the doubly-darkened firmament
> Of Time to come with all its burning stars
> At awful intervals. I thank thy power,
> Whose wondrous emanation hath poured
> Bright light on what was darkest, and removed
> The cloud that from my mortal faculties
> Barred out the knowledge of the Latter Times.

([1824] 1.1–13)

These lines represent the Spirit's knowledge as constituted in a darkened interior space, where the events the poem describes are produced as on a stage. But if the passage establishes the Spirit's knowledge of these events under the sign of *enclosure*—it is worth noting the figural sense of *grasp* in line one—it also seems to constitute them as objects that it illuminates from somewhere else. The Spirit is represented here both as enfolding a darkened interior space that it peoples with the objects of its knowledge and as illuminating objects of knowledge that are imagined as external to it. I shall argue that the light the Spirit pours forth becomes in Tennyson's poem a figure for the gaze; what we see implied even in this opening passage, therefore, is a split between the position assigned to the subject of knowledge and that assigned to the subject of the gaze. One might argue that this split is adumbrated even in the first part of this passage, where the Spirit's knowledge seems to encompass both figures who walk a dim stage and the stars that appear at intervals above, as if to watch them from the darkened firmament. It is certainly as watchers that they reappear at the poem's conclusion, "looking steadfast conscious / Upon the dark and windy waste of Earth" ([1824] 4.26–27).

If in this opening apostrophe the subjects of knowledge and vision appear to be separated, their figural identification is nonetheless the major undertaking of much of the poem, which seeks to combine them in the figure of the Spirit. This identification depends, here and throughout, on a double reading of the figure of light. Light is described as removing the cloud that from the speaker's faculties had "barred out the knowledge of the Latter Times" and as pouring on "what was darkest" ([1824] 1.11, 13). What does this second phrase refer to? Clearly both to a darkness *within* the eye and to a darkness in the landscape before it—just as the cloud in this passage anticipates both the clouds that obscure the landscape of the poem until its last section and, in its effect, the "dull Mortality" which the Spirit rebukes the speaker for allowing to "clog" his senses ([1824] 2.14). Under the sign of knowledge, the light that dispels this darkness thus figures a power both of *making visible* and of *seeing*, a power the poem later figures as the expansion of a mental eye to incorporate the things it sees:

> my mental eye grew large
> With such a vast circumference of thought,
> That, in my vanity, I seemed to stand
> Upon the outward verge and bound alone
> Of God's omniscience.
>
> ([1824] 2.23–27)

The expansion of the eye into the field of knowledge which this passage records and which the poem's opening paragraph prefigures takes place, however, literally under the eye of another. The passage just quoted is immediately preceded by the arrival of an angel, who tells the speaker, "Open thine eyes and see!" He obeys these instructions:

> I looked, but not
> Upon his face, for it was wonderful
> With its exceeding brightness, and the light
> Of the great Angel Mind which looked from out
> The starry glowing of his restless eyes.
>
> ([1824] 2.16–20)

As at the outset of the poem, knowledge is figured as illumination; here, however, it is explicit, as it is not at the outset, that this illumination also figures the gaze of another.

A reading of the text as a whole makes it clear that knowing and being seen are related throughout; knowledge is in fact represented here as a function of the *being seen seeing* that I have identified above with the gaze. Hence the appearance of clouds throughout the first section of the poem as a figure of blockage that obscures, not the speaker's vision, as in the passages quoted above, but the sun, moon, and stars, figured as sickly, bloody, or hidden eyes.[6] It would thus be wrong to read the access to knowledge of the second section as figured only, or even primarily, as a clearing of the speaker's sight. On the contrary, knowledge is the effect on him of someone else's gaze, which opens his eyes only to dazzle them.

If in this text knowledge is the function of *being seen seeing,* that function cannot itself be seen. It is of necessity constituted in the field of the Other and exists in the eye only as a blind spot or as a trace:

[The angel] looked into my face
With his inutterable shining eyes,
So that with hasty motion I did veil
My vision with both hands, and saw before me
Such coloured spots as dance athwart the eyes
Of those that gaze upon the noonday sun.

([1824] 2.4–9)

Each of the last two passages quoted has been organized around a moment in which the poet falls under the Angel's gaze, a moment that at once endows him with knowledge and establishes him in relation to the Angel as someone who does not see what sees him. In both of those passages, this moment has been figured as one of blinding illumination. And the moment of the flash of light that both blinds and illuminates appears in the central passage of this section of the poem as a figure for the moment that establishes the poetic subject as such:

Each failing sense,
As with a momentary flash of light,
Grew thrillingly distinct and keen. I saw
The smallest grain that dappled the dark Earth,
The indistinctest atom in deep air,
The Moon's white cities, and the opal width
Of her small, glowing lakes, her silver heights
Unvisited with dew of vagrant cloud,
And the unsounded, undescended depth
Of her black hollows. Nay—the hum of men
Or other things talking in unknown tongues,
And notes of busy Life in distant worlds,
Beat, like a far wave, on my anxious ear.

I wondered with deep wonder at myself:
My mind seemed winged with knowledge and the strength
Of holy musings and immense Ideas,
Even to Infinitude. All sense of Time

([1824] 2.27–50)

And Being and Place was swallowed up and lost
Within a victory of boundless thought.
I was a part of the Unchangeable,
A scintillation of Eternal Mind,
Remixed and burning with its parent fire.
Yea! in that hour I could have fallen down
Before my own strong soul and worshipped it.

This whole passage is a specimen of the sublime that culminates, conventionally enough, in a moment in which the speaker contemplates the strength of his own mind. Its final splitting of the subject to produce a moment of reassuring self-absorption finds its structural prototype in the lines immediately preceding, in which the speaker figures himself as a spark ("scintilla" [Lat.] = "spark") split off from its "parent fire" only to be immediately reabsorbed into it. The characterization of the fire as a parent in itself suggests the status of the spark as *objet a*. But what we have been thinking of in its root sense as a spark, a particle that can be split off from and then "remixed" with the fire from which it came, also appears literally as a "scintillation," or flash of light. As such it is cognate with that flash of light that a few lines earlier made it possible for the subject to see. In the movement between these lines there is a shift in the place the subject is imagined as occupying; what remains constant is that the flash, whether it is thought as marking the place of the subject or as constituting that place elsewhere, remains irreducible to that which the subject sees. In one instance it would only be visible where the subject is not; in the other the subject is dazzled by it. For this reason the speaker's claim to see everything depends upon the representation of the flash as already reabsorbed in the fire where it originated. Indeed, the text represents the moment when the flash is split off from the parent fire as one that does not exist in narrative time at all, and certainly not in the narrative time of the subject:

([1824]
2.46–48)

I was . . .
A scintillation . . .
Remixed and burning with its parent fire.

At the moment it is split off, then, the flash is irreducible not only to what the subject sees but also to the narrative of its own experience. The moment of this split is nonetheless constitutive of the subject, for which the flash can stand as the signifier of the Other's gaze or as that which signifies it to the Other but for which it can never signify anything proper to itself. The moment that closes this passage should thus be thought of, like the moment in which the speaker characterizes himself as a scintillation *already* remixed with a fire, as founded on a forgetting of the irreducible alterity of the signifier.

What we cannot remember, Freud says, we repeat. When Tennyson revised "Armageddon" in 1828, he retained the passage we have been discussing but added to it the following:

> A maze of piercing, trackless thrilling thoughts
> Involving and embracing each with each
> Rapid as fire, inextricably link'd,
> Expanding momently with every sound
> And sight which struck the palpitating sense
> The issue of strong impulse, hurried thro'
> The riv'n rapt brain, as when in some great lake
> From pressure of descendant crags which lapse
> Disjointed, crumbling from their parent slope
> At slender interval, the level calm
> Is ridg'd with restless and increasing spheres
> Which break upon each other, each the effect
> Of separate impulse, but more fleet and strong
> Than its precursor till the eye in vain
> Amid the wild unrest of swimming shade
> Dappled with hollow and alternate rise
> Of interpenetrated arc would scan
> Definite round—

([1828], from *T. Nbk 18* fol. 7v–8r)

>   I know not if I shape
> These things with accurate similitude
> From natural object for but dimly now
> Less vivid than a half forgotten dream
> The memory of that mental excellence
> Comes o'er my Spirit and I may entwine
> The indecision of my present mind
> With its past clearness, yet it seems to me
> As, even then, the torrent of quick thought
> Absorb'd me from the nature of itself
> With its own fleetness. Where is he, that, borne
> Adown the sloping of an arrowy stream
> Could link his shallop to the fleeting edge
> And muse, midway, with philosophic calm

Upon the wondrous laws which regulate
The fierceness of the bounding Element?

The first verse paragraph in this passage recalls the image of the earlier
text in which the sounds the poet hears "Beat, like a far wave," upon his
"anxious ear" ([1824] 2.39). Here the wave reappears, not initially as a
figure for what the poet perceives, but for the confused train of thoughts
that perception induces in him. As the figure is elaborated, this distinction
of perception from thought becomes increasingly blurred; the confusion
of the poet's thoughts itself comes to be represented by a problem of
perception, by the puzzle for the eye presented by intersecting systems of
waves on the surface of a lake.

In fact, the eye is at the center of this paragraph, which figures both
problems of thought and problems of perception in terms of it. In the
paragraph's last two lines, the eye's puzzlement before a confused pattern
of waves is described as its failure to "scan / Definite round." The logic of
the figure suggests that the definite rounds the eye attempts in vain to scan
are those of the waves on the surface of the water. But the slightly strained
use of *round* here in a substantive sense reminds us of the more normal
usage according to which the eye might be supposed to "scan . . . round"
its own place, the place of the perceiving subject. The indefiniteness of the
circles in the water spreads to the eye that looks at them and suggests an
indefiniteness in the arc of its trajectory through the world, an arc that is
itself a projection of the eye's own surface.

Indeed, it is as a projection of the eye's surface that we should read the
figure as a whole, in which the level surface of the lake is riven into
"restless and increasing spheres" by crags that have been split off from
their "parent slope."[7] The circle of the waves here expands like the sphere
of the eye in the passage we discussed above; it does so, moreover, under
the influence of an object that is split off from a parent, like the spark in
the "Armageddon" of 1824 (2.48). Perhaps more distantly, these restless
spheres also recall the "restless eye" of the Angel in the earlier version
(2.20), and the "restlessly" sparkling thunderbolts (4.16), which, I shall
argue below, constitute the final appearance in the first version of the poem
of the flash of light that we have been reading as the signifier of the gaze.

At the center of both the passages I have been discussing, in short, is
the eye's enrapture by an object that produces a rift in it, in a moment that
also appears as one of rapid dilation. It is this moment, at once traumatic
and constitutive for the poet-seer who is the subject of "Armageddon,"
that I have sought to align with the moment of what Lacan calls the split
between the eye and the gaze.

Like the passage from the 1824 version of "Armageddon," that which was added in 1828 ends with the poet's contemplation of the power of his own mind. In the passage from 1824, the split in the subject that is implicit in such contemplation appears as a split between the grammatical subject of the poem—the "I" of the text—and the "strong soul" before which he could have worshipped. The formulation of these lines, moreover, implies a temporal dimension to that grammatical split: If the "I" exists in the time of writing to act as the subject of the sentence "in that hour I could have fallen down / Before my own strong soul and worshipped it" ([1824] 2.49–50), we may ask in what time the strong soul exists that it is apparently no longer available for worship?

In putting this point as a rhetorical question, I repeat Tennyson's own gesture in the version of 1828, where he asks,

	Where is he, that, borne
([1828],	Adown the sloping of an arrowy stream
from *T.*	Could link his shallop to the fleeting edge
Nbk 18 fol.	And muse, midway, with philosophic calm
8r)	Upon the wondrous laws which regulate
	The fierceness of the bounding Element?

Where indeed? The second paragraph of the passage I have quoted from the 1828 manuscript repeats the pattern of self-absorption that we saw in the passage from the 1824 text, but with a far greater emphasis on its temporality. The faculty that literally absorbs the subject—so that the first person pronoun vanishes from it—is memory.

The most remarkable feature of this passage is the way it takes up and adapts the figuration of thought in the first paragraph as a disturbance on the surface of a body of water. Here, thought appears as a torrent into which the "I" can be absorbed:

	it seems to me
([1828],	As, even then, the torrent of quick thought
from *T.*	Absorb'd me from the nature of itself
Nbk 18	With its own fleetness.
fol. 8r)	

The surface here has been elided, and with it the figuration of the mind's turn upon itself in terms defined spatially—by the eye. If the first paragraph figured the subject's nonidentity with itself by the irreducibility to itself of the eye, here it is figured—and resolved—as a problem of time.

The time in question, as I have implied by suggesting that it is introduced into the 1824 version of "Armageddon" by its grammar, is in fact the time of writing: The second paragraph of the passage quoted from the 1828 text opens with one of the few explicit references in either version of the poem to the problems of writing down the experience it describes, as Tennyson complains of the weakness of memory to recapture the "mental excellence" described in the paragraph before. The function of this reference is to temporalize the moment of the rift between the subject and what signifies it by representing it as the difference between the subject of an experience and the "I" that subsequently signifies that subject in a text.

Close attention to the text, however, suggests the difficulty of assigning any specific temporal location to this difference. As I have remarked, the second paragraph opens by complaining of the dimness at the time of writing of the poet's memory for the "mental excellence" he has been describing. The difference between the dimness of memory and the mental excellence it seeks to recapture thus appears here to be situated in a certain lapse of time. But the passage goes on to suggest that the dimness initially associated with the time of writing was in fact already present at the moment of mental excellence the poet seeks to recall. The words "even then," which describe the poet's absorption by a "torrent of quick thought," imply that that moment was already characterized by the indistinctness that characterizes his attempts to remember it. Thought thus absorbs the poet, not *into* itself, but *from* itself. This passage represents the subject who thinks as already subject to that difference from his thought which it figures as the temporal difference for which writing and memory seek to compensate. The subject here can only be figured as always already remembering; that is why this passage, while insisting on the difference between the states of "clearness" and "indecision" in the poet's past and present mind, nonetheless refuses to assign a distinct moment to either of them.

The rest of this chapter will consider other passages and poems that deal with looking and remembering. I will attempt to articulate this account of the subject as established in a moment of writing that always comes after the fact with the account of it as established in the gaze of the Other that I analyzed above. The two accounts do not appear commensurable.

I have described the former as a revision of the latter; to describe their relation in these term is, however, already to accept the former's model of a textuality that incorporates a subject unfolding in time. The same is true a fortiori of the possible analysis that would refer these alternate readings of the subject to changes in Tennyson between the different recensions of "Armageddon" in 1824 and 1828. Aside from its theoretical limitation, this analysis would overlook the temporality marginally inscribed in the grammar of the 1824 version—and the spatial organization of the figure of 1828, which after all can supply no answer to its own question about the subject's place, "Where is he . . . ?"

I have been considering the negative moment that gives the subject sight in these poems primarily as a phenomenon of the surface, as a blind spot or as an opening in the body where time is marked by muscular contractions and dilations. I want now to read some passages in "Armageddon" as projecting this negative moment, or rift in the eye, into the field of the visible. But it should be noted that in considering the eye as a surface, we have already been considering it according to the logic of projection, which is in fact pervasive in this group of texts.

In geometry, a projection is the mapping of a figure (A) onto a plane (B) along imaginary lines (rays) passing through the figure from a single point (C). The points at which the lines intersect the plane construct a two-dimensional image of the original figure. I give a sketch of this process as figure 1. The operation of the eye, like that of every other optical instrument, depends upon this kind of mapping; thus in figure 2 I illustrate how it functions by casting an inverted version of such a projection onto its own interior surface (D) by passing rays of light through its exterior lens, at point C. My argument so far has been that the opening of the eye at point C, the eye as it appears to the Other, is necessarily irreducible to this projection.

This schema of the operation of the eye as producing internally the image of a hypothetical external projection makes possible perspective drawing, in which the picture is imagined as occupying exactly such a hypothetical position. However, classical perspective is further established as inscribing in the image a representation of the place of the eye that this schema excludes. Hence the vanishing point, to which the eye is drawn by the arrangement of the objects represented in the picture. I have diagrammed this effect in figure 3.[8] This function in painting is what Lacan refers to as "given . . . to the eye," and as bringing about "the abandonment, the *laying down,* of the gaze" (*Four Fundamental Concepts,* 101).

It is precisely to the lack of this function in the landscape of "Armageddon" that Tennyson refers when at the opening of his poem he describes it in terms that clearly reflect a concern with its relation to painting, as

([1824]   a huge plain whereon the wandering eye,
1.26–30)   Weary with gazing, found no resting-place,

> Unbroken by the ridge of mound or hill
> Or far-off cone of some aerial mount
> Varying the horizon's sameness.

This landscape is represented as a surface on which the eye travels and hence as already a projection; but it is nonetheless a landscape where the eye has no place and where it consequently labors under the burden of the gaze, a labor whose burdensomeness consists in that it is performed for the Other.

To speak of the moment of negativity in the eye as *projected* is strictly to use a false figure because the eye's function as a projector of a surface depends upon the elision of this moment. Nonetheless, this elided moment becomes in Tennyson's poem a lack, manifested in the poem's obsessive preoccupation with what cannot be seen or what it is taboo to see:

> Black, formless, unclean things came flitting by. . . .
> So shadowy, indistinct and undefined,
> It were a mockery to call them aught
> Save unrealities, which took the form
> And fashioning of such ill-omened things
> That it were sin almost to look on them.

([1824] 1.47–54)

This passage should be aligned with another, in which the moon rises and the speaker sees in its face the marks of the obscenities it sees:

> In the East
> Broad rose the moon. . . .
> Then with dilated orb and marked with lines
> Of mazy red athwart her shadowy face,
> Sickly, as though her secret eyes beheld
> Witchcraft's abominations, and the spells
> Of sorcerers, what time they summon up
> From out the stilly chambers of the earth
> Obscene, inutterable[9] phantasies.

([1824] 1.96–107)

This is the only passage in the poem where anyone but the speaker is represented as *seeing* anything—and what it imagines is that seeing can be thought of as marking; that what the moon sees—although with secret eyes—is somehow registered on her face. Given the taboo nature of what is seen in both passages, we could also say that this passage represents the inscription of a transgression on the face of the transgressor.

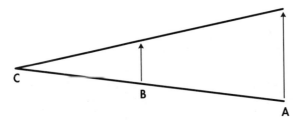

Fig. 1. Schematic diagram of projection

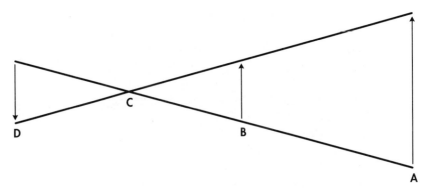

Fig. 2. Schematic diagram of the function of the eye

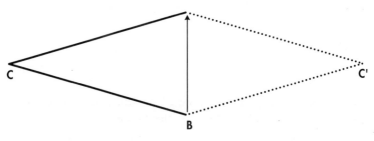

Fig. 3. Schematic diagram of classical perspective

I am arguing here that the lack in the subject's eye, the negative moment that subjects it to the gaze of the Other, can be represented when it is imagined as the object of a taboo whose transgression is recorded on the (imaginary) face of another like the subject.[10] I will try to make this formulation clearer by reference to a remarkable passage at the end of the poem. In recalling the passages just quoted, it reduces the strange figures the speaker has seen and imagined to a shadow on the face of the air:

> The sooty mantle of infernal smoke
> Whose blank, obliterating, dewless cloud
> Had made the plain like some vast crater, rose
> Distinct from Earth and gathered to itself
> In one dense, dry, interminable mass
> Sailing far Northward, as it were the shadow
> Of this round Planet cast upon the face
> Of the bleak air. But this was wonderful,
> To see how full it was of living things,
> Strange shapings, and anomalies of Hell,
> And dusky faces, and protruded arms
> Of hairy strength, and white and garish eyes,
> And silent intertwisted thunderbolts,
> Wreathing and sparkling restlessly like snakes
> Within their grassy depths. I watched it till
> Its latest margin sank beneath the sweep
> Of the horizon.

([1824] 4.3–19)

Here the opening lines figure the cloud not only as obliterating the plain but as giving it the appearance of an empty space. It is described as a blank, dewless mass that makes the plain look like a vast crater—in fact, like an enormous, dry, empty eye socket. The word *blank* is part of a pattern of allusion in "Armageddon" to the Invocation to book 3 of *Paradise Lost* (3.48), where it denotes the blank that the world presents to Milton's blind eyes—a denotation that is introjected in another relevant text, Coleridge's Dejection Ode, where the poet looks at the world with a "blank" eye.[11] This blank passes from text to text like the signifier as such, always signifying a lack in the subject, but a lack that has a significance for someone else, like Milton's "Book of Knowledge" (*Paradise Lost* 3.47), or Coleridge's eye, blank presumably only for the Other who sees it.[12]

How does one project a blank? Here, by imagining it as a mark on the face of another—in the text's remarkable figure, "upon the face / Of the bleak air" (4.9–10) It is on the face of the air that the cloud is transformed from a mantle that both covers the surface of the earth and makes it a blank, into a form of its projected image, its shadow. It is an image only in outline, however; an image whose substance is elsewhere.

The planet may be read as a figure of the eye; it is in any case the type of the *objet a,* constituted only in the moment when its lack can be read in another. The cloud that shadows it is thus made up, with the metonymic logic of the obsessional neurotic who can never give up enough to the Other, of a mass of split-off objects—a catalog, in fact, of the objects that have most preoccupied the poem: faces, arms, eyes and

> intertwisted thunderbolts,
> Wreathing and sparkling restlessly like snakes
> Within their grassy depths.

In the thunderbolts we recognize the flash of light that signifies the gaze. Here it appears in the field of the visible under a taboo.

The sign of this taboo, the snakes to which the thunderbolts are compared, focuses the relation between the thematic of the look I have been discussing in this poem and the thematic of gender, with which I want to align it, in this poem and several others. The snakes recall the "two huge serpents mating in the green forest" which, in Ovid, Tiresias sees and strikes with his staff (*Metamorphoses* 3.324–25). This transgression is punished by his transformation into a woman.

What are we to make of this peculiar allusion? At the moment in the poem when the eye sees the image of its own blank, or blind spot, Tennyson's thoughts turn to a sex change. In fact, the topic was already present. We have already discussed the passage that first figures the function of seeing as becoming visible, in which it appears as a bloody mark on the face of the female moon. And the poem's earlier representation of dark, formless shapes that it is forbidden to look at is itself marked by the combination of fascination and denial we associate with the little boy's attitude to the female genitals in his oedipal phase.

None of this, however, is to argue that in this poem the conception of the blind spot, or the rift in the eye, is determined by the Oedipus complex. On the contrary, I mean to suggest that the configurations of the Oedipus complex are a way of representing what can otherwise only be thought of as a lack in representation, in the field of what can be seen. These configurations depend, not only on the legible inscription of lack on the woman, but also on an imagined identification with her, which we may ventriloquize as follows: "She was like me, but now she is castrated. And if I transgress against the Law, I will be castrated too." Hence the bizarre recollection of the fate of Tiresias when what has hitherto been unrepresentable appears in the poem as the taboo. And hence, more generally, the recurrent mediation of the look in Tennyson's early poetry through a woman's loss, or through a lost woman.

In this reading, the moment of self-absorption I analyzed above represents the moment of the self's absorption into the Law, or of its absorption of the Law into itself—as the account of the moment in "Armageddon" suggests. For it will now be recalled that the relevant passage represents the subject as a spark absorbed into its "parent fire" and as absorbing the parent's authority into itself:

> I was a part of the Unchangeable,
> A scintillation of Eternal Mind,
> Remixed and burning with its parent fire.
> Yea! in that hour I could have fallen down
> Before my own strong soul and worshipped it.

([1824] 2.46–50)

In what I have already said about this moment, I have stressed its association with temporality. Now, as my ventriloquism above suggests, the Oedipus complex depends for its effect on a narrative—a sort of etiological fable about the woman's castration. This fable, moreover, is made possible by a temporalization of the difference with which we have been most concerned in this chapter, that between seeing and knowing.

In one of Freud's discussions of the termination of the oedipal phase in the male child, he describes the relation between the boy's first sight of the female genitals and the threat of castration: "When a little boy first catches sight of a girl's genital region, he begins by showing irresolution and lack of interest; he sees nothing or disavows what he has seen, he softens it down or looks about for expedients for bringing it into line with his expectations. It is not until later, when some threat of castration has obtained a hold upon him, that the observation becomes important to him: if he then recollects or repeats it, it arouses a terrible storm of emotion in him and forces him to believe in the reality of the threat which he has hitherto laughed at."[13]

The order of events described in this passage may be summarized as follows: first the little boy sees the female genital region but fantasizes there the penis which he had expected to see. Then he hears the threat of castration; and finally, when he "recollects or repeats" the earlier observation, he experiences "a terrible storm of emotion." Only at this final stage does he accept either the reality of the threat he has heard or that of the lack he has seen in the woman. The whole passage suggests a profound uncertainty about the status of knowledge, which it constitutes as doubly a recollection, both of the threat of castration and of the sight of the female genitals. And in the latter case this recollection is somewhat tendentious. As Freud remarks, the little boy may, on seeing the female genital region, see "nothing." But he remembers this nothing after the threat of castration as a *lack,* thus seeming to remember that he *already knows* of the possibility with which he is now threatened.

What this account imagines, then, is the possibility of making looking and knowing coincide by the deferred action of memory. But within it is retained an implied moment of looking as such, which memory is constituted as eliding, in which the look needs to be supplemented because it is always missing something.

II

In this account of the resolution of the male Oedipus complex, the little boy, after hearing the threat of castration, returns to ("recollects or repeats") the sight of the female genitals as a reader, equipped to (mis)interpret the signifying lack he rediscovers there. We may ask whether that reading is ever complete and whether it is somehow marked by the moment of blindness, of seeing nothing there, that initiates it.

On the question of completeness, Freud himself supplies an answer in the essay "The 'Uncanny,' " where he writes of the female genitals as being for the male one of those uncanny sites to which one feels one is constantly returning: "It often happens that neurotic men declare that they feel there is something uncanny about the female genital organs. This *unheimlich* [uncanny] place, however, is the entrance to the former *Heim* [home] of all human beings, to the place where each one of us lived once upon a time and in the beginning. There is a joking saying that 'Love is home-sickness'; and whenever a man dreams of a place or a country and says to himself, while he is still dreaming, 'this place is familiar to me, I've been here before,' we may interpret the place as being his mother's genitals or her body" (*SE* 17:245). Freud's confident interpretation of this dream as a regressive fantasy does nothing in itself to explain why the female genitals seem *unheimlich*. On the contrary, what it does do is to line up one form of male libido with sickness for home. That the genitals nonetheless seem *unheimlich* suggests that in the object of this libido there was something that would ensure its frustration; that it had, in a sense, taken frustration itself for its object.

To explain the both *heimlich* and *unheimlich* nature of the female genitals—and more generally of the *heim,* or home, as such—we may turn from the dream of having "been here before" in the passage I have been discussing to a moment earlier in the essay where Freud discusses another phenomenon of return. Here he is analyzing the uncanniness of involuntary repetition and gives as an example the sensation of repeatedly finding oneself involuntarily in the same place or situation: "From what I have observed, this phenomenon does undoubtedly, subject to certain conditions and combined with certain circumstances, arouse an uncanny feeling, which, furthermore, recalls the sense of helplessness experienced in some dream-states. . . . So, for instance, when, caught in a mist perhaps, one has lost one's way in a mountain forest, every attempt to find the marked or familiar path may bring one back again and again to one and the same spot, which one can identify by some particular landmark" (*SE* 17:236–37).

Let me note some of the differences between the experiences described in these two passages. One is of course the experience of a dreaming subject, the other of a waking one; this difference is, moreover, only emphasized by the fact that the second experience *recalls* certain types of dream—for to recall a dream is possible only when one is awake.[14] The moment of the uncanny in Freud is necessarily a waking moment; the uncanny feeling is itself figured as awakening in the second passage quoted. In fact, the idea of the uncanny as that moment when waking reality seems to recall our fantasies and thus to call into question our property in them is one that Freud develops at length later in the essay.

The other difference between the two experiences is that one of them seems to be determined by the subject's desire—his "home-sickness"— while the other is apparently determined by a logic exceeding that of the subject, which in this essay and in the contemporaneous *Beyond the Pleasure Principle,* Freud terms the compulsion to repeat. Moreover, where the logic of repetition appears in the second of these passages, it is not merely as a contrast to the logic of the subject's desire but specifically as that which frustrates it. For the concept of "home" appears in both of these passages, not just in the one that concerns the woman's genitals. As much as the man in love, the man lost in the forest wants to get home, or at least back to the "familiar" path that would take him there. The uncanny thus appears in this episode as an agency outside the subject that frustrates this wish.

The opposition of the familiar and the unfamiliar, of the *heimlich* and the *unheimlich,* organizes the episode of the lost traveler itself. Within this episode, though, in a repetition that itself partakes of the uncanny, there lies across this opposition the thematic of the mark. In the traveler's wanderings, it is the repeated appearances of the same spot, recognizable "by some particular landmark," that produce the uncanny effect. But what the traveler is looking for, and is prevented by this repetition from finding, is "the marked or familiar path." What distinguishes the mark that enables one to recognize the path from the mark that enables one to recognize that one has once again missed the path?

Any answer to this question will invoke a narrative. We may, for example, recognize a mark as marking a path because we can read in it the evidence of human agency; because we can tell how it got to be where it is. Or we may recognize it precisely because it marks the path, itself a figure for a narrative line, that will eventually, prospectively, get us where we want to be. The mark that repeatedly looms uncannily out of the mist, however, is unreadable, at least in the sense that it does not authorize any narrative. The traveler remains blind to its meaning, to adopt a figure that appears in the episode in the mist that Freud makes a point of mentioning and is moreover the topic of repetition in "The Sandman," the central text in the argument of his essay.

I previously argued, following Lacan, that the moment of the subject's look in "Armageddon" is always marked by a certain lack, a blind spot, that is established in a moment in which what Lacan calls the gaze is split off from the subject's eye and established in the field of the Other. I further attempted to show the recurrence in Tennyson's text of the projection of this blind spot as a lack in what the eye sees, which the subject recuperates under the sign of *knowledge*. The subject of knowledge remembers having seen but does not remember the moment of not seeing—a moment I will now align with the moment of the uncanny, as a moment that can be repeated but not remembered as something securely located in the subject's past and that comes around again and again, always as a surprise. That moment is recorded in "Armageddon" in the pattern of repeated involuntary contractions of the subject's body, which make of it a *watch*—which the Other watches, and which tells for the Other a time the subject itself cannot know.

In the rest of this chapter I want to pursue through a series of related texts dating from shortly after "Armageddon" the themes of waking, remembering, and knowing in their relation to the topics of gender and of place. As mentioned earlier, when Tennyson revised "Armageddon" for the last time, he incorporated the bulk of the 1828 version of the poem into his entry for the Chancellor's Gold Medal in 1829; the assigned topic was "Timbuctoo."[15]

Timbuctoo's existence had been known in Europe since the fifteenth century, when Portuguese explorers had returned with accounts of its extraordinary splendor. By 1618, according to Hugh Murray, Timbuctoo was already known in England as "that celebrated city . . . round which revolved all the commerce and splendor of interior Africa" (*Historical Account* 2:167).[16] This account of Timbuctoo lasted virtually until Tennyson's own time and was reinforced by the reports of its wealth with which Mungo Park, the Scottish explorer, returned in 1797 (Park, 215). Park, however, had not actually seen Timbuctoo, and subsequent descriptions of it proved somewhat different. Early in the next century, a sailor named Adams, who claimed he had been shipwrecked off West Africa in 1810 and taken to Timbuctoo as a captive, produced a description that corresponds more closely to Tennyson's disillusioned vision of "Low built, mud-walled, Barbarian settlements" ("Timbuctoo," l. 244): "The habitations of the principal people were . . . composed of wooden cases filled with clay and sand, and having all the rooms on the ground floor. The huts of the poorer class are framed merely of the branches of trees bent in a circle, covered with a matting of the palmetto, and the whole overlaid with earth. The mayor's house, or palace, is built in a square of about half an acre, enclosed by a mud wall" (Murray, *Historical Account* 1:491). Murray remarks of this account, that "in regard to its splendor . . . and to the state of the arts, it [Timbuctoo] certainly differs very widely from what we had been taught to expect" (1:503). In a later work, which Tennyson could not have seen in 1829 as it had its first edition in 1830, Murray questions the authority of this description,[17] but he also confirms its substance by the report of René Caillié, who returned from an expedition to Timbuctoo in 1828, the year before Tennyson's poem was written.[18]

This narrative of disappointed expectations forms the immediate context for Tennyson's "Timbuctoo" in 1829. That he should have chosen to adapt for this poem his 1828 version of "Armageddon" is not altogether as improbable as it seems. For the passage from the first part of the culminating vision of "Armageddon" that Tennyson adopted for his vision of Timbuctoo itself derives at least in part from the kind of travel literature about Africa that had fueled the legend of Timbuctoo—though its African allusions, which include descriptions of pyramids and of what W. D. Paden argues is a temple of the Sun, are in fact more appropriate to Egypt than to Timbuctoo's location in West Africa.[19]

One of the most intriguing qualities of Tennyson's text, as well as of the European ideas of Africa in the eighteenth and early nineteenth century that lie behind it, is a fascination with Africa as the site of imperial power. The city that Tennyson describes in the lines he appropriated from the end of "Armageddon" is clearly the center of an empire, whether it is meant to be Timbuctoo or the New Jerusalem, and the occupant of the throne at its center is evidently imagined as an oriental despot.[20] Its power appears in one figure in the accumulation of objects; it is

> A wilderness of spires, and chrystal pile
> Of rampart upon rampart, dome on dome,
> Illimitable range of battlement
> On battlement, and the Imperial height
> Of Canopy o'ercanopied.
>
>   Behind
> In diamond light upsprung the dazzling peaks
> Of Pyramids as far surpassing Earth's
> As Heaven than Earth is fairer. . . .
> . . . But the glory of the place
> Stood out a pillared front of burnished gold,
> Interminably high.

("Timbuctoo," ll. 159–72)

This repeated figure of an accumulation that exceeds comprehension may be termed the imperial sublime. Under another figure, the city's status as an imperial power is signaled by its association with the image of a luminous center, which casts light upon the space that surrounds it:

> Each [of the pyramids] aloft
> Upon his narrowed Eminence bore globes
> Of wheeling Suns, or Stars, or semblances
> Of either, showering circular abyss
> Of radiance.

(ll. 166–70)

Figures of imperial power as sublime at once in the scope and multiplicity of its objects and in its own extreme concentration seem to be a feature of late eighteenth- and early nineteenth-century writing on a number of topics—on Rome, for instance, as well as the Orient and Africa, particularly Egypt. Especially in English travel writing of the period, this fascination may be essentially nostalgic. In the empire that England accumulated at this time power was in fact not concentrated but dispersed among agencies of the Crown, trading companies such as the Hudson's Bay Company and the East India Company, and private societies of missionaries and adventurers such as the African Association, which underwrote Mungo Park's first expedition up the Niger toward Timbuctoo. The English fascination with the idea that the countries they were opening up for exploitation were already or had already been parts of an empire in which power was concentrated in a single person may thus be seen as an Imaginary response to the increasingly shapeless and decentered quality of the English empire itself.[21] It manifests a wish to confront an imperial power with a shape and a center that could be imagined as the specular opposite, both agonistic and reflexive, of England's own.

One instance of this wish's disappointment forms the historical context for Tennyson's "Timbuctoo." The poem's self-situation in this context signals its design of giving a history to the look, which in "Armageddon" had as its moment the end of history, a moment that will necessarily never be historical. So its history is constructed in "Timbuctoo" under the sign of a nostalgia that is both a nostalgia for an Imaginary center, and, in a sense, for history itself.

The material Tennyson adopted from the 1828 version of "Armageddon" to describe the vision of Timbuctoo remains organized according to the logic of the split between the eye and the gaze. This material ends, characteristically enough, with a moment in which the eye is overwhelmed when the poet looks to the city's center, where

> Stood out a pillared front of burnished gold,
> Interminably high, if gold it were
> Or metal more etherial, and beneath
> Two doors of blinding brilliance, where no gaze
> Might rest, stood open, and the eye could scan,
> Through length of porch and valve and boundless hall,
> Part of a throne of fiery flame, wherefrom
> The snowy skirting of a garment hung,
> And glimpse of multitudes of multitudes
> That ministered around it—if I saw
> These things distinctly, for my human brain
> Staggered beneath the vision, and thick night
> Came down upon my eyelids, and I fell.

(ll. 171–83)

These lines suggest two different readings. On one hand, following a trajectory I have already discussed, they express a growing perceptual confusion that culminates in a moment of blindness. As the poet's eye is drawn into the depth of the image, the vertiginousness of its descent and its inability to rest on any of the objects it encounters become figures for the poet's increasing uncertainty about what he sees. Eventually, the description of the eye's movement into the image is arrested as the poet wonders if he actually saw what he saw at all. In this reading the depth of the image holds for the poet a re-recognition of the difference—articulable only in retrospect—between seeing and knowing that one has seen. On the other hand, the passage describes the eye's movement toward a center which, however, it never quite reaches. A slightly vulgarized reading (see n. 20) will see this fascinating trajectory that is arrested at the skirt of a garment as directed toward the center of the city's power, toward its symbolic father, or in short, toward the phallus. The conjunction of these two readings suggests the insistent connection in Tennyson between the constitutive incompleteness of the look and a thematic of gender. Here the incompleteness of vision is apparently localized as an instance of blindness at the site of the phallus. As Tennyson sets material from "Armageddon" in the new context of "Timbuctoo," this blind spot is consistently projected as a castrative lack, not in the eye, but in its object.

The moment at the end of this passage where the poet's sight goes dark marks the end of the material Tennyson adopted from the 1828 "Armageddon." The nature of the added material suggests what I have called its design of giving a history to the moment of the look; it consists principally of an introductory meditation on memory and the encounter with the spirit of Fable that follows the passage I have been discussing and closes the poem.

The spirit restores the poet's sight and explains what will be the story of the city he has seen. Simply put, that story describes how a home—"this glorious home"—is changed by a look into a set of marks—"Black specks amid a waste of dreary sand, / . . . . How changed from this fair City!" (ll. 239, 243–45). To become the subject of this narrative, the city must be made a woman:

> Seest thou yon river, whose translucent wave,
> Forth issuing from the darkness, windeth through
> The argent streets o'the city, imaging
> The soft inversion of her tremulous Domes,
> Her gardens frequent with the stately Palm,
> Her Pagods hung with music of sweet bells,
> Her obelisks of rangèd Chrysolite,
> Minarets and towers? Lo! how he passeth by,
> And gulphs himself in sands, as not enduring
> To carry through the world those waves, which bore
> The reflex of my City in their depths.

(ll. 225–35)

If the city is represented here as a woman, it is visible as such only as a reflection in a river, which, strictly, is all the spirit in these lines invites the poet to see. To begin to understand this image, we may turn back a few lines to the moment when the spirit who speaks here first appears in the poem. He addresses the poet

> with a mournful and ineffable smile,
> Which but to look on for a moment filled
> My eyes with irresistible sweet tears.

His voice, speaking "In accents of majestic melody," sounds "Like a swoln river's gushings in still night / Mingled with floating music" (ll. 185–90). Herbert F. Tucker has wittily remarked that the poet here looks the way the spirit sounds ("Strange Comfort," 21), and it does seem true that the fullness of the poet's eye at this moment anticipates the fullness of the river that is invoked as a metaphor to describe the sound of the spirit's voice. The river here is a metaphor for a discourse that appears, by a half-hidden false figure, to fill the eye.

We may read the same false—or double—figure in the longer passage quoted above. For here too the river functions as a metaphor for a discourse. More specifically, it is an elaborated figure for the temporal status of myth, one of the main concerns of Tennyson's poem as a whole. Like myth, the river rises from the darkness (1. 226), from an unknown origin, passes current in the world for a while as a medium of representation, but ultimately survives only as something buried, or under erasure. This is in brief the story Tennyson tells of myth in his nostalgic references to Atlantis, Eldorado, and the Islands of the Blessed in the far West during the opening paragraphs of the poem.

The middle phase of this narrative, however, requires some further explanation. If we accept the river's vanishing beneath the sands as figuring the way myths lose their authority in the course of time, Tennyson's account makes it clear that this is the effect and in some sense the repetition of a loss that is already the burden of myth itself. The waves bury themselves because even before they vanish they have ceased to be the medium of the city's reflection. Furthermore, there is an analogue to this doubling of loss in the account of myth that Tennyson gives at the start of the poem. An attentive reading of the lines on Atlantis, for instance, shows that their nostalgia is not for the city of Atlantis as such but for its memory:

> thou wert then
> A centred glory-circled Memory,
> Divinest Atalantis, whom the waves
> Have buried deep, and thou of later name
> Imperial Eldorado roofed with gold:

(ll. 20–27)

Shadows to which, despite all shocks of Change,
All on-set of capricious Accident,
Men clung with yearning Hope which would not die.

As these lines describe the loss of hope, they also describe the loss of loss
itself. The moment with which they are concerned is the moment when
something one had thought lost turns out never to have existed, or in
which the object one thought one had lost turns out always to have been
already lost.

The figure of the river at the end of the poem displays something of
the same difficulty in locating an originary moment of loss as is implied in
this account of nostalgia for the legend of Atlantis. We have seen how the
disappearance of the river beneath the desert was motivated by a prior
disappearance, which was already the burden of the river, or of the
discourse which we have taken the river to figure. The river, so the spirit
says, buries itself

as not enduring

(ll. 233–35)   To carry through the world those waves, which bore
The reflex of my City in their depths.

What was the status of this lost reflection, for the memory of which
the waves become the medium? The poem's reference to it here recalls, in
both vocabulary and structure, its earlier account of Atlantis, "whom the
waves / Have buried deep" (ll. 22–23). The moment the spirit of Fable here
represents as the lost object repeats another moment by which the poem
represented the loss of a *prior* object. To the extent that the river may be
read as figuring a discourse that is always situated in time, these two
moments are in fact congruent; both figure by a city's engulfment the
situation of the object signified by a discourse that always constitutes what
it signifies as temporally prior to it. The logic of such a discourse dictates
that what it signifies is always figured as lost.

Clearly, however, this reading of the river in the spirit of Fable's
speech as a figure for the temporality of legend—a sort of narrative of
narrative—is incomplete. If the river exists as a spatial metaphor for the
temporal displacement of language, it is also a surface that reflects an
image. As such, it is part of a logic of representation from which temporality is specifically excluded. A reflection has no story—there is no
time between it and its original.

In fact, this doubleness of the figure of the river appears within it as a
problem. For if we accept the spatial displacement of the river's waters as a

metaphorical representation of the displacement of language through time, then the inapplicability of this metaphor to reflection appears in the fact that a reflection, of course, does not move with the water in which it appears but remains where it is, in a place constituted as such only by virtue of the reflection's relation to its original. If the reflection in this passage remains where it is, of what does the text record the loss?

The spirit asserts that the river buries itself because it cannot endure "To carry through the world those waves, which bore / The reflex of my City in their depths" (ll. 234–35). The text's figure for that place where the loss of the reflection is specifically registered is one of *depth*. Again, this figure poses a problem. For a reflection, except in a certain specialized sense, does not have depth; it is on the contrary a phenomenon of the surface, constituted in the liminal plane that divides one substance from another.

In the double reading we have been giving it, the figure of the river is another staging of the split that constitutes the subject in "Armageddon" and "Timbuctoo." Like the surface of the eye, the surface of the river here brings an image into being in a place that is liminal to the movement of a discourse, in which the image can only be signified as the site of a loss. In this reading, the passage is an elaborated figure for the absolute separation that prevails between the place of the eye, or the moment of the look, and the place and time of the signifier. What signifies the subject's look in these texts is always lost to the eye—that is why the river here buries itself in a blind alley.

Notwithstanding the split implied between the place of a reflection and the depth of the medium on whose surface it is produced, the spirit asserts that the waves of the river "bore" the city's reflection in their depths (l. 235). Although a phenomenon of the surface, reflection nonetheless opens up to the eye what is known as a virtual space, coextensive with the space occupied by the medium on which it appears. The reflection of the city will appear only to the eye of someone looking on from a specific position above the river; only from that position will its virtual space appear to be borne in the river's depths. This is the position that the poet is here invited to assume: "Seest thou yon river . . . ?" (l. 225).

Implicit in this passage, then, is a moment in which the reflection of the city becomes the river's burden, or in which the place of the eye would coincide with the place of the signifier. This moment has no place for the subject and no time in its history; it constitutes the field of the Other. The poet is invited to assume a position from which he can see what the Other sees and from which, but only after the fact, he can see the signifier that lets him know that the Other did indeed see.

> Lo! How he [the river] passeth by,
> And gulphs himself in sands, as not enduring
> To carry through the world those waves, which bore
> The reflex of my City in their depths.

(ll. 232–35)

The knowledge that the reflection is somehow recorded in the depths of the river, that it becomes a signifier for another subject, is derived from the phenomenon that, later, the river buries itself.[22] The signifier that allows the subject to know in retrospect that the Other has seen is here the river's engulfment in the sand—in fact, the Other's very blindness.

Through the mediation of the signifier, the poet in this passage encounters another subject, whose time, however, he has already missed. This missed encounter will define for us the subject's experience of the Other.

Here the missed encounter is mediated by the gaze. This passage invites the poet to see Timbuctoo as the gaze's object, from the place in which the Other sees it—even if he recognizes the invitation too late, as he awakens to the knowledge that the signifier that constitutes the gaze remains in the field of the Other, where it can be read only as signifying loss. It is because the city appears as the object of the gaze that the poet is invited to see it only in reflection, as it would appear from another place, which becomes for him, before he can reply to this invitation, the place of the Other.

Moreover, it is as the object of the gaze that Timbuctoo becomes a woman, and the object of the male desire that Freud, in the passage I quoted earlier, facetiously calls "home-sickness."[23] The city is the "glorious home" of Fable (l. 239). Its depths—which in an earlier passage opened an epistemological crisis according to whose logic the subject's eye pursued a center that always just eluded it—are here by a false figure made to coincide with the depths of the river, which I have read as figuring the knowledge of the Other. In its reflection the city's depths appear as filled up. And the motif of the hanging object, which earlier figured the momentary arrest of a metonymic chain of contiguous objects, reappears in the "Pagods hung with music of sweet bells" (l. 230), not in a relation of contiguity to that from which it hangs, but as filling it with sound.

This passage thus describes the constitution of the object of desire, in a missed encounter with the gaze, as the gaze's object. But it also describes the institution of the gaze as a signifier in the field of the Other. That is why the poet's desire in this text, insofar as it must be mediated by the signifier, runs after it into a blind alley; because the gaze in this poem always looks at another place, in another time, what the eye sees is never "home." For this reason, the eye appears at the end of the spirit of Fable's speech in the disembodied form of "keen *Discovery*" (l. 240), and arrives too late to see the glorious city, which it transforms into a set of marks that only signify to it its own homelessness.

This is the narrative of disappointed expectations that organizes Tennyson's account of Timbuctoo. I have tried to show, however, that the desire of the eye is instituted in his text in a moment that can appear in narrative only as a missed encounter, or as an encounter that is missed by narrative as such, which stands in relation to it as the river stands to the reflection that appears on its surface.

I want now to argue that in "Timbuctoo"—and in certain related texts as well—Tennyson's principal figure for the encounter with the gaze is memory. I have already noted the peculiarity of the opening lines of the poem, where memory appears not as the agent but as the object of a certain nostalgia. We may now specify this nostalgia a little further as a nostalgia for something that has been lost to narrative—that is to say, for Atlantis or a Paradise in the West as something of which one could say, "Once, I could have gone there, even if I can no longer." It is a nostalgia that is articulated from the position of someone who knows that Atlantis and the paradisiacal islands in the West were always fictions, or effects of the signifier, which never had a place in the subject's own narrative time. Memory is in one sense the name Tennyson gives to the agency that once represented these places which now turn out to be irreducible to his narrative. More characteristically, however, memory is a metonymy that designates the places themselves; it is in this sense that Tennyson writes of Atlantis as having been "A centred glory-circled Memory" (l. 21).

The motif of the glory, or nimbus, which appears in this line is elaborated at greater length in the lines that invoke the Islands of the Blessed:

> Where are the infinite ways . . .
> Whose lowest deeps were, as with visible love,
> Filled with Divine effulgence, circumfused,
> Flowing between the clear and polished stems,
> And ever circling round their emerald cones
> In coronals and glories, such as gird
> The unfading foreheads of the Saints in Heaven?
> For nothing visible, they say, had birth
> In that blest ground but it was played about
> With its peculiar glory.

(ll. 46–56)

We find in these lines the figure of the full depth that I have discussed in the context of the closing lines of the poem; here the islands' depths are filled "as with visible love" by a divine effulgence, which we may describe as condensing into the glories that surround everything that is visible.

There is an insistent connection in these lines between the glory and the notion of the visible. Glories both surround everything that is visible and themselves appear as making visible something that, like love, is not normally so. As an optical phenomenon, a nimbus may surround either a luminescent object seen through a refractive medium or a nonluminescent object that is lit from a source not visible to the observer. In its earliest appearances in Christian iconography, which derive from Greek and Roman art, the glory surrounds only representations of the persons of the Trinity and may be interpreted as figuring the divine light proceeding from them. Somewhat later, representations of the Virgin Mary and of the saints began also to be adorned with glories, which require a somewhat different reading. Tennyson's text certainly represents the glories that surround everything in the Western islands, as well as those that surround the saints, as deriving, not from a light shining out of the objects they encircle, but from a light that shines on them from somewhere else. This light, the "Divine effulgence" (l. 49), is typologically the light of God's eye, of which the glory is then the visible sign.

The nostalgia of these lines, and implicitly also that of the description of Atlantis as a "glory-circled Memory" (l. 21), is directed toward a moment in which the humanly visible world was also visible to God. And, it is in relation to a god who does not see that Tennyson constructs his poem's most highly charged figure for memory's loss. He describes how men cling to Atlantis and Eldorado as memories,

> As when in some great City where the walls
> Shake, and the streets with ghastly faces thronged
> Do utter forth a subterranean voice,
> Among the inner columns far retired
> At midnight, in the lone Acropolis,
> Before the awful Genius of the place
> Kneels the pale Priestess in deep faith, the while
> Above her head the weak lamp dips and winks
> Unto the fearful summoning without:
> Nathless she ever clasps the marble knees,
> Bathes the cold hand with tears, and gazeth on
> Those eyes which wear no light but that wherewith
> Her phantasy informs them.

(ll. 28–40)

I have argued that the subject's look is constituted as giving something up to the Other in a moment that, possessing a certain rhythm, is for that reason all the more without a story. But I also argued that this figuration of the look in "Armageddon" is nonetheless at certain moments made to authorize a narrative, which I identified with the narrative of the Law. What enabled this transfiguration was a projection, in which the blind spot that the eye gives to the Other appeared in the field of the object as the signifying lack that authorizes the Law's story. I do not intend to privilege either of these figurations over the other; inasmuch as the function and position of the eye are unthinkable outside the logic of projection, we cannot represent it in terms of the first of them without being implicated in the second. This fact gives the body of texts I have been discussing their peculiar instability and inconclusiveness.

Here I have been centrally preoccupied with the narrative that "Timbuctoo" assigns to what it represents as the object of the gaze. This narrative should be identified with what I have just called the narrative of the Law; it takes its departure from the construction of the woman as such and traces her transformation from a home into a mark on a surface. Most remarkable, however, is the poem's insistence on the fictitiousness of this narrative. My reading has tried to show how Tennyson's text makes the woman the object of the gaze and its mediator for the subject; but I have also shown with what specificity the text exposes this figuration as a fiction, and the narrative which proceeds from it as one that derives from a moment that for the subject has always been missed.

Earlier I suggested that the rhythm of contraction and dilation according to which Tennyson figures the moment of the look in "Armageddon" constructs the subject as marking the time of the Other. This representation of the subject I aligned with the subject of the uncanny. The place of the Other in this view would be constituted in the place from which these marks might be read, and read once and for all, in a time when it would not be necessary to repeat them.

I would like now to return to the last passage quoted from "Timbuctoo," for I wish to argue that it is unreadable from the place and time of the subject in a sense that may help to explain the unreadability of the rhythm to which I have just referred. This description of a catastrophe striking a city is paradigmatic for the catastrophes that overtake the other cities in the poem—Atlantis, Eldorado, Timbuctoo itself—and thus for the loss of what it calls memory. These lines are also an allegory of waking. In a city at midnight something begins to breach the walls. Voices are heard from underground, and the temple lamp, which we may read as figure for the nocturnal illumination of the dream, "dips and winks" (l. 35).

If this passage allegorizes the breaking of sleep and of the dream, it does so from within the dream itself. The subject that wakes is not yet present to itself as awake. That is why the voices that break into the city's sleep still speak from underground, why the faces that throng its streets still appear ghastly, or spectral, and why the light still burns, albeit fittully, at its center. This passage, then, records a dream of waking, like the one that Freud analyzes in chapter 7 of *The Interpretation of Dreams* as manifesting the desire to go on sleeping (*SE* 5:509–10).[24]

Such a dream poses the question What wakes us? We wake *to* an alarm, to a voice, to a knocking at the gate, but the agency of our waking remains inaccessible in our dream. What would Tennyson's subterranean voices have said if the dreamer in this passage had remained asleep to hear them? This question can never be answered, because they are in their essence precisely what wakes the subject up. For the subject, these voices will remain perpetually underground.

When we wake, we pull ourselves together. We know that now we are awake, whilst then we were dreaming; if we are so inclined we may remember our dreams and subject them to analysis. But in this dream there appears something that remains irreducible to this pulling together because it does not answer either to the wishes of the dreamer or to the objects to which the dreamer awakes.

This moment of the breaching of the dream is in Tennyson's text the fullest representation of what I have been describing as the moment of the missed encounter. If the moment of the rift in the eye institutes what is given to the Other in the field of spatial representation, this, I would argue, is a corresponding moment with respect to time. The moment of waking is a mark in the subject's time that is legible only from elsewhere.

It is remembered, however, as a loss. When the dreamer in Tennyson's text wakes up—if the dreamer may be said to be *in* this passage, in which he is not yet present—something seems to remain behind in the dream, even if it appeared in the dream itself only as its breach. I would argue that this is the moment that "Timbuctoo" tropes as memory, which it constitutes always in retrospect, nostalgically, as a moment before the poet thought of his own time as discontinuous with the time of the dream.

The situation of this memory, which for the waking subject symbolizes that moment in the dream that can only be figured as loss, is inscribed in Tennyson's figure of the pale priestess. In the elaborate metaphor that organizes this passage, her "deep faith" (l. 34) figures man's faith in the memories of Atlantis and Eldorado. The structure of infinite regress I have discussed in the poem's representation of memory, however, makes her situation a double one. For as a personification of what under the name of memory is figured as lost, she stands at the center of the city and will suffer whatever catastrophe its waking visits upon it. But as a personification of that waking agency for which memory's object is figured as lost, she herself wakes and tries to rouse to wakefulness a god who nonetheless remains in sleep.

This figure ends by establishing for the poet a position of knowledge. He knows that the god the priestess seeks to wake has never woken; she herself will in consequence be lost along with her city. In this double sense, his knowledge is founded on a woman's loss. But as we have seen, that loss tropes a moment, or an agency, which is irreducible to the field of knowledge and which continually recurs. That is why the woman whose loss weaves it into knowledge must never sleep. Even in the place of the dream she wakes, since she must represent what breaches the dream to the waking subject. Her insomnia is the price this poem pays for knowledge. In this respect her function prefigures that of the women we shall discuss in the next chapter—Mariana, the Lady of Shalott, and the Hesperides— insomniacs all, whose insomnia defends a particular space against something it could not accommodate.

III

The concern with memory that we have traced in Tennyson's transformation of "Armageddon" into "Timbuctoo" is apparent in a number of other poems and manuscript fragments written around the same time, 1827–30. One thinks of the "Recollections of the Arabian Nights," and the "Ode: O Bosky Brook," of "In deep and solemn dreams," of the manuscript fragment "Memory [Ay me!]," and of *The Lover's Tale,* the long unfinished narrative poem that Tennyson worked on in 1827–28 and at intervals subsequently until 1833. Many of these texts assign to memory the same double status it had in "Timbuctoo," where it designates both a place that is lost and that which represents that loss to the poet. In many of these texts, too, this double status is dramatized in the person of a woman.

Thus in the "Ode to Memory" that Tennyson published in 1830, we find that the figure of Memory is divided in two. On the one hand the poet calls upon her to return to him like the morning and illuminate the darkness in which he finds himself, while on the other it turns out that this darkness is itself brought on by Memory's appearance in another guise:

Strengthen me, enlighten me!
I faint in this obscurity,
Thou dewy dawn of memory.

(ll. 5–11)

II

Come not as thou camest of late,
Flinging the gloom of yesternight
On the white day; but robed in softened light
Of orient state

Memory is invoked here as a figure who brings illumination when she appears at night but who, as she appears to the waking poet during the day, darkens his sight.

As Tennyson abandoned the mode of "Armageddon," a poem that from its very inception seemed to mark for him as a dead end the totalizing gestures that resolve the High Romantic sublime, the moment of waking becomes in his poetry the characteristic figure for the establishment of the subject as one who sees. And always, the eye awakens as owing a certain debt—the figure is from the "Ode to Memory":

Large dowries doth the raptured eye
(ll. 72–74)   To the young spirit present
When first she is wed.

When the eye is joined to the spirit, it yields something up—and becomes a woman. Sometimes that debt is a crippling one and the poet awakens only to darkness and to a sense of nostalgia, as indeed at the opening of this ode and at the end of "Timbuctoo," and in certain passages of *In Memoriam*.

But elsewhere the moment of waking is eroticized under the characteristically Tennysonian figure of the glimmer. In a number of later texts—such as "Tithonus," the "Conclusion" to *The Princess,* and the lyric "Now Sleeps the Crimson Petal"—the flash of light we have analyzed in "Armageddon" is revised as a half-light that makes things, not more, but less distinct. It illuminates a moment in which only the poet wakes, while the rest of the world is asleep, and in which the peculiar evanescence of the objects before his eye, which seem to shimmer and to flit away at the edges of his field of sight, appears as a visible sign that no one else sees them. The light of the dawn—or of the moon, when the poet wakes alone at night—marks, in a mark that is not a mark, the sleep of the Other and illuminates the moment of a peculiarly Tennysonian eroticism.

We shall return later to this figure in a reading of "Tithonus." I want now to turn to a poem that joins the moment of waking to that of the end of the world in a way that sums up this chapter. The text is short enough to be quoted in full:

The Kraken

Below the thunders of the upper deep;
Far, far beneath in the abysmal sea,
His ancient, dreamless, uninvaded sleep
The Kraken sleepeth: faintest sunlights flee
About his shadowy sides: above him swell
Huge sponges of millennial growth and height;
And far away into the sickly light,
From many a wondrous grot and secret cell
Unnumbered and enormous polypi
Winnow with giant arms the slumbering green.
There hath he lain for ages and will lie
Battening upon huge seaworms in his sleep,
Until the latter fire shall heat the deep;
Then once by man and angels to be seen,
In roaring he shall rise and on the surface die.

The Kraken in this text has generally been rather vaguely read as a
figure for repression (Ryals, *Theme and Symbol,* 66; Lourie, 11); indeed, as
it grows and incorporates other creatures hidden in the half-light, it recalls
Freud's descriptions of the way the repressed wish, as it seeks expression,
attracts to itself the libido originally attached to other objects than its own,
with the usual result that this libido too falls under repression.[25] But if we
accept this reading, we need to turn it on its head and argue that what is
repressed here is repression as such—or, to put it in other terms—that this
text is not an instance of the proliferation of tropes that opens the sublime
but of the negation of trope, or of the negative sublime.

The Kraken represents the systematic denial of all those differences,
splits, and turnings away that I have argued in this chapter constitute the
Tennysonian subject. Its time is unmarked by waking, and even its sleep is
"uninvaded" by dreams (l. 3). Perhaps most uncannily, it does not wake to
eat, thereby denying what is perhaps the child's most elementary experience of the time it lives as a time that is not its own.

But the Kraken is figured as unmarked not only in terms of the
poem's representation of its time. The surface of its body bears none of
those rifts that situate the part-objects that serve the subject as signifiers.
Because it neither sees nor is seen, the Kraken is not subject to the logic of
the gaze. Nor, one might argue, does it have a mouth, since it feeds by
"battening upon huge seaworms" (l. 12), in a process that is described in
terms that designate growth without suggesting ingestion. Certainly, the

absence of eyes and mouth would explain the indistinctness of the limits of the Kraken's body—its "shadowy sides" (l. 5)—for the difference between what is seen and what is eaten must have a peculiar force for the small child in marking the difference between what is inside and what is outside its body.[26] Indeed, in its representation of the sponges that grow over the Kraken and of the seafloor, with its grottoes and cells, the poem displays a recurrent concern with structures that show no distinction between inside and outside; their interiors are conceived only as involutions of their exterior surfaces.

If the Kraken is represented in this poem as exempt from the elementary structures that establish the place and time of the subject in the Symbolic, these structures nonetheless appear with a vengeance at the poem's conclusion. The Kraken will wake to be seen—and to be seen moreover on a surface—as what has been hidden beneath it in the depths. In a certain sense, then, this text is an allegory of entry into the Symbolic order, in which the Kraken's sleep would figure as a deeply nostalgic representation of the body before its subjection to the logic of the signifier.

In another sense, however, the Kraken occupies a position in this text analogous to that of the "subterranean voice" (l. 30) in "Timbuctoo"— which is ultimately also that of all the other buried or submerged objects we saw in that text. It is the position of the object that can appear in history only as lost, or in the Kraken's case, like the subterranean voice's, under the sign of death. The Kraken wakes, furthermore, to a history that has unfolded for ages over its sleep, as a mark of that history's limit. This double reading of the Kraken opens to question a concept we have perhaps taken too much for granted—that of the mark. The Kraken may be read as a representation of the mark as that which itself has not been marked. Here it signifies because, although it appears only once, it has been sleeping— marking time—all along. But as Freud's essay on the uncanny implies, the mark can only be constituted as such by its iteration. Writing on Freud, Jacques Derrida has written that "to be a mark and to mark its marking effect, a mark must be capable of being *identified,* recognized as the same, being precisely *re-markable* from one context to another. It must be capable of being repeated, re-marked in its essential trait as the same. This accounts for the apparent solidity of its structure, of its type. . . . This iterability is thus that which allows a mark to be used more than once. It is more than one. It multiplies and divides itself internally" ("My Chances," 16).

"The Kraken" expresses a wish that the mark would awaken only once—that it was not always the mark of a prior awakening.

II

The Place of Voice

With its ability to scan through a complete list of phonetic transcriptions in a matter of minutes, the computer is an incomparably more versatile rhymester than the live poet with his dying brain cells and deteriorating memory.

(Rosalind Fergusson, Introduction to *The Penguin Rhyming Dictionary*)

I

The Skipping-Rope

Sure never yet was Antelope
　　Could skip so lightly by.
Stand off, or else my skipping-rope
　　Will hit you in the eye.
How lightly whirls the skipping-rope!
　　How fairy-like you fly!
Go, get you gone, you muse and mope—
　　I hate that silly sigh.
Nay, dearest, teach me how to hope,
　　or tell me how to die.
There, take it, take my skipping-rope,
　　And hang yourself thereby.

"The Skipping-Rope" was among the new poems Tennyson published in 1842, and it continued to appear in editions of his poems until 1850, after which it was not reprinted in his lifetime. A reader of the first edition who for some reason took the trouble could have deduced from the pronouns that the poem represents a dialogue between a skipping woman and her somewhat listless suitor; in the modern standard edition this deduction is confirmed by a headnote that quotes an unpublished draft beginning "While Annie whirled the skipping-rope, / Said Harry standing by . . ." (*Poems* 2:85). But the main source of the poem's nervous good humor cannot thus be found from internal evidence. For Ricks's headnote also tells us that Tennyson wrote the poem in the end of his copy of John Walker's *Rhyming Dictionary* and that he took his rhymes in *ope* from its index.

The index to Walker's *Dictionary* consists simply of lists of rhyme words, alphabetically arranged, without even the sketchy definitions included in the main body of the work. It thus appears to generate language without discourse by a process of purely mechanical differentiation. In so doing, it subverts any assumption that sense precedes language, in a way that seems to have driven Tennyson to produce "The Skipping-Rope" as a half-joking reaction. As such, the poem claims to naturalize the alphabetic series of the dictionary by supplying for its rhyme words the context necessary to reoriginate them in the dialogue and in the play of desire between its two characters.

Ricks's headnote aptly cites Tennyson's much later reply to the question of Francis Turner Palgrave: "Did he ever use a rhyming dictionary? He had tried it in earlier days, but found it of little use: 'There was no natural congruity between the rhymes thus alphabetically grouped together' " (*Memoir* 2:496). The appeal here to a category of naturally congruous rhymes is an odd one. What kind of rhymes would these be? Behind this appeal lies another, not to an empty category of natural rhymes, but to a category of rhymes produced by the poetic imagination, which Tennyson wants to endow with a power of *conferring* naturalness denied the purely mechanical production of the dictionary.

Such an appeal is implicit in Tennyson's practice in "The Skipping-Rope." Here, in spite of choosing his rhymes arbitrarily from a dictionary, he succeeds in producing something like poetic discourse by displacing his sense of their incongruousness onto the characters who speak them. Hence the poem's pairing of a skipping, antelopelike woman with a mopey, would-be hopeful lover. The poem thus naturalizes the mechanical production of difference in its rhymes, but only at the cost of a preoccupation with sexual difference. The proliferation of different rhymes in *ope* (and in *oop, op,* and *up,* which Walker lists as "allowable rhymes" [338] for *ope*) is resolved into what is, in this context, a much more reassuring scenario of tension between different sexes.

We shall see later how the process of displacement that is wittily, if defensively, foregrounded in "The Skipping-Rope" is in more veiled forms powerfully at work in many of Tennyson's greatest early treatments of sexual tension. But first let us consider further what could be meant by the whirling of the skipping-rope itself, the figure that opens and closes the play of sexual difference. It does so, moreover, as itself an image of play; and as such it has two specific characteristics particularly worth noting here. One is that it is repeated; the other is that its repetitions enclose a space for a playing woman, in which she can remain, though continually at risk, for as long as her agility will sustain her there.

Different kinds of enclosed space are a recurring motif in Tennyson's early poetry, and, like the space enclosed by the whirling of the skipping-rope, they are characteristically constituted by repetition or doubling and usually more or less at risk. They are frequently inhabited by women, as in "The Hesperides," "The Lady of Shalott," and "Mariana." Even in early poems less obviously akin to "The Skipping-Rope," Tennyson tends to represent interior space as somehow constituted by doubling. This seems to be so in texts as diverse as, for instance, "The Two Voices," in which the double appears as a threat, and as "O Darling Room," with its mysterious second bed.

In "The Skipping-Rope," moreover, repetition does not simply constitute space but specifically the space of the subject at the origin of discourse. The play of the skipping woman in the poem may be read as a figure for Tennyson's own play with rhyme. I have suggested that anxiety about the proliferation of difference in the rhyming dictionary was the poem's occasion; this anxiety generates the energy it invests in representations of autoeroticism and repetition. The poem's own rhymes thus transform the dictionary's mechanical production into repetition, as the word *skipping-rope* itself returns to rhyme with itself three times.

The play of the skipping-rope in this text figures the play with rhyme that opens out the space of the speaking subject. In so doing, however, it figures it not just as repetition but as repetition without articulation. There is no mark between any one of the rope's turns and the next; its trajectory could only be sounded as a string of vowels—*o o o o o*. This figuration shows what is at issue in its appearance here, for the articulation it denies is one of the elemental forms of linguistic difference. Derrida has written that articulation is "the becoming-writing of language"; and he goes on to argue that this "becoming" does not come after the origin of language but is on the contrary constitutive of it:

(Of Gram-
matology
229, 232)

Language could have emerged only out of dispersion. The "natural causes" by which one explains it are not recognized as natural except in so far as they accord with the state of nature, which is determined by dispersion. This dispersion should no doubt be overcome by language but,

for that very reason, it determines the natural condition *of language. . . .
In truth, dispersion will never be a past, a prelinguistic situation in which
language would certainly have been born only to break with it. The
original dispersion leaves its mark within language . . . : articulation,
which seemingly introduces difference as an institution, has for ground
and space the dispersion that is natural: space itself.*

We have already seen how the play of the woman's skipping-rope
figures a play of rhyme in which difference would not occupy the originary and constitutive position it had in the dictionary but would be subordinate to a notion of natural congruity predicated on the continuity of poetic
discourse. The passage just quoted from Derrida suggests that the play of
rhyme can achieve this naturalization only when difference has been
effaced at its origin in space itself; hence this poem's fantasy of a space
without dispersion or difference, enclosed by the whirling of the skipping-
rope. Such a space can, however, only be a fantasy, as indeed many of
Tennyson's early poems show. In "The Lady of Shalott" the space of the
subject at the origin of discourse turns into a space *within* the subject, while
in "The Two Voices" the dream of the subject's hearing its own speech has
become a nightmare in which it is constituted as two voices radically at
odds. Even in the present relatively sketchy text, the skipping-rope,
initially a figure for an idealized repetition enclosing a space without
difference, eventually, when repetition has been breached, introduces a
threat of hanging—a return of articulation that would be final.

In this reading, the poem represents the discourse of two kinds of
desire, the relations between which are ambivalent. The man's desire is
for the woman constituted as other; like the poem as a whole, his
discourse exists in the space opened up by sexual difference. The
woman's desire, on the contrary, is for a self that is constituted by
repetition, figured in the whirling of the skipping-rope. If the uneasy
intensity of the poem's representation of sexual difference is determined
by the casting-out of difference from language, its representation of
autoaffectionate play is a figure for the language thus produced. What
"The Skipping-Rope" can show us is that these two kinds of discourse
are related as, respectively, the anxious and the wishful versions of the
same fantasy. But the displacements and suppressions that produce them
here can also be found under various elaborations and revisions as the
necessary preconditions of discourse in some of Tennyson's most powerful early poetry, where indeed the play of autoeroticism and sexual
difference is a recurrent theme.

II

If "The Skipping-Rope's" appeal for the critic is founded on the evidence we have for its origin, the perhaps more respectable appeal of "The Hesperides" has a lot to do with its impenetrability. In the song of Hesperus' daughters, Tennyson produces discourse whose function is not to open out meaning but to protect a mystery. In a very literal sense, this is a poem against dispersion; Hanno, hearing the Hesperides' song, sails on by without paying attention. Language, as Tennyson represents it, is not a commodity for export—and the question of trade is relevant to this text, for the historical Hanno was a Phoenician, a member of the most active trading nation of the ancient world.

The possibility "The Hesperides" refuses, that the golden apples could be taken from the garden and made into objects of exchange or signifiers, Tennyson describes in "Œnone," a poem contemporary with "The Hesperides" in which he tells the story of the judgment of Paris. Here, the golden apple has become an index of desire, inscribed with the words "For the most fair," which Paris is to award to one of three goddesses. The story's catastrophe is Paris's choice of Aphrodite, for which she rewards him with Helen, whose abduction leads to the Trojan War.

The poem is narrated by Paris's first love, the nymph Œnone. She speaks on the slopes of Mount Ida, where the judgment took place, and addresses the mountain as her mother. Her narrative is framed as an extended lament over Paris's desertion; and, such is the closeness of her relation to the landscape in which she speaks, that in her account of his transgression, it becomes virtually a transgression against the landscape and against nature itself. At the end of the poem Œnone describes the ruin of the glen where she stands to fix the blame for it on the golden apple and on the goddess of strife, who had maliciously first produced it as a prize:

> I wish that somewhere in the ruined folds,
> Among the fragments tumbled from the glens,
> Or the dry thickets, I could meet with her
> The Abominable, that uninvited came
> Into the Peleian banquet-hall,
> And cast the golden fruit upon the board,
> And bred this change.

(ll. 217–23)

The golden apple introduces transgression against the natural because it represents the differential, denatured structure of desire and, more generally, the fact of writing. In the scene of Paris's judgment, desire is not naturally attached to its object but is constituted as a written sign, referring only to other signs, and available for arbitrary exchange. The goddesses thus compete, not to induce the affect of desire in Paris, but to possess the apple, which signifies that affect. And Paris, seeing nothing odd in this, does not adjudicate between the goddesses but among the gifts—of power, wisdom, and love—they offer him in exchange for it. The question of which goddess is actually—naturally—the fairest is not possible here; fairness becomes a quality constituted as possession of the apple bearing the inscription "For the most fair." For all the participants in the judgment, the apple as signifier usurps, replaces, the affect of desire or the quality of desirability it claims only to represent. Similarly, if from the perspective of Paris, Helen is the ultimate object of desire in this scene, she too is represented by a formula constituted as pure difference: "The fairest and most loving wife in Greece" (l. 183). Like the desire of the goddesses, Paris's desire can define its object only as the sign of value, or only in terms of exchange with other objects.

This proliferation of difference in "Œnone" is introduced by writing in the form of an inscription on the golden apple; it ends in the Trojan War, which Cassandra foresees at the poem's conclusion: "A fire dances before her, and a sound / Rings ever in her ears of armèd men" (ll. 260–61). But in "The Hesperides" the apple is uninscribed; and the catastrophe that is to result from its inscription is part of the world the sisters shut out of their garden: "The world is wasted with fire and sword, / But the apple of gold hangs over the sea" (ll. 104–5). The poem represents a fantasy of the sign before writing, which is to say of meaning and value without difference, as categories in a nature that they would constitute, rather than as arbitrary and exchangeable marks upon a nature that always, as in "Œnone," vanishes beneath them.

Like "The Skipping-Rope," then, "The Hesperides" defends the possibility of naturalized language against the proliferation of difference. In an important essay, G. R. Stange has seen that the poem's principal theme is the relation of the production of the Hesperides' song to the growth of the fruit on their tree. He quotes at length from the first section of their song, ending with the lines:

> For the blossom unto threefold music bloweth;
> Evermore it is born anew;
> And the sap to threefold music floweth,
> From the root

(ll. 30–37)

> Drawn in the dark,
> Up to the fruit,
> Creeping under the fragrant bark,
> Liquid gold, honeysweet, through and through.

Stange comments on this passage that "the conception by which the burgeoning of the fruit depends on the charmed music of the Hesperides and they, in turn, draw their vitality and find the source of their song in the root and the tree, is a figure of the connection among the artist, his art, and his inspiration." Later, this connection becomes a unity: "The root, the bole, and the fruit are the elements of a living unity . . . [that] not only symbolizes the process of growth and the nature of artistic creation, but also suggests the ancient distinctions among body, soul, and spirit, as well as the organic principle of multiplicity in unity" (Stange, 103, 108–9). And in fact, living unity is the implicit subject of the first of Stange's claims as well as of the second. In his initial account, the unity of the tree and the fruit is constituted in the Hesperides' song, which he paradoxically identifies with both. In his analysis, the song both grows out of the tree like the fruit and fosters the growth of the fruit like the natural vitality of the tree.

What is at issue in the poem as Stange reads it is thus not so much the notion of a language whose living unity is derived by analogy with nature as that of a language whose undifferentiated unity constitutes it as the natural. As Stange sees, what grows naturally in the garden of the Hesperides is language; it is, in his terms, a "garden of art." His analysis goes on, however, to transform this insight into a discussion of Tennyson's views on the morality of art. For him, the poem is finally an "assertion of a desire to retreat from purposive moral activity" (Stange, 111); and it is this moralized reading that has established the terms in which much of the subsequent discussion of the poem has taken place.[1]

It should by now be possible to evolve a more sophisticated account than Stange's of the determinants of what is, after all, a rather stranger text than his reading allows. If "The Hesperides" is like "The Skipping-Rope" in defending a fantasy of naturalized language, it does so, also like "The Skipping-Rope," by producing language as autoerotic repetition. Indeed, the erotic charge that the Hesperides' song attaches to the regularity of its own rhythm, and its insistence on the sleeplessness of its singers, give it the quality of a masturbatory fantasy:

> If ye sing not, if ye make false measure,
> (ll. 23–25)   We shall lose eternal pleasure,
> Worth eternal want of rest.

The same quality extends, moreover, to the poem's representation of the production of language in the growth of the golden fruit, which also fairly clearly figures masturbatory activity—let me recall the passage that Stange quotes:

> the sap to threefold music floweth,
>
> From the root
>
> Drawn in the dark,
>
> Up to the fruit,
>
> Creeping under the fragrant bark,
>
> Liquid gold, honeysweet, through and through.

(ll. 32–37)

In connection with this poem, it is worth noting Stephen Marcus's analysis of the economic basis of Victorian fantasies about masturbation, in which he takes as an exemplary text William Acton's *The Functions and Disorders of the Reproductive Organs* (1857). He concludes his discussion of Acton on adolescent masturbation as follows:

> *[According to Acton,] in the masturbating boy, "the large expenditure of semen, has exhausted the vital force." The continent boy, however, has "not expended that vital fluid, semen, or exhausted his nervous energy, and his youthful vigor has been employed for its legitimate purpose, namely, in building up his growing frame." . . . The fantasies that are at work here have to do with economics; the body is regarded as a productive system with only a limited amount of material at its disposal. And the model on which the notion of semen is formed is clearly that of money. Science, in the shape of Acton, is thus still expressing what had for long been a popular fantasy: up until the end of the nineteenth century the chief English colloquial expression for the orgasm was "to spend." . . . Furthermore, the economy envisaged in this idea is based on scarcity and has as its aim the accumulation of its own product.*

(Marcus, 21–22)

Against this background we can see in the perpetual generation of "liquid gold" and in the delight that "Hoarded wisdom" (ll. 37, 48) brings in Tennyson's garden the record of what Marcus would describe as a fantasy of unlimited production that bears nonetheless the traces of a strong prohibition against masturbation.

The possibility that the song includes material originating in auto-erotic fantasies is a useful one because it opens up an explanation, not only of its hothouse eroticism, but also of the sense that this eroticism depends upon the fantasized evasion of a taboo. It is explicit throughout that the song and the pleasure it produces require secrecy—that "Out of watching, out of wiles, / Comes the bliss of secret smiles" (ll. 77–78). Oddly enough, one of the powerful defenders of this secrecy seems to be the father, who is repeatedly exhorted to "watch, watch, night and day" (l. 68). In this respect, as in others, Father Hesper is the wishful inverse of the father we all suppose ourselves to have in childhood. Instead of being a continuously watching figure who prevents his children from gratifying their desires, he is here a watcher entirely subject to their will, whose attention and whose wrath they can continuously direct away from them. The result of this inversion is that the father becomes, within the garden, an aged and curiously insubstantial figure, characterized chiefly by his "silver hair" and "silver eye" (l. 44), who is apparently incapable of any action or speech that might even momentarily interrupt his daughters' continuous outpouring of song.

The anxiety induced by the autoerotic activity embodied in the Hesperides' song is not, however, entirely suppressed. It is rather cast out of the garden to reappear in displaced form in the disturbingly threatening imagery the singers use to describe the world outside. This world, they sing, is "wasted with fire and sword"; and their father is exhorted to watch specifically "lest the old wound of the world be healèd" (ll. 104, 69). It is hard not to see in this bizarre line an externalization of castration anxiety, which the autoeroticism invested in the song would at once defend against and intensify. In the most schematic reading, the song's repetitions and numerations would amount to the multiplication of phallic symbols and repeated assertions of the presence of the phallus that accompany the return of castration anxiety, while the "old wound," which the song itself sustains, would at once reassuringly externalize the threat of castration, while paradoxically implicating the song itself as the transgression with which it originates.

At this level, it should now be clear, the fantasy material in this text derives from a specifically male autoeroticism. Here, as in "The Skipping-Rope," Tennyson distances himself from his own wish to find autoerotic gratification in the production of language by displacing a representation of its fulfillment onto female characters. The greater elaboration of "The Hesperides" makes the nature of this displacement clearer than it was in "The Skipping-Rope," where less psychic material is engaged. In the masturbatory content of "The Hesperides" we can see some of the taboo material that makes such a displacement necessary.

We now need to ask how a text whose essential subject is language comes to be so powerfully overdetermined by masturbatory fantasies. It is certainly true that the fantasized economy of bodily fluids that, according to Marcus, organized Victorian notions of masturbation bears a marked affinity to the economy of the signifier as Tennyson represents it in "The Hesperides" and "Œnone." Both structures are constituted around fantasies of the natural origin of the sign; in the passage Marcus quotes from William Acton, semen is figured not simply as money but also as deriving its value from its specifically natural function of "building up [the] growing frame" rather than as the subject of dissemination and exchange. At work here are fantasies, not only about the function of semen, but about that of money as well.

Still, the availability of an analogy between contemporary wishes about the economy of the body and Tennyson's fantasy of the natural production of poetic discourse does not of itself explain why that analogy should have been so important in determining the text of "The Hesperides." To put it another way, it does not seem necessary that the wish to identify language as an autoerotic object, which we have already seen in "The Skipping-Rope," must necessarily be associated, as it is here, with a purely genital autoeroticism and with the taboo which that eroticism calls up.

I have argued that a central mechanism in the text's dealing with taboo material is its displacement of the consequent anxiety away from the place where this material is represented, in the song and garden of the Hesperides, and onto a world at large against which the song is specifically a defense. To pursue the question of why the notion of a taboo that has to be defended against appears here at all, I want to consider in more detail the poem's principal representation of this world outside the garden, in the character of Zidonian Hanno. Hanno has very little place in the canonical reading of the poem that was initiated by Stange's essay, and yet its account of his journey and of his swerve away from the voices that he hears is surely one of the strangest things about it.

In the *Periplus,* Tennyson's source for the explorer's name and itinerary—though not for an encounter with the Hesperides—Hanno sailed south along the west coast of Africa until he ran short of provisions, whereupon he turned around and returned to his starting point in Carthage. It is hard to imagine Tennyson's Hanno doing likewise. His journey to "the outer sea" (l. 13) sounds much more like that of Ulysses, who announces his purpose "To sail beyond the sunset, and the baths / Of all the western stars, until I die" ("Ulysses," 60–61). Moreover, the Dantean Ulysses, who took the journey Tennyson's character anticipates in these lines, followed a route very similar to Hanno's, sailing out beyond the Pillars of Hercules and then turning south. But that story ends, of course, with Ulysses' death when a vast wave overwhelms him and his ship.

The idea of death as a sea voyage into the west, which Tennyson found in Celtic mythology, as well as in Dante and Classical sources, seems to have held an enduring fascination for him. It figures not only in "Ulysses" but also in "Morte d'Arthur" and in *In Memoriam* 103, as well as in the late poem "Merlin and the Gleam" (1889). In "The Voyage of Maeldune" (1880), a similar voyage ends, not with the protagonist's own death, but with his reconciliation to his father's—a theme also implicit in "Ulysses," "Morte d'Arthur," and *In Memoriam,* each of which has at least partly at issue the son's response to the death of a father figure.[2] I want to argue that the account of Hanno's voyage in "The Hesperides" belongs to this group of texts. We have already seen that the song of the Hesperides is produced at the expense of the father within the garden; I want to show now that outside it, the attenuated figure of Hesper has his double in Hanno, in whose ambiguous fate the defensive measures necessary to produce the song find their fullest representation.

In the opening lines of the poem, Tennyson lists not only the places Hanno passed by on his journey but also, more oddly, the sounds he did not hear:

> The Northwind fallen, in the newstarrèd night
> Zidonian Hanno, voyaging beyond
> The hoary promontory of Soloë

(ll. 1–8)
> Past Thymiaterion, in calmèd bays,
> Between the southern and the western Horn,
> Heard neither warbling of the nightingale,
> Nor melody o'the Lybian lotusflute
> Blown seaward from the shore.

The catalog of place-names comes from the *Periplus,* but the sounds have a source closer to home. They refer in a concise shorthand to two of Keats's odes, "To a Nightingale" and "On a Grecian Urn," both written in the spring of 1819. In each of these odes, a wishful version of poetic inspiration is figured by one of the sounds to which Tennyson alludes—in the former, by the song of the nightingale, and in the latter, by the music of the piper represented on the urn as a "happy melodist, unwearied, / For ever piping songs for ever new" (ll. 23–24). In a loose paradox, the melodies Hanno does not hear recall the unheard melodies of the "Ode on a Grecian Urn."

If Tennyson records in this passage a swerve away from the figurations of Keats's spring odes, he attempts in the song of the Hesperides itself, which Hanno does hear, to achieve what Harold Bloom would call transumption of the later "To Autumn."[3] For "To Autumn" is itself a swerve away from the achievements of the spring of 1819. Keats wrote it that September, in a period when it seemed that he had not the means to continue writing poetry, and just as he was deciding that, for a second time, he would have to give up his plan for an epic on the Hyperion story. The poem is a crisis lyric, whose closest contemporary analogue is Shelley's "Ode to the West Wind," in which the poet works through a period of blockage to a renewal of the poetic gift. The question "Where are the songs of spring?" in "To Autumn" should, as Helen Vendler has implied (604–5), be read as Keats's nostalgia for the inspiration of the preceding April and May—a nostalgia that finds its rebuke in the lines which follow.

Hanno is Tennyson's version of the Keats of "To Autumn." Having passed the song of the nightingale and the music of the pipes, he hears, not the music of autumn, but the song of the Hesperides. For Hanno, the song is a phenomenon of the limit; it is the last thing he hears before he vanishes, for the purposes of the poem, into the "outer sea" (l. 13). And from Tennyson's point of view, the music of autumn which the Hesperides' song replaces was for Keats a phenomenon of the limit in a precisely analogous sense. In 1830 Tennyson could have known nothing of *The Fall of Hyperion,* and so for him, even more obviously than for us, "To Autumn" was the last great achievement of Keats's life. When in "The Hesperides" he came to write his own revisionary version of Keats's text, the liminal song of its final stanza consequently returned as a song marking the limit of Keats's own life.

Song actually is constituted in a liminal moment in "To Autumn"; it marks the limit, however, not of the poet's life, but of the figural proliferation of the poem's opening stanzas, and, if it comes to that, of Keats's own earlier poetry. The poem's first two stanzas have as their subject the overliteralization of figural language as a defense against time—an overliteralization that is most ironically represented by the bees at the end of the first stanza. The work of its third, and last, stanza is finally to reveal its earlier specificity of representation as an agent of blockage, as we discover when autumn's voice is finally released, and the stability and particularity of the scenes represented in the first part of the poem dissolve. If the opening stanzas seem to recoup something from the imminence of loss in the richness of present experience, in the last Keats finds that present experience is itself constituted as loss and that what has appeared as its richness was already a richness of figurality that in the final lines reaches its limit and the hidden source of its power.

In "The Hesperides" Tennyson takes his central image of the golden apple from the first part of "To Autumn." The fruit in his poem—which

(ll. 101–3)

> clustereth mellowly,
> Goldenkernelled, goldencored,
> Sunset-ripened above on the tree

—recognizably derives from the fruit filled "with ripeness to the core" of "To Autumn" (l. 6). But where in Keats the apple represents a figurality that claiming too much for itself, seems to block poetic utterance, in Tennyson, as we have seen, the apple stands for an utterance that precedes figurality. This naturalizing misreading of an ironically excessive figuration opens Tennyson's defense in "The Hesperides" against the voice at the end of "To Autumn," which constitutes itself as figurality's limit.

This revision seems to me the central determinant of the text of "The Hesperides." By its epigraph Tennyson's poem situates itself in the garden of "Hesperus, and his daughters three" to which the Attendant Spirit ascends at the end of *Comus,* where a limitless spring and summer are perpetually combined in a day that never ends (ll. 984–91). It is on Milton's figure for unending day, the sun that "never shuts his eye" (l. 978), that Tennyson tropes when he imagines the endless wakefulness of his Hesperides. But if the setting of his poem and its figuration of the Hesperides' apples as perpetually ripe echo Milton in seeming to exclude the notion of the liminal from the garden, the compelling influence of Keats nonetheless makes that notion his text's dominant obsession. The apple, which Milton doesn't mention, is itself an autumnal fruit. And Tennyson's poem insists that it grows at sunset, in a liminal moment:

(ll. 89–92)

> the western sun and the western star,
> And the low west wind, breathing afar,
> The end of day and the beginning of night
> Make the apple holy and bright.

The perpetual ripeness of the apple is a perpetual suspension in a liminal time and place.

The notion of the liminal that Tennyson's poem casts out of its representation of poetic discourse reappears in its characteristic figuration of the garden where language is produced as standing at the limit of something else. Hence the ambiguous ending of Hanno's voyage, which marks the garden as standing at the limit of the world. And hence the forebodings of apocalypse that pervade the poem's characterization of the world outside the garden—forebodings that are, moreover, themselves linked to its weird representation of its own discourse, the Hesperides' fruit, as preceding and constituting the limits of consciousness as that which can be known: "If the golden apple be taken / The world will be overwise" (ll. 63–64).

I read "The Hesperides," in short, as anxiously revising Keats's representation in "To Autumn" of song as a figure for figurality's limit, which comes into being only by assuming for its burden its own emptiness in the face of death. The power of this representation is that it closes off the possibility of subsequent figural language; in consequence, "The Hesperides" begins by claiming its own priority to Keats's text, representing, in the figure of Zidonian Hanno, Keats himself as a belated quester to whose quest the Hesperides' song marks a limit. This subversion of its precursor text is the specific transgression against the father that Tennyson's fantasy of naturalized language must suppress. In this reading, the silence of Father Hesper, besides representing the wishful suppression of anxiety called up by masturbatory fantasies, also marks Tennyson's suppression in his text of the voice of Keats. In fact, it seems that the poem's suggestions of masturbatory guilt should be read as its playing out of a transgression whose real origin is the origin of Tennyson's poetic self.

In certain of its configurations, then, "The Hesperides" bears a marked resemblance to "The Skipping-Rope." Here, as in "The Skipping-Rope," Tennyson's investment in a representation of poetic discourse as autoerotic repetition derives from a fantasy of a naturalized language in which significance would be inherent in signs rather than constituted in the relations between them. In both poems, this fantasy is preserved by a displacement that excludes difference from the origin of language and represents it elsewhere obsessively intensified. In "The Skipping-Rope" the difference suppressed in language reappeared as exaggerated sexual difference; in "The Hesperides" it reappears most markedly as difference between the inside and the outside of the garden in which the sisters sing.

All the same, the text of "The Hesperides" is clearly far more richly overdetermined than that of "The Skipping-Rope." The ambivalence in "The Skipping-Rope" toward autoerotic repetition as both suppressing and proliferating difference represents itself in "The Hesperides" as a transgression of the taboo against masturbation and plays itself out in terms of ambivalence to the father who institutes this prohibition. This representation is, however, also determined by the poem's origin in difference from a prior text, as a troping on Keats's "To Autumn." The poem's investment in autoerotic repetition is specifically an investment in suppressing this origin and in effacing in itself the traces of its precursor; in consequence, the Hesperides sing before a wishfully weak and silent father.

III

Freud's late essay "Femininity," published in *New Introductory Lectures on Psychoanalysis,* is tonally a remarkably uncertain text, affording repeated instances of tendentiousness, misogyny, and a certain anxious defensiveness. All these appear in the notorious passage where he discusses the origin of weaving in women's need to conceal their lack of a penis:

> *Shame, which is considered to be a feminine characteristic* par excellence *but is far more a matter of convention than might be supposed, has as its purpose, we believe, concealment of genital deficiency. We are not forgetting that at a later time shame takes on other functions. It seems that women have made few contributions to the discoveries and inventions in the history of civilization; there is, however, one technique which they may have invented—that of plaiting and weaving. If that is so, we*
>
> (SE 22:132)   *should be tempted to guess the unconscious motive for the achievement. Nature herself would seem to have given the model which this achievement imitates by causing the growth at maturity of the pubic hair that conceals the genitals. The step that remained to be taken lay in making the threads adhere to one another, while on the body they stick into the skin and are only matted together. If you reject this idea as fantastic and regard my belief in the influence of lack of a penis on the configuration of femininity as an* idée fixe, *I am of course defenceless.*

Throughout his essay, Freud treats woman's castration as a fact about her body and about its relation to the male body which she must inevitably discover and which will determine the course of her development from the moment of discovery on. But in the story Freud tells about this development it is characterized at virtually every turn by resistance to the supposed fact that is its central determinant. Such resistance has its first instance in penis envy: "The girl's recognition of the fact of her being without a penis does not by any means imply that she submits to the fact easily. On the contrary, she continues to hold on for a long time to the wish to get something like it herself and she believes in that possibility for improbably long years" (*SE* 22:125). Resistance can also appear as a refusal of psychoanalysis itself: "A man of about thirty strikes us as a youthful, somewhat unformed individual, whom we expect to make powerful use of the possibilities for development opened up to him by analysis. A woman of the same age, however, often frightens us by her psychical rigidity and unchangeability. Her libido has taken up final positions and seems incapable of exchanging them for others" (*SE* 22:134–35). And finally, the notion of women's resistance might be said to provide the essay's point of departure in that it begins by representing femininity as posing a particularly difficult problem, or a point of persistent resistance to understanding: "Throughout history people have knocked their heads against the riddle of the nature of femininity. . . . Nor will *you* have escaped worrying over this problem—those of you who are men; to those of you who are women this will not apply—you are yourselves the problem" (*SE* 22:113).

Freud's account of the origin of weaving may be read as affording a paradigm for all of these forms of resistance. In this account, the woven fabric functions as a means by which woman resists the gaze and conceals her castration. Freud himself has no hesitation in cutting the knot and reading this resistance as itself a sign of the lack that it seeks to conceal. But even as he does so, he reinscribes the resistance he has thus overcome as his audience's resistance to his own discourse. The paragraph closes with Freud professing himself to be "defenceless" against the charge that his "belief in the influence of the lack of a penis on the configuration of femininity"—a belief that constitutes the central argument of his essay—is the result of fixation. Like the queen's purloined letter in Poe's story, woman's secret seems here to be all the better hidden for being set in plain view.

Freud's discourse insistently makes the woven fabric a phenomenon of the threshold. It is instituted on the threshold between nature and culture; "nature herself," Freud writes, provides the model that it imitates. That model itself derives from the advent of puberty, the liminal moment of adult sexuality, and indeed from the threshold of the vaginal orifice. Further, Freud represents the woven fabric as the material form of shame, a characteristic that is itself ambiguously natural to women ("a feminine characteristic *par excellence*") and an instance of cultural determination ("far more a matter of convention than might be supposed"). In this passage, Freud's essay thus flirts with the possibility that as it enters the cultural order, the female body does so not only as the site of a lack but also as primordially veiled, endowed in its origin with a defense that would always prevent that lack from being seen. In spite of its project of solving "the riddle of . . . femininity," Freud's essay constitutes woman as the site of a defense that is apparently irreducible.

Tennyson's "The Lady of Shalott" also reads a woman's weaving as a

defense against what I shall argue is a castrative lack.[4] The poem constructs a narrative in which the Lady can become visible as a body only
under the sign of loss. Further, as Geoffrey Hartman and others have
shown us, this body is a textual body (Hartman, *Saving the Text,* 110;
Joseph, 9); in the 1832 version of the poem, the Lady's body appears at the
poem's close with an explanatory verse lying on it, while in the 1842
version this text is reduced to the inscription on the prow of her boat. In
both versions, however, the poem ends with a reading of the Lady's
textualized body. Its narrative thus aligns the loss that it represents as
constitutive of textuality—briefly, the loss of voice—with a loss that
constitutes the condition of a woman's visibility.

In two of the best readings the poem has attracted, this narrative is
seen as articulating a critique; they interpret the Lady's death not primarily
as a loss but as the demystification of an illusion that cannot coexist with
the textuo-historical conditions in which the poem sets itself. Geoffrey
Hartman has claimed the poem as an instance of how art can "burn
through, in its cold way, the desire for self-definition, fullness of grace,
presence . . . [and] expose the desire to own one's own name." He thus
argues that the poem's close reduces the Lady in death to "what she was
without knowing it in life: a floating signifier" (*Saving the Text,* 110). In
the course of a much more elaborated argument, Isobel Armstrong has
read the Lady's death as Tennyson's critique of a specific understanding of
the socially integrative power of poetic mythology, an understanding she
terms "narcissistic" and identifies primarily with Arthur Hallam.

These essays work in widely divergent theoretical idioms; nonetheless, having traced the particular forms of critique they see in Tennyson's
poem, they each note the disabling or ineffectual quality of the knowledge
this critique produces. Here is Hartman: "The trouble with Tennyson is
that his poetic dream-work seems at first no work at all. . . . Poem and
lady remain immaculate though web, mirror, or spell may break. Such
impassibility is perhaps part of the infection, an unresolved narcissism of
festering lily or psyche. Yet this tension between specular and poetic is
precisely what fosters the illusion of completeness and so the attractive
fetish we call a poem" (*Saving the Text,* 111). And in somewhat similar
terms, Armstrong draws to the close of her reading with the claim that the
poem's "language both frees and kills, able to reconceptualize the Lady's
choiceless imprisonment in opposition but not able to *effect* change. . . .
The Lady may sing a song of liberated insight, but she dies as she sings.
This is an aestheticized politics indeed" (99–100).

For both of these critics, the demystifying project of "The Lady of

Shalott" reveals the position it constructs for the lady as an impossible one. And for both of them this revelation has—no further effect at all. Why? Hartman implies that the poem's status as an aesthetic object—its immaculateness—identifies it as itself a defense against the demystification it has effected. Such a paradox would certainly explain the idleness or irresolution that he attributes to Tennyson's "poetic dream-work"; what it does not explain is the function or motive of such an apparently self-canceling labor. Nor, in my view, does Armstrong's richly historical account answer this question.

Ultimately, the question is not one that bears only on Tennyson. At least from Ovid to Freud, Western narratives about women have compulsively reproduced the motif of weaving as a form of woman's work that at once compensates for or conceals their castration and at the same time renders it legible. Such narratives always invoke the woven fabric for the purpose of unraveling it, or more strictly imagine it as self-unraveling, as always inevitably undoing its own effects. As we shall see, the Lady of Shalott' tapestry may be read as an instance of this structure.

I argued in chapter 1 that the Freudian account of the institution of the castration complex in boys is structured not only by the difference of gender but also by the difference between seeing and knowing that makes it possible for this institution to be understood as a narrative of demystification. It is possible to read the veil, apparently so extraneous to his argument, that Freud brings into the essay "Femininity" as marking precisely this second difference. Freud's theory requires that woman not be *self-evidently* castrated; her castration can only be known when the sight of her genitals has been supplemented by the word of the Law, and it is because of the knowledge-generating function that this narrative confers upon it that the Law is able to use the castration complex as its primary support. If castration were self-evident or naturally visible (as of course no fact is), it could not have its function of underwriting the Law. Hence the necessity for Freud to hypothesize, precisely at the limit or threshold of the natural, a veil that would make of castration a fact always already hidden.

The institution of the castration complex is for Freud a narrative of demystification. It ends with a subject who finally knows the difference between men and women. But this knowledge of difference is itself founded on the difference between the sight of the female genitals and the word of the Law. In all of the discourses we have just touched on, the woven veil, marking difference and differing from itself in its proper function, appears as the figure of this difference within knowledge—a difference by which knowledge will remain marked, never more so than at the moment when it claims to lift the veil that nonetheless determines its structure. Hence what Hartman and Armstrong read as the flight of Tennyson's poem into an aesthesis that reproduces the structure of the Lady's web—an aesthesis whose culminating instance is the lovely but silent face of the dead Lady.

At this point, before we return to the poem's ultimate fixation on the Lady's fetishized body, I want to resume the argument I made above about "The Skipping-Rope" and "The Hesperides." There I claimed that Tennyson deployed gender difference, and specifically the difference between the inside and the outside of the enclosed place of woman's discourse, as a way of containing what Derrida taught us to understand as the dispersion that is constitutive of language. We may resume by considering the representation of space in "The Lady of Shalott" as what lies outside the place where voice speaks, indeed as the external other of voice. This text is concerned from its opening with space and its articulations. Into its representations of space voice irrupts, in contrast to the profusion of quoted song in "The Hesperides," only rarely, and characteristically as a more or less uncanny arrival.

Space is literally mentioned twice in "The Lady of Shalott," once at the beginning of the poem and once at the end, as if the poem were itself a mirror, opening out space and the double of space on its two sides. In both cases it is a space that is opened up by gazing, and in both cases it is implicitly introduced as the figure of a silence that needs to be filled up by speech. At the beginning of the poem we learn that on the Lady's island

(ll. 15–18)
> Four gray walls, and four gray towers,
> Overlook a space of flowers,
> And the silent isle imbowers
>   The Lady of Shalott.

The space here is specifically a silent space, constituted and delimited by walls that are figured as looking in at it. From outside the walls, other lookers also gaze at this space:

(ll. 6–9)
> up and down the people go,
> Gazing where the lilies blow
> Round an island there below,
>   The island of Shalott.

Shalott is thus represented, as it were, as pure exteriority; in the proliferation of objects in space that locates it, each turns out to enclose something else—the lilies lying round the island, the island enclosing the walls, the walls the space of flowers, and the flowers the Lady. In sharp contrast, the Lady figures in the beginning of the poem only as interiority; unavailable to sight, she manifests herself only as a voice, which itself is audible outside her island only as an echo of the pure self-presence it figures within it.

It is, moreover, precisely in terms of this dislocation instituted at the outset between inside and outside, or between voice and image, that the poem goes on to tell the Lady's story. Her eventual fate is to become herself an image, a surface without an interior or a voice, when her body floats into Camelot:

> A gleaming shape she floated by,
> (ll. 156–58)   Dead-pale between the houses high,
>   Silent into Camelot.

And it is upon this dislocation that the poem insists with the pathos of Lancelot's final remark upon the Lady's face; for the convention of the prosopopoeia, by which the invocation of a face metonymically calls up a voice, here reminds us of the voice's absence, making the force of the line purely nostalgic.

The nostalgia for voice that informs these last lines is not, however, so heavy as it was in the poem's first published version, when it ended, not with the speech of Lancelot, but with the written message of the Lady:

> "The web was woven curiously
> ([1832] ll.   The charm is broken utterly,
> 177–80)   Draw near and fear not—this is I,
>   The Lady of Shalott."

The irony of this ending, of the writing announcing the presence of the woman on whose corpse it is inscribed, was pronounced by John Stuart Mill to be "lame and impotent" in his review of the original publication (Jump, 89). When, after the appearance of this review, Tennyson revised the poem for republication in 1842, he seems to have set out to supply the lack Mill discerned in the original version by replacing the Lady's text with the spoken comment of Sir Lancelot. Interestingly, in the revised version voice is again figured as inserting itself into a silent space opened up by the specular relation:

> Lancelot mused a little space;
> He said, "She has a lovely face;
> (ll. 168–71)   God in his mercy send her grace,
>   The Lady of Shalott."

The poem's most complete representation of voice as speaking in the face of a silent specular opposite is of course its description of the Lady herself in her tower. Here the dislocation of sight and sound is instituted by the curse that forbids her to look out and see where the sounds that reach her might come from. Her gaze is fixed on silent representations of the outside world in her weaving and in the mirror that she uses to produce it.

The effect of these silent representations is to make of the Lady's situation a powerful myth of consciousness in which the self's awareness of itself as a voice is radically separate from its perception of the exterior as a silent image. This image is in its turn dislocated from any sounds outside the self, of whose origin it can only be a shadow. Sounds from outside thus appear to consciousness in this myth as radically other; and indeed, the only sounds the poem actually represents as reaching the Lady in her tower in its first two sections are intimations of death, in the music of the funeral that passes her by (l. 68).

In the course of Tennyson's text, representations of the specular image and of space come to be characterized not simply as silent but also as empty in a way I have identified as specifying the absence of a speaking voice. When at the end of part 2 the Lady says, "I am half sick of shadows" (l. 71), she is articulating the pathos of this absence in a moment that is cognate with the beginning of the Soul's unrest in "The Palace of Art," which "divided quite / The kingdom of her thought" and eventually leads to her ultimate complaint: "No voice breaks through the stillness of this world: / One deep, deep silence all!" (ll. 227–28, 259–60).

In the course of both of these texts, then, the place of the speaking subject is constituted in a specular relation with a silent opposite. And in both texts this configuration becomes unstable at a moment when the subject experiences the image's silence as making it empty or shadowy, and articulates its lack in a complaint. For it is at the moment that she experiences what she sees as shadowy that the Lady says she is "*half* sick"; that is to say, experiences a division in the place from which she speaks, just as at the corresponding moment in "The Palace of Art" the Soul is "divided quite." And finally, in both texts the moment the subject complains of a lack in the image introduces a movement that undoes the configuration we have been discussing and leads to the subject's displacement—to the Soul's departure from her palace and the Lady's descent to Camelot.

To simplify this constellation of related events, we may say that at a certain moment in "The Lady of Shalott," what had appeared as a differ-

ence between the places of voice and of representation, or between interiority and exteriority, is transformed into a difference within the notion
of place as such. And as the text unfolds, the difference the Lady initially
experiences as internal to herself is repeated in her tapestry and in her
mirror in the register of the image.

When the Lady's web falls apart and her mirror cracks, these lose
their function of representation as they become metaphors for her own
division as a subject. At this moment their relation to the Lady changes
from one of specular opposition to one determined by the logic of a
figure. Eventually, the strange image of the second stanza of part 4
suggests that for the Lady a purely specular relation with the object has
become impossible:

> And down the river's dim expanse
> Like some bold seër in a trance,
> Seeing all his own mischance—
> With a glassy countenance
> Did she look to Camelot.

(ll. 127–31)

In this remarkable figure the landscape and the Lady's face both seem
dimly to reflect a self that has somehow been lost.

If the appearance of a break in the field of representation subjects it to
the logic of figuration, we would nonetheless be mistaken to assume that
we can read "The Lady of Shalott" as a narrative of the introduction of
figurality into a place from which it had hitherto been absent. Moreover,
we would also be mistaken to assume that we can read the break that
appears in the Lady's tapestry simply as a figure for a psychological
division that appears at a particular moment in *her* narrative. On the
contrary, I want to argue that place in this poem is always already divided
and that the specular opposition between the places of voice and representation in which it installs the Lady is its principal defense against this
difference—a defense that is reestablished at its conclusion over the Lady's
dead body.

The poem makes it clear enough that the Lady weaves in her tower as
a defense against a curse that has already been spoken. And if we press the
figure of the weaving that is the principal instrument of that defense a little
harder than we have so far, we can say that the rift that opens the
figuration of the subject at the end of part 3 is in fact always present in her
web. For if it is the function of weaving to produce the illusion of
representation without rifts or spaces, this illusion is itself constituted in
the diacritical differences between the woven threads, differences that

insist on the very space it is weaving's function to close up. The unraveling of the Lady's tapestry thus only opens out the differences that had always been its means of signification.

The Lady's weaving is introduced as a defense against a curse, whose nature the poem leaves obscure. I quote the moment of its introduction:

> She has heard a whisper say,
> A curse is on her is she stay
>   To look down to Camelot.

(ll. 39–45)

> She knows not what the curse may be,
> And so she weaveth steadily,
> And little other care hath she,
>   The Lady of Shalott.

What might be the burden of this whisper? When Tennyson took the Lady's story from Thomas Roscoe's translation of novella 81 of the *Cento Novelle Antiche,* he added so many details as to virtually transform the story; he also changed the name given to the Lady from "Scalot" to "Shalott" because, according to his note in the Eversley Edition (quoted in *Poems* 1:387), it was "a softer sound." The change softens the name by replacing the consonantal stop of its first syllable with the sibilant *sh,* so that the newly coined word opens as an invitation to whisper—an invitation that is apparently taken up by the reaper in the preceding stanza, who mysteriously whispers it alone under the moon.

I suggest that this whispered name, the name by which the Lady is known which is still not her name, is the curse under which she lives.[5] For no one's name is really their own; Lacan's dictum has it that by virtue of the proper name, the subject is the slave of a discourse in the universal movement of which it already exists at birth (*Ecrits,* 495. This passage is slightly mistranslated in the English of *Ecrits: A Selection,* 148). The poem signals this fact by giving the Lady the name of a place; by making her naming a *placing* of the subject in a space that precedes it. And the constitution of this space as difference, as well as being the burden of the Lady's curse, is in effect that of the poem, in which the repeated rhyme *Shalott / Camelot* determines the whole scene of its representation.

The space in which this poem is set is thus the space of language, or of what Lacan would call the Symbolic order. And it is precisely as a defense of the subject against this space that threatens to claim it that the poem represents the myth of consciousness I have described above. Its principal features are the production of the subject as a voice to which space is always eternal, and of space, most explicitly in the Lady's tapestry, as an extension from which language, and the possibility of signification constituted diacritically or as difference, are wishfully excluded.

The name *Shalott* thus at once denotes a place whose interior figures an imaginary interiority in the face of the Symbolic order and, by naming it, institutes that interiority as itself an epiphenomenon of the Symbolic. This contradiction becomes apparent when, in the last moment before she leaves her island, the Lady inscribes herself "The Lady of Shalott" on the boat that is to carry her away. In this moment, what I have argued is the force of the Lady's name as that which both asserts the place of the subject and effects its displacement finds a full representation in the poem's narrative.

And what of the landscape where this representation unfolds? I suggested above that this landscape is determined by the repeated rhyme of *Shalott* and *Camelot*. There is a general connection in Tennyson's early lyrics between his fascination with the compelling force of rhyme and other patterns of phonic play and his tendency to represent landscape by a profusion of details. The effect of these habits is to insist on the materiality of both landscape and language—on the sense in which neither is to be read as a representation of a prior object—while denying the totality of either as an object in itself. Tennyson's language and landscape both take their meaning as they bear the traces of a force that manifests itself in the proliferation of minimal differences. As in "Mariana," this force is often figured as an absent or shadowy other; it is in effect the coercive force of the signifier itself.

We have seen that in "The Lady of Shalott" the play of the signifier breaches the representations of the Lady's web and of her mirror, and that this moment repeats the division of the subject that the poem figures at the end of part 2. But this moment also repeats the configurations of the landscape of the opening stanzas, which lies on either side of a river that divides it, just as the Lady's mirror is divided from side to side by a crack:

> On either side the river lie
> Long fields of barley and of rye,
> That clothe the wold and meet the sky;
> And through the field the road runs by
> To many-towered Camelot;
> And up and down the people go,
> Gazing where the lilies blow
> Round an island there below,
> The island of Shalott.

(ll. 1–9)

In its representation of space this whole passage prefigures the image of weaving that is literally introduced in the poem's description of the Lady. This is so most clearly in the instance of the fields, which are described as cloths lying over and repeating the contours of the ground beneath them, in a figure that transforms the visible surface of the landscape itself into an image of a prior object. But the Lady's weaving is also, and perhaps more strangely, prefigured in the way the extensions within the landscape of the road and the journeys of the people who travel along it come to be represented as very much like the interlocking warp and woof in a woven fabric.

The figure by which a road is described as running through something appears innocent or conventional enough; its force becomes clearer in the next stanza when it recurs in a description of "the wave that runs for ever" (l. 12) by the Lady's island. There is a peculiar displacement in this line whereby the notion of running is transferred from the moving water of the river to the stationary wave through which it passes. More abstractly, it is transferred from the *substance* of moving water to a *structure* that is visibly constituted only in the disruption of the water's motion.

As through this wave, so through all the landscape of "The Lady of Shalott" there runs a structure that, while determining it, can only be represented in it as its disruption. It is this quality of the text's representation of landscape that makes the Lady's web its best exemplar. For, as I have argued, what is at issue in the figure of the web is the distinction in it between representation and the structure of woven threads in which representation is constituted but which can only appear in it as its dissolution, as a breach. And if the poem's narrative records in the tapestry the undoing of representation, and of extension as an object of representation, and their exposure as epiphenomena of a structure of difference, the poem's first lines imply that this undoing has already taken place in their representation of landscape. In the description of the road and of the people who travel along it, extension is not represented as distance between specifiable places but figured as the mechanical production of structural difference, both in the account of the people as going "up and down" and—if I can now claim for the line its full force as an anticipation of the threads that run through the Lady's tapestry—in the figure of the road as running through the field.

In the way it describes landscape, as well as in the way it uses rhyme, this text insists on the relations of the signifier that run *through* representation such that these relations appear in its own representations as breaches and discontinuities. There is, in fact, in the poem's account in its second stanza of the wind that shimmers through the landscape, making the leaves it touches whiten and quiver, a momentary register of the uncanniness specifically of what both passes through representation and eludes it:

(ll. 10–13)

> Willows whiten, aspens quiver,
> Little breezes dusk and shiver
> Through the wave that runs for ever
> By the island in the river.

The notion of one thing passing "through" another is forced in these lines literally beyond the point of representation—how can wind pass *through* a wave?—by a wind that is, however, figured as the agent of representation in a scene that it invisibly works to tint and animate.

Tennyson added the little breezes to the opening section of the poem when he revised it for republication in 1842; they appear there as a prefiguration of the autumn wind that introduces the last section's narrative of the Lady's death. The wind, and to a lesser extent the river, in the opening section of the poem figure the materiality of the signifier as that which *runs through* representation, as threads run through a tapestry, and which can appear in it only as a breach. It is thus apt, in this last section of the poem, after the Lady's tapestry has disintegrated, that on the level of the poem's representation of landscape, the river and the wind should introduce the notion of strain:

(ll. 118–20)

> In the stormy east-wind straining,
> The pale yellow woods were waning,
> The broad stream in his banks complaining.

The figuration in these lines of strain against limits is accompanied by the introduction of voice into the poem's landscape. Until the last section, this landscape has always appeared in a hush, which is emphasized rather than broken by the whispering of the reaper and by the funeral that passes, like the wind itself, "*through* the silent nights" (l. 66, emphasis mine). Most obviously, of course, the force of voice as something that is out of place in this landscape is demonstrated in the song of Lancelot, which I shall discuss in more detail below. The song introduces the transformation of the last section, in which the river complains in its banks, and the whole space through which the Lady passes fills with noises:

(ll. 136–44)

> Lying, robed in snowy white
> That loosely flew to left and right—
> The leaves upon her falling light—

Through the noises of the night
    She floated down to Camelot:
And as the boat-head wound along
The willowy hills and fields among,
They heard her singing her last song,
    The Lady of Shalott.

At the level on which this text is a narrative about the Lady, the
sounds that fill the space around her, like the destruction of her mirror and
her web, register her emergence from the shadows she had complained of
in part 2. As these shadows were figured as silent, so here they open into a
space that can be figured as filled with voice, and coterminous with it.

Here, the space into which the text opens out, a space filled with
sounds among which the Lady's voice has its own place, is opened out for
her by desire. Tennyson's well-known comment on the poem makes this
clear: "The new-born love for something, for some one in the wide world
from which she has been so long secluded, takes her out of the region of
shadows into that of realities" (*Memoir* 1:117). How are we to understand
this desire that opens out space? Tennyson's hedging about its object—he
speaks of the Lady's love "for something, for some one in the wide
world"—is symptomatic. What the Lady sees when she turns away from
her mirror and looks out of her tower is not Lancelot but a metonymy—or
rather, a pair of metonymies: "She saw the helmet and the plume" (l. 112).
And in the description of Lancelot that makes up the bulk of this section of
the poem he is figured entirely by an accumulation of metonymy—of
details about the things he wears and the objects that hang from him and
about his horse and its accoutrements. Perhaps the most remarkable of
these contiguous objects that constitute the poem's image of Lancelot is his
shield, which literally stands for him, bearing as it does the picture of "A
red-cross knight [who] for ever kneeled / To a lady" (ll. 78–79).

This last item, like the helmet and its feather that burn "like one burning flame together" (l. 94) is not only a metonymy for Lancelot but also a
metaphor for desire itself. These figures are the poem's only allusions to
Lancelot's adulterous and ultimately frustrated love for Guinevere, which,
as Tennyson's prose source makes clear, is the reason why the Lady's love
is in turn doomed to frustration.

The energy of condensation and displacement, the two primary
processes that correspond to metaphor and metonymy, that goes into this
passage is not a matter of coincidence. In this text, where the play of
figurality is at once opened up and wishfully resolved as echoing and

reflection, Lancelot appears in a blaze of reflected light and sings a song constituted as self-echoing. At the beginning of part 3 we learn that as he rode by

(ll. 75–77)
>The sun came dazzling through the leaves,
>And flamed upon the brazen greaves
>   Of bold Sir Lancelot.

This reflected flaming is the dominant motif of the description that follows: his shield sparkles, his bridle glitters, his saddle shines, and his helmet and its feather burn in the sunlight. All of this reflection culminates in the moment when he flashes into the Lady's mirror both as a reflection and as a re-reflection from the river that flows by her island.[6]

All of this reflection repeats—mirrors—the effect of Lancelot's figuration by a proliferation of metonymy, an effect of the vanishing of the signified behind an infinite regress of signifiers, which is again repeated in the poem's representation of the song in line 107. As John Hollander has pointed out, Lancelot's song is the phonic equivalent of his flashing into the Lady's mirror ("Tennyson's Melody," 685–86):

(ll. 105–8)
>From the bank and from the river
>He flashed into the crystal mirror,
>"Tirra lirra," by the river
>   Sang Sir Lancelot.

"Tirra lirra" here echoes itself, and is echoed again in the word *river,* a word that is itself the echo of the "river" that ends the last line but one.

Lancelot's song then echoes and reechoes in the poem's rhyme scheme (in the words *river* and *mirror*) in the same way his image is reflected and re-reflected in the river and the mirror before the Lady. But it is an echo in another sense as well. It comes from Autolycus' song in act 4 of *The Winter's Tale:*

(4.3.9–12)
>The lark, that tirra-lyra chaunts,
> With heigh, with heigh, the thrush and the jay!
>Are summer songs for me and my aunts,
> While we lie tumbling in the hay.

Both the season and the erotic content are relevant, as Hollander points out. Also relevant is the lark, which, like Lancelot, sings "In the broad day-light . . . unseen" as Shelley puts it in lines from "To a Sky-Lark" (19–20) that are themselves heard at one remove in "The Lady of Shalott."

In its allusiveness, moreover, Lancelot's song is typical of the whole section of the poem that describes him, which is full of literary echoes. He appears in a veritable catalog of allusions to romance, numbering among his ancestors Chaucer's Squire and Spenser's Redcross Knight as well as Autolycus.

In Lacan's reading of Freud, the object of desire is always produced as a metonymy, by the same process of continual displacement that characterizes Lancelot as he appears to the Lady: "The enigmas that desire seems to pose for a 'natural philosophy' . . . amount to no other derangement of instinct than that of being caught in the rails—eternally stretching forth towards the *desire for something else*—of metonymy" (*Ecrits: A Selection,* 166–67). In this view, the phallic stage of sexuality is one of the moments when this signifying chain is suspended—petrified, as Lacan says, in the fascinating image of the fetish.

In this sense, the plume on which the Lady fixes her gaze, this passage's final metonymy for the object of desire, has the function of the phallus. Like the phallus, the plume not only bears a metonymic significance but is also a metaphor for the desire of the father—in this case, of all the poetic fathers who appear here in the text as echoes. As such, it also bears the significance of the phallus that enforces on the son the oedipal prohibition that makes his desire always a trope, a "desire for something else."

Lacan uses a text of Browning's as an epigraph to the Discourse of Rome: " 'Flesh composed of suns. How can this be?' exclaim the simple ones."[7] The burden of part 3 of "The Lady of Shalott" is that the sun, which appears in line 75, can never become flesh but can only be reflected by it; that sons can never be their fathers' flesh but only figures of it; that the son's desires are always tropes of the father's, themselves already tropes.

In "The Lady of Shalott," as in "The Hesperides," what is spoken as desire is also a sense of poetic belatedness that brings with it an anxiety that what one thinks of as one's own language and desire may only be tropes on one's father's. The Lady of Shalott both embodies and defends against this knowledge. She embodies it because desire takes her, I have claimed, from a region of representation, not into a region of reality, but into a region of tropes, where her voice appears as the voice of a belated Romantic quester. This movement is allegorized in the poem by the way Lancelot, the object of her desire, appears as a figure who is not represented but described in figures of deferral, and of course by the way in which her desire opens a breach in the representation that it had hitherto been her function to produce.

But, like the Hesperides on their island, the Lady also represents for Tennyson a defense against a desire that articulates itself as a compulsive production of texts whose meaning is always constituted as difference and as the deferred meaning of prior texts. I have argued that the Lady initially embodies in the poem a fantasy of a discourse constituted as pure interiority, without difference, to which space would always appear as a silent exterior. In this fantasy voice and space each appear as the other's other, the difference between them guaranteeing the absolute self-presence of speech in one dimension and place in another. I suggested, however, that this fantasized articulation of space and voice seems to be on the verge of breaking down at certain points where spatial differences appear as displaced versions of differences within the poem's text. This breakdown occurs only in the Lady's web, not in the text, which ends by reasserting the articulation of voice and representation over the dead body of the Lady. This reassertion takes place then at the expense of the Lady, who feels the lack that is the burden of all of Tennyson's tropes as a sexual lack and the difference that constitutes their meaning as sexual difference. If her desire fixes on the phallus, it is because it is the signifier that opens sexual difference, here the difference between Lancelot and herself. And it is this sexual difference that, as in "The Skipping-Rope," makes it possible for the poem to end, prevents it from being an infinite series of echoes and differentiations, by making it possible for it to cast out in the figure of the Lady the desire that nonetheless produces it as a text.

As a figure who sings without being seen, the Lady of Shalott at the beginning of the poem owes something to Keats's nightingale. The language Tennyson uses to describe his unseen Lady at the end of the poem's first section echoes the romantic diction of the pivotal seventh stanza of Keats's ode, from which he remembers words like *casement* and *fairy,* while the weary reaper who hears the Lady's song derives both from the figure of Ruth amid the alien corn and from Wordsworth's solitary reaper, who is herself the precursor of Ruth as she appears in Keats's poem.

"The Solitary Reaper" influenced Tennyson directly and through Keats, not only in "The Lady of Shalott," but also in "The Hesperides" and elsewhere. Here I want to notice a problematic in Wordsworth's poem that is central to that influence. "The Solitary Reaper" presents itself as the record of an encounter with a woman singing in an unknown language, whose song Wordsworth describes himself listening to and then bearing away in his heart. A note that Wordsworth appended to the poem at its first publication, however, represents it as the result of a different kind of encounter: "This Poem was suggested by a beautiful sentence in a MS Tour in Scotland written by a Friend, the last line being taken from it *verbatim.*" Is this a poem about an encounter with a voice or with a text? And what, specifically, are we to make of the ambiguity that the note introduces into the last line, which seems to figure a moment of experience recaptured as *resonance*—"The music in my heart I bore, / Long after it was heard no more"—but which must also be read as Wordsworth's recapture of the experience as a *transcription.*

In effect, these alternate readings of the last lines raise the question of how to figure the production of lyric affect that is in any case central to the poem in other ways as well. Even in the body of its text "The Solitary Reaper" incorporates both moments that seem to record a speaking voice—"Will no one tell me what she sings?" (l. 17)—and moments in which the poem seems not to quote a speech but to transcribe an inscription. As Geoffrey Hartman has remarked, the opening of the poem, with its invitation to the traveler to "Stop here, or gently pass!" (l. 4) is a variant of the apostrophe to travelers that was for classical poets and their eighteenth-century successors a convention of the literary epitaph or commemorative inscription (*Wordsworth's Poetry*, 12). Unlike the more conventionally lyric outburst, quoted earlier, this line presents itself, not as the record of a voice, but as always having been an inscription—an inscription, moreover, with something distinctly elegiac about it; one that, far from recording a voice, would mark the place of a voice's absence.

Does "The Solitary Reaper" thus record the presence of a voice or its absence? I suggest that the reaper and her song are made the subjects of the poem in an attempt to answer this question, which nonetheless is never completely closed; for the poem's paired references to singing and reaping are not accidental:

(ll. 25–28)
> Whate'er the theme, the Maiden sang
> As if her song could have no ending;
> I saw her singing at her work,
> And o'er the sickle bending.

Although the reaper sings as though her song could have no ending, reaping itself surely thematizes ending in this poem. It appears, moreover, as a technique of repetition, which inscribes and reinscribes its mark upon the landscape in the places where it cuts down the grain. And the significance of that mark is the fullness of a harvest that is always gathered elsewhere, appearing in the reaped field only as an absence.

Reaping in this poem occupies the place of writing, and the reaper's force as a source of lyric affect lies in the play between the fullness of her voice and the absence she inscribes on the fields around her, an absence that may be most fully present in the text in its intimations of her death, both in the opening stanza and in the ominous impersonal construction of the last line's reference to her voice, "after it was heard no more." What is interesting about this text for my purposes is the way the reaping woman becomes a figure in whom voice and writing can be separated; in whom the possibility of a song without articulation—that would "flow" from something—can be represented by splitting articulation off from it under the sign of *technique*. The result of this separation is that the category of the origin, or referent, of discourse is powerfully installed in the poem in the context of the reaper's song, but only as a category of indeterminate content and as a focus of the poem's anxiety.

One way of putting the question posed by the ambivalence of "The Solitary Reaper" is to ask whether memory should be figured as a voice or as an inscription, or, to put it another way, whether one can remember a voice. It is a question to which Keats's negative answer, with all its implications as a critique of Wordsworth's poetic, is formulated in the "Ode to a Nightingale." Here the nightingale's song, which that of Wordsworth's reaper had been supposed to surpass ("The Solitary Reaper," 9–12), is constituted from the beginning of the poem as that which induces forgetfulness, and which, in the last lines, is itself forgotten: "Fled is that music:—Do I wake or sleep?" (l. 80). The difference between the two poems' claims could not be made clearer than in the contrast between this ending and Wordsworth's final couplet: "The music in my heart I bore, / Long after it was heard no more."

Another way of articulating the same difference is to note that Wordsworth's poem begins with a placing of the voice that he hears and with the constitution of that place as something that can be looked at. In Keats's ode the voice of the nightingale is experienced as a displacement, indeed as a loss of place, which is figured as a fade-out of the visual.

What kind of a voice is Keats writing about that can manifest itself only as forgetting and displacement? The answer to this question is that he is writing about prior texts and about the tropes that he performs on them to hear them as voices. For the voice we hear in a text is always displaced, never has a visible origin, and can only be produced precisely as a forgetting of textuality. It is not an accidental irony that the "Ode to a Nightingale," perhaps the most densely allusive of the major Romantic texts—a poem that remembers not only Wordsworth, but also Shakespeare and, most vitally, Milton—should take as its theme hearing and forgetting.

Keats's principal source for the ode was the Invocation to book 3 of *Paradise Lost,* where Milton figures himself as the nightingale that "Sings darkling, and in shadiest Covert hid / Tunes her nocturnal Note" (3.39–40). The word *darkling* here has a double force, in that it figures Milton's blindness, the theme of the invocation, not by making the nightingale blind, but by situating it in a space where it not only cannot see but cannot be seen. It thus in part displaces the notion of blindness away from the subject and onto a space in which the subject is constituted.

When Keats writes "Darkling I listen" (l. 51), what he listens to is the Miltonic nightingale. His line transforms the Invocation's figure for Milton's production of *Paradise Lost* into a figure for Milton's relation to Keats. It would be wrong, however, to read this relation as one in which Keats is figured as hearing Milton, or hearing "Milton's darkling," as John Hollander has suggested (*The Figure of Echo,* 90). On the contrary, Keats hears Milton's nightingale by virtue of *not* hearing Milton's *darkling;* for if in this line the song remains the nightingale's, so that Keats hears it as belonging to another subject, the *darkling* refers to Keats himself as a subject, and appears as his own.

This slide is possible only because of the double force of *darkling* noted above. In a sense, the word *darkling* is itself darkling in that it always hides the subject to which it ostensibly refers by denoting a space in which that subject vanishes. If for Milton's bird to sing darkling means that whoever hears it must also be darkling, then *darkling* is clearly not a property of either the speaking or the listening subject in the same way that speaking and listening are proper to them. It is, on the contrary, a property of a space where speakers and listeners vanish in a discourse of which darkling is a part that can never be proper to them.

It is this space, the space of discourse without a subject, which I provisionally designate as the space of the text, which Keats and Milton have to forget in order to figure themselves as singing or as listening. This space, moreover, is occupied by other texts than theirs—for instance, the texts of *A Midsummer Night's Dream* and *King Lear,* in which the word *darkling* raises the question When can we stop reading Keats's or Milton's "darkling"? The same question is raised by Keats's "viewless wings of Poesy" ("Ode to a Nightingale," l. 33) which recall the "viewless wings" on which Milton figures himself as hurried aloft in the fragmentary poem "The Passion" (l. 33) but which also seem to derive from the "viewless winds" of Claudio's speech in *Measure for Measure,* which are indeed, not only viewless themselves, but like "darkling" also delimit a space where the subject vanishes to itself:

Ay, but to die, and go we know not where;
. . . . .
To be imprison'd in the viewless winds
And blown with restless violence round about
The pendant world.

(3.1.117–25)[8]

That Keats and Milton forget the space of a discourse in which the speaking subject vanishes to represent themselves as listening or singing is in fact the burden of the figure of the nightingale. For in the legend of Philomela, the song of the nightingale is itself a forgetting of the cycle of transgression and revenge that makes up her story.[9]

In the classical narrative Philomela is abducted and raped by Tereus, the Thracian husband of her sister Procne. To conceal his crime, Tereus cuts out her tongue and has her kept under guard in an isolated cell. After a time, however, Philomela manages to get word to her sister of what has happened by means of a tapestry—in Ovid's account, by "weaving purple signs (purpureasque notas) on a white background, she . . . tells the story of her wrongs" (*Metamorphoses* 6.576–77). Having read the tapestry, Procne releases Philomela, and together they take their revenge on Tereus by killing Procne's son by him and serving the son to the father as food. When Tereus finds out that he has eaten his son, Itys, he rises to kill the two women, but is prevented from doing so when all three of them are transformed into birds.

This transformation restores Philomela's voice and makes possible the closure of the story. But it does so not in such a way as to answer her wish to speak of her wrongs, or of her pleasure at having avenged them, but by having her and the other characters forget them. In this sense, the end of the story repeats the silencing of Philomela—a point Ovid makes clear when, echoing his earlier description of Philomela's web, he writes that on the bodies of the birds she and her sister have become, there appear in red the "marks of their murderous deed (excessere notae)" (6.670). Like Philomela's rape, the murder of Itys cannot be spoken; is represented only by a mark.

These marks, which are the other of voice, and which, to acquire song, the characters have at the end of the story to forget, can simply be said to signify writing as such. Like the written text, they always speak for a subject who is absent and hidden—Philomela in her prison, and Itys in the body of his father. There is, however, more to be said about them than that. The story of Philomela is, among other things, a fantasy of the institution of gender, in which Philomela's mutilation is an imaginary staging of the woman's castration. Ovid's account makes this clear enough: "He seized her tongue with pincers, as it protested against the outrage, calling ever on the name of her father and struggling to speak, and cut it off with his merciless blade. The mangled root quivers, while the severed tongue lies palpitating on the dark earth, faintly murmuring; and, as the severed tail of a mangled snake is wont to writhe, it twitches convulsively" (6.555–60). The purple mark in Philomela's weaving thus signifies the absence of the phallus, as indeed do the bloody marks she and Procne bear at the end of the story. For the markings of the birds that the characters turn into are clearly marks of gender; instead of the stains that Ovid describes on the women's feathers, Tereus as a hoopoe bears the phallus, extravagantly multiplied: "Upon his head a stiff crest appears, and a huge beak stands forth instead of his long sword" (6.672–73).

On their bodies, then, these birds bear marks that signify gender. As signifiers, moreover, they function only diacritically, in relation to one another. That is to say, the phallus, the privileged signifier of this narrative, has significance only as a mark of difference in a syntactic field that also includes its absence. It is the institution of this field that psychoanalysis represents in the castration complex, in which seeing the female genitals precipitates the male child's internalization of the Law of the father. One could argue that this effect has as its analogue in the Philomela story Tereus' devouring of Itys, an event that should be read as the *inverse* of the plucking out of Philomela's tongue and hence as guaranteeing the father's possession of the phallus whose lack in women is figured in Philomela's mutilation.

In this reading of the Philomela story, as in the fantasies surrounding the male castration complex, the play of signifiers that constitute gender would be a text whose author is the father. The force of this reading in a patriarchal culture would be to explain the insistence in these texts of Milton, Keats, and Tennyson of allusions to specific, male precursors. But in another reading the marks that appear on the birds at the end of the story have no author; they constitute a text whose logic is opposed to the logic of the subject as author of his or her own discourse and whose author can only appear to the subject as Other.

It is as a forgetting of the discourse of the Other, whose marks she nonetheless bears on her body, that Philomela's song is finally produced. And it is by forgetting this discourse, and by forgetting Philomela herself, that the nightingale sings also in Milton and, more explicitly, in Keats. Although indeed, the figure of Ruth in the "Ode to a Nightingale," who, I have noted, derives from Wordsworth's solitary reaper, should also be read as the nightingale's Other; as the type of a Philomela who cannot forget, and stands silent, in tears, far from home.

I have already argued that the phallus appears as a privileged signifier in "The Lady of Shalott" in the description of Lancelot and that its force as such is registered in the gap that opens up in the Lady's web when she looks out her window. In this reading, material deriving from the castration complex figures entry into the Symbolic and Tennyson's relation to his poetic fathers.

But such a reading of the poem forgets that the gap in the Lady's weaving is there from the beginning and makes possible its significance. Moreover, if it comes to that, the fathers too are always there, and they appear in this poem most powerfully, not in the figure of Lancelot, but precisely in this woven space that always has something missing. The Lady's weaving tropes both on the space in which the solitary reaper works and on the web of Philomela, the space of discourse that Keats forgets when he hears the nightingale. If Tennyson's poem appropriates these figures under the sign of *enclosure,* such that the Lady weaves and sings within her tower while the reaper remains outside, and inside the casement that in Keats is charmed open by the nightingale singing outside in "faery lands forlorn" (l. 70), it is to produce the fantasy of a place that the subject can call its own whose undoing the poem finally represents. So that indeed the tapestry that appears in this poem as a defense against the Other's discourse, as it appears for example in the curse that she bears, turns out always to have had that discourse as its burden. And so it is that the Lady of Shalott, the producer of the tapestry, becomes the burden of the poem, which thus can finally utter only her death.

IV

There is a widespread critical consensus that the peculiar excellence of "Mariana" lies in the force of the landscape the poem describes as a symbol for the state of her consciousness. This consensus dates at least from John Stuart Mill's discussion of the poem in 1835, which he introduces by praising Tennyson's "power of *creating* scenery, in keeping with some state of human feeling; so fitted to it as to be the embodied symbol of it, and to summon up the state of feeling itself" (Jump, 86). Arthur Hallam's remarks in his well-known review of *Poems, Chiefly Lyrical* on Tennyson's "vivid, picturesque delineation of objects, and the peculiar skill with which he holds all of them fused . . . in a medium of strong emotion"

(Jump, 42), although not applied by Hallam specifically to "Mariana," have often been cited in connection with the poem by more recent critics (Ricks, *Tennyson,* 75–76; McSweeny, 38).

Mill's and Hallam's comments combine a Coleridgean understanding of the synthetic power of the symbol with a distinctly Victorian sense of the role of affectivity—feeling—in producing this power. They enable us to identify the large theoretical stakes in understanding the relation between representation and expression in Tennyson's poem. The poem stages this relation in the first instance as a matter of form: The difference between representation and expression corresponds in it to the distinction between stanza and refrain, and more generally to the distinction between the extensiveness of the discourse of the poem's speaker and the radical impoverishment of Mariana's. What in this poem has enabled readers to see these discourses as fitted to one another or as fused in the medium of a single emotion?[10]

One answer to this question is that of Dwight Culler, who has asserted that "it is out of . . . inner music . . . that the poem arises, and one feels that Mariana is less an emanation of the moated grange than the grange is an exhalation of her consciousness. For although the grange is described by the poetic speaker, only the refrain being put into Mariana's mouth, one has the impression that the entire poem is spoken by Mariana" (42).

Culler wants in this passage both to align "Mariana" with and to distinguish it from "Claribel," a poem Tennyson published with "Mariana" in his 1830 volume. Claribel appears in his argument as the "spirit of the place" the poem describes (Culler, 41) and as the singer of the melody the poem announces itself in its subtitle ("A Melody") as recording. For Culler the poem's melodic quality is inseparable from its character as a description of a place. The melody, he writes, elaborates "the mournful sounds of an English churchyard . . . into a musical composition" (40–41). There are, however, theoretical problems involved in assuming that language can in any consistent way reproduce natural sounds. Moreover, evidence exists that these problems concern Tennyson throughout the poems published in 1830.

Culler's reading of "Claribel" asserts an equation of Claribel's voice, the sounds of the place where she is buried, and the melodic qualities of Tennyson's text. But this equation is clearly not a literal one; it is a figure developed under the sign of Claribel's name. It is the force of the figure of prosopopoeia, which endows objects with human faces and voices, that makes us read the verbal patterns which constitute Tennyson's text and the sounds which that text describes, as signifying Claribel's voice. The pathos of the poem derives from our discovery in the middle of the second stanza that this figure is a fiction—that the woman whose voice we imagine ourselves to hear under Claribel's name is in fact buried in the place the poem describes.

In "Mariana," too, Culler describes the text as the record of a single voice: "Although the grange is described by the poetic speaker . . . one has the impression that the entire poem is spoken by Mariana" (42). Here too the text's status as a description of a place is inseparable from the its voice; but the relation that Culler asserts between the poem's speaker and its place is the reverse of what he described in "Claribel." There Claribel was a "spirit of the place" the poem described; here the grange rises as an "exhalation" of Mariana's consciousness. The figure of breath, however, organizes his account of both texts and provides the principal ground for both readings. Thus Claribel, as spirit, sings a song that ends up providing the melody of Tennyson's text; and thus Culler's remark that the grange is an exhalation appears in apposition to his description of the poem itself arising out of an inner music (42).

I have argued that the pathos of "Claribel" depends on our discovery that this authorizing figure is a fiction; that whatever the melody of the poem might be, it is not a record of a living voice. In "Mariana," even if the place of voice is not, as in "Claribel," occupied by a funeral inscription, the figure is nonetheless problematic. It is so not least because the text itself is emphatic that it does not only record a single voice. It presents itself as quoting Mariana's speech in its refrains alone, which begin in every stanza with the words "she only said . . ." If we take this reiterated limitation literally, what do we make of its splitting-off of the burden of Mariana's discourse from the place that, in Culler's view, constitutes its breath and music? Whose breath would be in question there?

This question becomes more pressing when we consider the authority for Culler's reading of the poem, Tennyson's note in the Eversley Edition, in which he recalls that his "*moated grange* . . . rose to the music of Shakespeare's words" (quoted in *Poems* 1:205). But if the "inner music" that Culler mentions in his discussion of this note comes from Shakespeare, how does the grange become an exhalation of Mariana's consciousness? And, to return to Tennyson's note, when he remembers "the music of Shakespeare's words," what music is he thinking of? The passage from *Measure for Measure* to which the poem alludes is a passage of not noticeably musical prose which ends "There, at the moated grange, resides this dejected Mariana" (3.1.264–65). These are the lines that Tennyson either misremembered or deliberately altered when he produced his poem's epigraph: "Mariana in the moated grange." With the addition of an un-stressed syllable, this would be a line of iambic pentameter; with its alliterated *m*'s and the movement of its vowel sounds from back to front it certainly has a better claim to be called musical than the Shakespearian line it recalls. To whose music, then, does the grange rise?

The impossibility of an adequate answer to this question alerts us to the *allegorical* nature of the relation between place and voice in this text. In a seminal essay whose terms seem pertinent here, Paul de Man has rebuked readings of Romantic allegory that are founded on an aesthetic of the symbol:

> *In the world of the symbol it would be possible for the image to coincide with the substance, since the substance and its representation do not differ in their being but only in their extension. . . . Their relationship is one of simultaneity, which, in truth, is spatial in kind, and in which the intervention of time is merely a matter of contingency, whereas, in the world of allegory, time is the originary constitutive category. . . . it remains necessary, if there is to be allegory, that the allegorical sign refer to another sign that precedes it. The meaning constituted by the allegorical sign can then consist only in the* repetition *(in the Kirkegaardian sense of the term) of a previous sign with which it can never coincide, since it is of the essence of this previous sign to be pure anteriority.*

("The Rhetoric of Temporality," 207)

The notion that Mariana's grange occupies a place that is coextensive with a voice has formed virtually every reading of Tennyson's text. But the problems that arise when one tries, as we say, to place that voice begin to suggest that it is in fact always elsewhere; that the illusion of a voice in the place that this poem represents is produced by misreading as a symbol a figure that is actually allegorical.

It is not hard to see that the commentaries that read Mariana's grange as embodying, respectively, a music and a voice depend for their authority on its allegorical status. Underlying Tennyson's remark that the "*moated grange . . .* rose to the music of Shakespeare's words" is the legend of the city of Troy rising to the music of Apollo, a legend that preoccupied Tennyson throughout his career. It is, for instance, central to the *Idylls of the King,* where Camelot is built to music ("Gareth and Lynette," 271–74); and it also appears in texts closer to the period of "Mariana," such as "Tithonus," "Œnone," and the fragment not published until 1931 but written about 1830, whose refrain asks of the city of Ilion, "When wilt thou be melody born?" ("Ilion, Ilion," ll. 2, 9, 19). Culler's awareness of the allusion in Tennyson's note, I suggest, determines his use of the figure of an exhalation to describe Mariana's grange. The figure is anticipated in "Œnone," where Œnone compares her own song to that which built Troy:

(ll. 38–41)
> Hear me, for I will speak, and build up all
> My sorrow with my song, as yonder walls
> Rose slowly to a music slowly breathed,
> A cloud that gathered shape.

Culler's figure has another source, however, which is not in Tennyson at all but in Milton's description of the building of Pandaemonium in book 1 of *Paradise Lost*—a description that itself draws on the story of Apollo's building of Troy:

(1.710–13)
> Anon out of the earth a Fabric huge
> Rose like an Exhalation, with the sound
> Of Dulcet Symphonies and voices sweet,
> Built like a Temple.

In Tennyson's own note on his poem, then, and a fortiori in the interpretation it suggested to Culler, Mariana's grange is read as signifying music or breath, not by virtue of its representation of either, but because of its relation to a chain of prior texts. Music, breath—these are figures of the presence in an utterance of its author whose place we must have found if we can hear the music of her voice or feel her breath. In the poems discussed earlier in this chapter these figures, particularly the figure of music, had the force of wishes; in "Mariana," a bleaker text, they are clearly fictions. In "Mariana," the place of the poem's music and breath is elsewhere, in texts constituted, as de Man would have it, in "pure anteriority."

In "The Lady of Shalott," the Lady's name was given as the name of the place where she sings, the place, in short, of her voice. But I argued that in "The Lady of Shalott" the name had a double force as what denominates the place of the subject while also displacing that place, constituting it diacritically in a discourse whose burden is the death of what it names. The same double movement is clearer in "Mariana," where Mariana's name appears at the head of the text as the referent of the personal pronoun that resonates throughout its refrain, a referent that authorizes us to read the text in quotation marks as the expression of a human psyche. This authority is, moreover, apparently the stronger in that Mariana's name alludes to that of a character already represented in Shakespeare's *Measure for Measure*.

But precisely the fact that Mariana's name appears only at the head of Tennyson's text draws attention to its status as a supplement that only by a process of continual back-reference enables the poem to constitute its refrain as human utterance. In this poem the fact that names constitute the origin of discourse only by virtue of being inscribed elsewhere than at that origin is made peculiarly clear—the more so if we consider more closely the poem's relation to *Measure for Measure*. Does the name Mariana, taken in conjunction with Tennyson's epigraph, denote the character represented in Shakespeare's play and so establish that character as the subject of the poem? The literal-minded answer is surely no; Shakespeare's Mariana never wishes to die or says any of the things she does in Tennyson's poem. Moreover, as Christopher Ricks has remarked, the happy ending of *Measure for Measure* poses something of a problem for "Mariana." If Shakespeare's play describes an outcome, Tennyson's poem refuses one— an equivocal situation, as Ricks points out (*Tennyson,* 50).

In fact, Mariana's name, which seems to give an authorizing context for the poem's refrain, is itself a quotation—or misquotation—out of context. As the name of a speaking subject, a name is always taken out of the context of another discourse where it already appears—a paradox that Tennyson explores in a number of poems besides "Mariana," perhaps most notably in "Ulysses," where the problematic relation of Ulysses' name to its appearance in the *Odyssey* is figured by his finding himself literally out of place. He has become, he says, a name; and it is as such that he can have no place:

> I am become a name;
> For always roaming with a hungry heart
> Much have I seen and known. . . .
(ll. 11–21)   I am a part of all that I have met;
> Yet all experience is an arch wherethrough
> Gleams that untravelled world, whose margin fades
> For ever and for ever when I move.

We know that "Ulysses" is an elegy, both from Ulysses' own hope to reach "the Happy Isles, / And see the great Achilles, whom we knew" (ll. 63–64) and from Tennyson's note that "the poem was written soon after Hallam's death, and it gives the feeling about the need of going forward and braving the struggle of life perhaps more simply than anything in *In Memoriam*" (quoted from the Eversley Edition, *Poems* 1:613). But if "Ulysses" thus describes the completion of the work of mourning, which Freud explained as the withdrawal of cathexes from the lost object of desire, it does so in the voice of one who himself speaks from the dead, not only because it is so that Ulysses speaks in canto 26 of the *Inferno,* the poem's principal source, but also because he speaks in Ithaca as a revenant, one who has returned from a journey to the underworld and who has himself been given up for dead. One of the contexts for Ulysses' name, which marks him as out of place in Ithaca, is the context of death.

"Mariana" is a poem engaged with the same problematic of context, but it represents a place where the dead can speak only "from without" ("Mariana," l. 68), and where they figure in consequence only as absences, as phantoms; in fact, only as figures. Mariana waits for her lover as Penelope waited for Ulysses, but there are no revenants in this poem. "Mariana" is nonetheless not an elegy; the repeated complaint "He cometh not," with its predicative force, would not be used of someone who could be thought of as dead.[11]

But if Mariana cannot think the death of her lover, the poem is nonetheless extravagant in its echoes of texts about the dead. Tennyson himself, in a note to the lines "Waking she heard the night-fowl crow: / The cock sung out an hour ere light" (ll. 26–27), recalled the ballad "Clerk Saunders" from Scott's *Minstrelsy of the Scottish Border,* where the ghost of the dead Clerk Saunders appears at the window of his betrothed "an hour before the day," when "cocks are crowing a merry midnight" and "wild fowl are boding day" ("Clerk Saunders," ll. 60, 73–74). The most immediate source for "Mariana," however, is Keats's "Isabella," in which Isabella too is visited by the ghost of her dead lover.

Harold Bloom has written of "Mariana" that "what reverberates in Tennyson's ear are a few lines from 'Isabella': 'She weeps alone for pleasures not to be; / Sorely she wept until the night came on . . . / And so she pined, and so she died forlorn'" (*Poetry and Repression,* 149). Bloom is certainly right to locate in "Isabella" the essential precursor of "Mariana," but his use of the figure of reverberation to describe its influence on Tennyson is characteristic of his idealization of voice throughout his discussion of the poem, particularly in his account of Mariana herself, whom he describes as "herself a poetess," concluding with the rhetorical question "In the final stanza, what is the poplar but the High Romantic aeolian harp, or Mariana's song gathered together in its condensed glory?" (151, 153).

I have already argued the difficulties involved in constituting Mariana as a speaking subject, as the author of a song, in this text. Bloom is right to see in the poplar a version of the Romantic figure of the aeolian harp, but if, as he appears to, we take that figure in the High Romantic poets to have claimed a correspondence between the wind blowing through the harp and the poet's song, then I would argue that it appears here under a considerably bleaker revision than he allows. Tennyson's poplar appears first as a mark, then as a shadow, then, in the last stanza, as making a sound "to the wooing wind":

> The sparrow's chirrup on the roof,
>> The slow clock ticking, and the sound
> Which to the wooing wind aloof
>> The poplar made, did all confound
> Her sense.

(ll. 73–77)

The word *aloof* in this description of the poplar's sound makes it into a figure of erotic frustration, even though the passage's syntax leaves the subject of this frustration radically ambiguous. Is it the wooing wind that holds itself aloof from the poplar or the poplar from the wind? If the sound the poplar makes confounds Mariana's sense, the position of the word *aloof* in this passage confounds the sense of the text.

That position is determined, not only by the rhyme scheme of the stanza, but also by the appearance of its *aloof-roof* rhyme in the text of "Isabella," in a passage describing the ghost of Lorenzo, her lover:

> Strange sound it was, when the pale shadow spake;
>> For there was striving, in its piteous tongue,
> To speak as when on earth it was awake,
>> And Isabella on its music hung:
> Languor there was in it, and tremulous shake,
>> As in a palsied Druid's harp unstrung;
> And through it moan'd a ghostly under-song,
>> Like hoarse night-gusts sepulchral briars among.

(ll. 281–96)

> Its eyes, though wild, were still all dewy bright
>> With love, and kept all phantom fear aloof
> From the poor girl by magic of their light,
>> The while it did unthread the horrid woof
> Of the late darken'd time,—the murderous spite
>> Of pride and avarice,—the dark pine roof
> In the forest,—and the sodden turfed dell,
>> Where, without any word, from stabs he fell.

Lorenzo's shadow in this passage speaks a desire, and what it desires is to speak as if it were not a shadow. An identical nostalgia is central to Keats's own rhetorical stance in the poem, as this account of his relation to his source in Boccaccio suggests:

> O eloquent and famed Boccaccio!
>   Of thee we now should ask forgiving boon,
> And of thy spicy myrtles as they blow,
>   And of thy roses amorous of the moon,
> And of thy lilies, that do paler grow
>   Now they can no more hear thy ghittern's tune,
> For venturing syllables that ill beseem
> The quiet glooms of such a piteous theme. . . .
> But it is done—succeed the verse or fail—
>   To honour thee, and thy gone spirit greet;
> To stead thee, as a verse in English tongue,
> An echo of thee in the north-wind stung.

(ll. 145–60)

The conjunction in this passage of the figure of the music of a stringed instrument with its displaced echo in the north wind duplicates the organizing figures of the passage describing the voice of Lorenzo's ghost, quoted above. Here, however, the "ghittern's tune" that figures the literary romance of Boccaccio is represented as prior to its echo in a wind that under the metaphor of a change of climate introduces the notion of translation. In fact, this figure only repeats the metaphor of a change of place embodied in the word *translation* and in the figure of metaphor itself, whose Greek name, denoting the transference of sense from one place to another, was actually translated as the Latin *translatio*. The wind here is, then, not simply a metaphor but an irreducibly metaphorical metaphor of metaphor as such, while the text's account of Boccaccio's melody represents a nostalgia for romance as an articulation of desire that would precede metaphor.

The same nostalgia is at work in the poem's account of the speech of Lorenzo's ghost, which, like Boccaccio's text, appears under the figure of a stringed instrument. But Lorenzo's speech is already displaced; it is the speech of a shadow, a catachresis that Tennyson remembers when he writes about the shadow of the poplar in "Mariana."[12] The index of this displacement is the wind, which here appears not as bearing the echo of a prior music but as the burden, or undersong, of Lorenzo's voice. It figures a sound that, in Keats's word, mourns *through* the tremulous music of the ghost's speech, like a wind that blows somewhere else, among "sepulchral briars" (l. 288), in the place of death.

This wind, which stands for an irreducible figurality, becomes the wooing wind of Tennyson's final stanza. *Wooing* in this passage signifies, among other things, the sound of the wind as it blows, a sound we would perhaps normally write "whooing." A similar onomatopoeic sense of the word appears in another poem Tennyson published in the same volume as "Mariana," in which the speaker addresses an owl he has heard the preceding night:

I

Thy tuwhits are lulled, I wot,
   Thy tuwhoos of yesternight,
Which upon the dark afloat,
    So took echo with delight,
    So took echo with delight,
      That her voice untuneful grown,
      Wears all day a fainter tone.

II

I would mock thy chaunt anew;
    But I cannot mimick it;
Not a whit of thy tuwhoo,
    Thee to woo to thy tuwhit,
    Thee to woo to thy tuwhit,
      With a lengthened loud halloo,
      Tuwhoo, tuwhit, tuwhit, tuwhoo-o-o.

("Second Song: To the Same," ll. 1–14)

"To woo" in this text marks the absence of the voice being wooed; it signifies a desire that it frustrates precisely by virtue of its status as a signifier. But even to say so much is to imply that desire can precede the signifier; in fact, as this text shows, it cannot; it is rather constituted in the moment that it is frustrated, in the moment that the sound of the owl becomes *wooing*—even though Tennyson's wish to the contrary is figured in the poem's representation of Echo, who, having been taken with delight by the owl's voice, now pines away in its absence. She occupies, indeed, the place of all the deserted women I have discussed in this chapter, as allegorical representations of voice's desire to hear itself, pining away under the burden of their own allegorization.

    The wooing wind in the last stanza of "Mariana" is, then, a figure for a desire that is essentially figural; that cannot be thought as belonging to a subject who could speak it but is constituted only in the signifier arbitrarily assigned to the noise of the wind. In this harsher text than the "Song," far

from calling up its echo, this noise calls up the sound of the poplar that
confounds Mariana's sense. How could it be otherwise? To begin with, can
we avoid confounding the sound of the poplar with the sound of the wind?
Each produces sound only by its resonance with the other; in Tennyson's
description of the poplar sounding "to the wooing wind," the word *to*
denotes not the interlocution of distinct voices but the logic of supplementarity that we invoke when we speak of a text set to music. It is out of a
scene governed by this logic that "Mariana," like the other texts discussed
in this chapter from "The Skipping-Rope" on, constitutes a drama of
frustrated desire.

That drama is constituted in these lines in the resonance of the words
wooing and *aloof,* a resonance I would argue is the burden of the figure in
which they appear. This resonance is not in its immediate origins entirely
arbitrary; the rhyme of *aloof* and *roof* in this stanza is drawn from a stanza of
"Isabella" that I have already quoted. The rhyme word from Keats that
Tennyson does not quote is *woof,* from a line that figures Lorenzo's ghost
as unthreading "the horrid woof" (l. 292) of Isabella's brothers' plot. The
aim of this plot was to prevent Lorenzo from seeing or speaking to
Isabella; the moment of its unraveling is the moment when he returns and
speaks to her from the dead. It is a moment Tennyson remembers in "The
Lady of Shalott" when the Lady's tapestry unravels when she sees and
hears Lancelot. But I have already argued that in "The Lady of Shalott" the
phenomenon of presence in this moment is a function of what Lacan calls
the Imaginary, and that the desire which produces it, which seems to undo
the web of signification that he names the Symbolic order, is itself a
phenomenon of the differences and deferrals which that web produces.
Indeed, in "Mariana," Keats's *woof* echoes only in the *wooing* of the wind;
the word that in Keats designated the plot against desire here not only
designates desire itself but also constitutes its origin in its own absolutely
deferred origin as a signifier. In this text, the place of that origin is thought
as the place of the dead.

There is another reason for aligning the last stanza of "Mariana" with
part 3 of "The Lady of Shalott" besides their common reference to a
passage from "Isabella." Most, Mariana loathes the hour

(ll. 78–80)
> When the thick-moted sunbeam lay
> Athwart the chambers, and the day
> Was sloping toward his western bower.

In "The Lady of Shalott," of course, Lancelot appears burning with the
reflected light of the sun, while Hanno, the figure who passes by the island

of the Hesperides, does so in the course of a journey to the west and hears their song as it comes to him "from a slope / That ran bloombright into the Atlantic blue" ("The Hesperides," ll. 8–9).

In an important discussion focused on "Morte d'Arthur" but discussing a number of other texts as well, W. D. Paden has shown the recurrence in Tennyson's early poetry of a figure he identifies as the transmigrating sun-god of the Helio-Arkite mythography devised in the early nineteenth century by G. S. Faber to explain the origin of all pagan religion (78–79). Prominent in the life cycle of this deity, or Great Father, is his vanishing at the end of his life to an island paradise in the distant west, a theme whose importance to Tennyson I have already noted. Whether or not Paden is right to assert the figure's origin in Tennyson's reading of Faber—a point on which there is no external evidence—the pattern of imagery he describes undoubtedly exists and can be found in many texts he does not cite as examples. Among these I would list "The Lady of Shalott" and "The Hesperides," and also "Mariana," with its barely personified day sloping past Mariana's chamber to his bower.

I would argue that the solar associations of the men who glance through these texts have less to do with the mythography of Faber than with the Keats of "Hyperion" and "To Autumn" and, to a lesser extent, the Shelley of "Prometheus Unbound," "Epipsychidion," and the "Hymn of Apollo." But what concerns me here is not the figure's immediate source or sources but rather its more general significance in Tennyson as the sign of a male desire that always turns away and on whose turning, or troping, they themselves turn.

I have argued that Tennyson's different representations of place in the Hesperides' island and the tapestry of the Lady of Shalott each turn out to bear the mark of the father's taboo. Under different revisions, they figure the mother's body, the place from which male desire is constituted as a turning away. Freud insists throughout his work, in a way that is itself almost fetishistic, on the importance of the *sight* of the female genitals as the event that must occur to underwrite the castration complex in the male child.[13] This view has a certain explanatory force with respect to the recurrence in Tennyson of women like the Hesperides and the Lady of Shalott, whose discourse depends on their remaining unseen; it will also serve to introduce what I take to be the thematization of looking in "Mariana."

Dwight Culler asserts that we see in this poem through Mariana's eyes, that it is "her perception of the grange, the phenomenology of it, that we are given" (52). Even on its own terms, however, the phenomenology

that produces the received account of the text's unity can do so only by
virtue of a symptomatic omission. Consider the placing of the shadow in
the following lines:

> And ever when the moon was low,
>   And the shrill winds were up and away,
> In the white curtain, to and fro,
>   She saw the gusty shadow sway.
> But when the moon was very low,
>   And wild winds bound within their cell,
>   The shadow of the poplar fell
> Upon her bed, across her brow.

(ll. 49–56)

If the phantasmagorical quality of the shadow projected on the curtain in
the first part of this stanza, like the similar figure in part 2 of "The Lady of
Shalott," marks Mariana's sense of an erotic lack, the shadow that falls on
her brow in the second part is a mark on Mariana herself. It is impossible to
see a shadow on one's own brow, or even feel it, if it is a shadow cast in
moonlight. The placing of the shadow here constitutes Mariana, not as a
subject, but as the object of someone's gaze; it undoes any possible
conception of her as pure interiority by endowing her with an exterior, a
surface, on which shadows can fall.

The shadow falls on Mariana as she lies in bed at once like an erotic
fantasy and like the figure of a curse, and it should be aligned with the curse
that falls on the Lady of Shalott, which in that poem literally has the
burden of displacing the Lady from a privileged interiority and constituting her as the object of the male gaze. In "Mariana," however, the gaze is
not represented and has indeed been systematically misrecognized by the
poem's critics. We read it only through the mediation of the shadow on
Mariana's brow, a mark that itself refers to the poplar that marks the waste
around the grange. This chain of mediations establishes the gaze in this
text as a phenomenon of the Symbolic, constituted in the signifier, rather
than one that would observe the logic of presence and representation.

It is in the sense that it establishes Mariana as the object of a readerly
gaze that this scene is a staging of the male child's sight of the female
genitals. The shadow that falls on Mariana is the mark of an absence, and
the poplar that casts the shadow can be read as figuring the phallus insofar
as it figures what she is missing (see Gunter, 65). It is important, however,
that the poplar is itself represented as a mark; it stands here for the phallus
constituted as a signifier, the authorizing signifier of the Law of the Father,
which is indeed established as a system of signifiers, or a text, whose

author is always the dead father of Freud's *Totem and Taboo*.[14] Insofar, then, as we can bring the desire to which the poplar gives voice in "Mariana's" last stanza home to anyone, it would thus be to the father of the Law, whose sun sets at its close.

When Mariana appears as a surface on which a shadow falls, she enters into the logic of a figure that organizes much of the poem's description of the landscape around her, which is consistently represented as a surface that has been overgrown, marked, or obliterated. Consider the poem's first stanza:

> With blackest moss the flower-plots
> Were thickly crusted, one and all:
> The rusted nails fell from the knots
> That held the pear to the gable-wall.
> The broken sheds looked sad and strange:
> Unlifted was the clinking latch;
> Weeded and worn the ancient thatch
> Upon the lonely moated grange.

It is not hard to read this stanza, with its moss and its worn thatch, and its entrance opened by a latch, quite precisely as a representation of the vaginal region. Such a reading is, moreover, strengthened by the long history of the allegorical topos of the erotic garden, a topos in which a garden with a woman at its center frequently becomes a figure for her body (as, for instance, in *The Faerie Queene* 3.6.43–44). It is indeed this topos that Paul de Man, in the essay cited earlier, discusses as an exemplary instance of allegory. One could argue that this selection is not accidental; that the deferral of signification that constitutes allegory will in male discourse necessarily find its exemplar in the female body.

For it would be wrong to imagine that when we have read the landscape of "Mariana" as an allegory of the female body under a male gaze we can stop reading, as the scene of this gaze is itself allegorical of the Law, upon whose prior institution under the sign of the phallus its intelligibility depends. It is for this reason that the scene's significance is, according to Freud, deferred in the male child until the traumatic resolution of the Oedipus complex by the threat of castration—which would, however, itself be unintelligible without the child's prior knowledge of sexual difference. The intelligibility of the castration complex thus depends not only upon a signifying difference but also upon its own deferral; it cannot be thought except as coming after an event whose significance it constitutes only in retrospect. Like that of allegory, its institution is essentially temporal.[15]

In spite of the logic of the surface that connects them, there is a difference between the figure of the shadow that falls on Mariana and the figures of overgrowing and encrustation that characterize the landscape around her. We can consider this difference under the figure of *thickness*. A shadow has no thickness; we can see through it, and, more to the point, we can read it. The shadow of the poplar refers precisely to the poplar outside Mariana's room; the scene figures a reading of the woman's body after the castration complex is established, as bearing a legible mark that places the phallus elsewhere, presenting itself as an absolute lack.

The stratifications that dominate the poem's landscape, on the other hand, are transparent in neither the literal sense nor in the figural sense of legibility. They are, in a term that appears three times in the text, *thick*. This term describes in each case an object, or an area of darkness, that, far from denoting to the gaze another object, simply blocks it. Thus we have the "blackest moss" that thickly crusts the flower-plots of the beginning of the poem, and the "thickest dark" (l. 18), which alone meets Mariana's gaze at the one time when she looks out her window. And finally we have the motes of "the thick-moted sunbeam" (l. 78) in the final stanza. Particularly if we recall Christ's question in the Gospel of Matthew, "Why beholdest thou the mote that is in thy brother's eye, but considerest not the beam that is in thine own eye?" (7:3),[16] we will read the sunbeam as figuring a gaze that, peering into Mariana's room, is both interrupted and marked by what it sees there. And if the beam seems like a strangely phallic figure for the gaze, that is because it figures the gaze by which the son internalizes the Law of the Father and confirms the possession of the phallus in himself.

What, then, of these motes, which are thick in exactly the sense that they figure a blockage of the gaze, a mark that it cannot read? The phrase "the thick-moted sunbeam," moreover, opens out a pun for which I would claim a central place in the poem as a whole. For Mariana's grange is of course the "moated grange"; the phrase appears twice in the body of the text (ll. 8, 32), and also in the epigraph, where it implicitly asserts for itself a certain generative force with respect to what follows. The moat here is a figure of enclosure, a mark that closes off meaning, under the signs of voice, consciousness, place. It is the figure in this text that makes it legible in terms of an interior where the subject can be constituted.

The motes of the last stanza, however, which appear when the interior of the grange is figured as an object of regard, are precisely not legible in terms of interiority, being constituted purely as marks. The homophony of *mote* and *moat*, I would argue, suggests that one of the things at issue in this text is the possibility of reading interiority—of reading Mariana's grange as "moated" rather than "moted."

The difference between the two possibilities for reading posed here—which I would align with the difference I have described between the marks on Mariana's landscape and the shadow that falls on her brow—must be thought of as an effect of deferral. I have argued that signification in the castration complex is such an effect; in this respect the castration complex is paradigmatic of reading as such. Our reading of a word, or of a text, is inevitably the deferred effect of the letter constituted as a mark. In an often-cited passage from *The Interpretation of Dreams,* Freud writes that "in a psycho-analysis one learns to interpret propinquity in time as representing connection in subject matter. . . . Two thoughts which occur in immediate sequence without any apparent connection are in fact part of a single unity which as to be discovered; in just the same way, if I write an '*a*' and a '*b*' in succession, they have to be pronounced as a single syllable '*ab*.' "[17] But the "single unity" that Freud reads in the letters *ab* must in fact always be a deferred effect: we can read the letters as signifying a sound only after we have determined whether they are followed, for instance, by the letter *e*—or indeed by the letter *c,* which would here open up an elementary chain of signifiers: "*A B C D E F G* . . ." The law of reading is then a law of deferral, and the function of spatial metaphors of meaning, such as voice and interiority, is consequently to repress the time of reading, also a time of writing, in which they are nonetheless constituted.

It is because it is haunted by the time of reading that "Mariana" is among Tennyson's least idealizing allegories of voice. Each of the figures I have read as introducing into the text the logic of a readerly gaze is in effect a figure of a present in which reading is deferred, a present arrested in the letter. This is true of the figures of stratification that dominate the poem's description of its landscape, and of the moment marked by "thickest dark" (l. 18) when Mariana looks out of her window. But it is clearest in the figure of the shadow, which appears in different configurations, as the shadow that falls on Mariana's brow and as the shadows that the dust-motes cast in the sunbeam of the last stanza. The text makes it clear that the poplar casts its shadow on Mariana and that the sun shines in her window only at specific times; indeed, in the last stanza it is not the sunbeam that Mariana loathes but the hour that it marks. Her grange is thus figured as a sort of large-scale sundial, or moondial; as a mechanism for registering the passage of time.

This fact leaves us with two irreducibly different ways of reading the poem. On the one hand we can read it as an allegory—whose paradigm would derive from the moment when the male child introjects the Law of the dead father and so learns after the fact—*nachtraglich*—to read the body of his mother. In such a reading the body would speak, even if in a voice not its own, its own lack. This reading would account for a great deal in the text; but it cannot account for what must be called its insistence on the letter, on a mark whose legibility is infinitely deferred, and whose present is the present of reading and of writing, a present of the mechanically repeated inscription of an unfathomable difference.

I began this chapter by arguing that the repetition in the Hesperides' song is in essence autoerotic and that it enacts a pleasure in discourse that reproduces a narcissistic pleasure in the products of the body. That Tennyson adopts for this hoarded production the figure of accumulated money, however, should alert us to the possibility that it belongs to a signifying chain that opens out beyond the subject in which it ostensibly originates. And indeed, in "The Lady of Shalott," where, under the figure of weaving, repetition initially also establishes the space of the subject, it finally acquires a very different value. Weaving here eventually appears as the product of a machine and as the figure of a discourse in which the subject appears, not at the origin, but as a diacritical mark, a discourse whose burden is finally the death of what it names. In both poems, then, repetition constitutes what fills up the subject, but it also opens out a movement of the signifier in which the subject is only a cipher. This was also the ambivalence of the skipping-rope in the rhyme discussed in the chapter's opening pages.

The place of the subject in these texts then depends upon a repetition that, I have argued in my discussion of "Mariana," establishes it as a place in an allegory. In "The Rhetoric of Temporality," Paul de Man characterized the repetition that constitutes allegory as Kirkegaardian, a characterization that makes allegory depend on the phenomenology of a subject who understands it as the reading or writing with a difference of something that has been written before.[18] But there is a movement in these texts, most notably in "Mariana," that insists on the essential illegibility of what they repeat; on the impossibility of imagining a subject who could ever produce meaning out of their repetition. This repetition, I have argued, is the repetition of the letter, a repetition to which Freud gave, among others, the name of the death drive.

III

Metaphor and Displacement

Metaphor, then, always carries its death within itself.　(Jacques Derrida)

Ultima Multis.　(Inscription on a sundial, quoted by Walter Benjamin)

I

THE "SONG (A spirit haunts the year's last hours)" that Tennyson published in 1830 may help us to recapitulate certain points we have already made while at the same time opening a topic that our argument has hitherto evaded: that of metaphor as a figure that evades place, topos, or topicality as such. Like the daughters of Hesperus, the Lady of Shalott, and Mariana, the spirit of this poem talks to himself. And, like them, he does so in an enclosed garden whose very enclosure functions as a metaphor for the extravagant inwardness of a speech that is imagined as being without intention or referent.

There is a paradox in the idea that the place where the spirit speaks can be a metaphor for the properties of his speech. For metaphor, as we have seen, is the trope of displacement, or of the transference of meaning from one place to another. Consequently, to the extent that the place in which the spirit speaks is in Tennyson's poem a metaphor for the condition of his speech, to that extent the poem has already subjected his speech to *displacement*. And there is a certain sense in which the place of the speaking subject in this text is in fact potentially multiple. The words of the poem are not those uttered by the spirit. Their syntax assigns them to another subject whose place is, however, defined by the deictic "these . . . bowers" ("A spirit haunts," l. 2) as being the same as his. This subject, moreover, addresses a "you" who is situated, if slightly less definitely, in the same place as the spirit: "At his work you may hear him sob and sigh / In the walks" (ll. 5–6). The shifters (e.g., "you" [l. 5], "my" [l. 16]) that designate these possible positions for the subject in relation to the poem's discourse can clearly designate an infinite number of actual subjects. Who is the "I" that utters this discourse? And if that question seems a simple one, to whom is it addressed? To a third party, besides the spirit and the poem's speaker, in this now increasingly crowded garden? Or to the unlimited number of its possible readers?

The syntax of this text thus constructs a fixed number of possible positions for the subject, all of which it situates in the same place—the garden where the spirit speaks and works. Semantically, however, the poem's pronouns designate an indeterminate number of subjects for each of these positions—and it is possible to think of the subjects thus designated as occupying the same place only if the notion of *the same* is thought of as itself in some sense multiple. For instance, it is possible to consider the poem as representing a speaker and an auditor in the same place. It is also possible to think of it as asserting that the poet and the reader occupy the same place. But these two possible—indeed necessary—readings appeal to notions of the same that themselves differ from one another.

The difference between them is simply the putative difference between the literal garden the text represents and the metaphorical garden of rhetorical flowers that is the text itself. I want to argue that the poem's project is to enact the dissolution of that difference in the moment that Derrida's "White Mythology" describes as the end of metaphor, its return to the literal: "Metaphor, therefore, is determined by philosophy as a provisional loss of meaning, an economy of the proper without irreparable damage, a certainly inevitable detour, but also a history with its sights set on, and within the horizon of, the circular reappropriation of literal, proper meaning" (*Margins,* 270). I shall also want to show, however, that this enactment of a return to the literal in the poem is itself determined by metaphor, which thus survives itself, continuing to operate even at its own end.

Leaving aside for the moment the topic of metaphor narrowly defined, it is not hard to see in this text a formal insistence on the notion of return. Its principal figure for closure is the image of the flowers, which, hanging over the earth, are represented as on the verge of dissolution, but also as hanging over their place of origin, on the verge of a return to it:

(ll. 9–12
and 21–24)

Heavily hangs the broad sunflower
    Over its grave i' the earth so chilly;
Heavily hangs the hollyhock,
    Heavily hangs the tiger-lily.

The bowing down of these flowers is moreover represented as the "work" of the spirit (l. 5); we may identify this work with the technical work involved in the writing of the poem. Specifically, these flowers in suspense, which the spirit bows down over the earth to which they are about to return, not only make up the poem's refrain but also figure the linked motifs of suspense and return that define refrain as such.[1]

We can say, then, that the flowers in this text are the site of a set of effects involving both the institution and the deferral of closure as a form of return. We can also say that these effects are produced by a labor analogous to the poetic labor of elaborating a refrain. But the force of the flowers in this text is not simply as the vehicle for its reflections on one of its own formal devices. In accordance with an iconographic convention of long standing, they convey claims about the devices of its rhetoric as well.

If work in this poem is what initiates the return of the flowers to their graves, and the return of its form upon itself, work stands in this respect in contrast to the text's representation of voice and, more generally, to the notion of interiority that is signified by the concept of the spirit itself. The spirit is represented as belonging to a single time and place and as speaking and hearing itself speak in that time and place. In accordance with the logic of this representation, the notion of communication, or of the transmission of meaning from one place to another, appears not under the sign of voice but as an effect of the forms of work we have been analyzing. We thus find in this text another version of the opposition we have already seen, for instance in "The Solitary Reaper," between meaning as single and present to itself in the place and time of its origin and the *technique* by which it is communicated. I have argued that, under the sign of technique, this poem thematizes its own formal devices; I want now to show that its central concern with the technical is, however, with rhetorical technique, or, more specifically, with the technique of metaphor.

While the first stanza of Tennyson's poem is principally concerned with the spirit and with his place and time, the second does not refer to the spirit at all but describes the air in which he dwells:

(ll. 13–20)

The air is damp, and hushed, and close,
As a sick man's room when he taketh repose

> An hour before death;
> My very heart faints and my whole soul grieves
> At the moist rich smell of the rotting leaves,
>   And the breath
>   Of the fading edges of box beneath,
> And the year's last rose.

This stanza follows from the first as the elaboration of the metaphor that is etymologically encoded in the word *spirit,* deriving as it does from the Latin "spiritus," or breath. I here elide the question of whether this elaboration is a movement *into* the realm of metaphor or a *return* from a metaphorical notion of the spirit to the literal idea of breath that underlies it. In fact, I want to argue that this formulation of the question is inadequate to Tennyson's poem, in which to frame a metaphor is also and at the same time to return to the literal. With this caution we can say that the dominant image of the poem's second stanza is a metaphor for the figure of the spirit in the first.

Along with the shift in the poem's topic of representation in its second stanza, there is a shift in its affective center from the spirit to the lyric subject as such. This subject is represented as wholly given up to a grief induced by the smell of the rotting leaves in the garden around him. If we can say that the shift in the site of affect in the poem is an effect of communication, then it is clear that this effect is ordered by the logic of metaphor. Because the spirit can metaphorically become the breath which the poet breathes in, we read his grief in the second stanza as the same grief that makes the spirit sob in the first. The circulating air of the second stanza should thus be read as a metaphor for the circulation of metaphor itself in the communication of affect.

Moreover, what the speaker in the second stanza breathes in are the smells of rotting leaves and fading flowers, smells that are the effects of the spirit's work in stanza 1. This poem thus figures flowers and plants as becoming metaphors by virtue of the spirit's work upon them. We may align it, therefore, with the poetic tradition in which flowers and plants figure the products of rhetorical technique. This conventional figure appears, for instance, in "The Poet," another poem of Tennyson's 1830 volume, where the poet scatters his thoughts abroad "like the arrow-seeds of the field flower." Whereupon,

> Where'er they fell, behold,
> (ll. 19–24)   Like to the mother flower in semblance, grew
>   A flower all gold.

But what marks this text's deeply belated relation to that tradition is its insistence that the proper metaphor for the end of metaphor is death. The metaphor that arrives at its destination in this poem is of necessity a dead letter, which is to say one that fails to arrive at its destination except as an absence, a trace, a smell of decay. That is why the dialectical irony of Tennyson's poem makes the spirit it describes both a figure like the poet in the passage I have just quoted, who disseminates his thought like someone sowing flowers, and a sort of heavily sedated Guyon, who tears down the flowers in the garden of art.

The central structuring metaphor of "A spirit haunts" is an implied equation between its formal and rhetorical turns and returns and the imminent turn of the year. I have already argued that these turns are themselves metaphorically identified as sharing properties with the place the poem represents and with the flowers that grow there. So we can further identify the flowers that turn down over their graves as metaphors also for the year that has turned toward its close, in a final turn that, like that of the flower, is also equally a return to a beginning. This metaphor, I suggest, determines Tennyson's combination of the time and the place where his poem is set.

And yet there is a motif in the poem that its metaphors do not encompass. That is the motif of work, or of what I have discussed as technique. The poem elaborates a series of metaphors that describe metaphor itself by analogy with changes that belong to nature, such as the return of flowers to the earth and their subsequent decay. But it represents these changes as the result of work, as though the flowers required an additional pressure, beyond that of their own heaviness, to return them to the ground. The work of the spirit thus stands, not quite in a relation of analogy to natural processes, but rather in a relation of supplementarity. The extent to which the spirit's work is an anomaly in the poem is marked by its disappearance from the second stanza, where the poem's figures appear to resolve themselves into a moment of full lyric interiority. This moment appears under the sign of "repose" (l. 14); in it the work of formal elaboration apparently vanishes in the moment of pure affect that is ideally its product.

The figure of repose itself, however, betrays a temporal dislocation which suggests that something, at least, still works here. The air in the garden, the poem tells us,

> is damp, and hushed, and close,
> (ll. 13–15)   As a sick man's room when he taketh repose
> An hour before death.

It is impossible to say with certainty that one *is* in the last hour of a sick man's life; one can only know in retrospect when one *has been so.* In its proleptic inscription of the certainty of death into this figure, the poem exerts on it a pressure analogous to the pressure exerted by the spirit upon the stalks of the flowers in the first stanza. For the repose this text seeks, the repose of the figure that has fully returned to its proper sense, nature apparently supplies no proper metaphor. Even in the moment of meta-phor's return upon itself, a certain supplemental labor, a labor of the supplement, still continues.

It is hard to write about this short poem without resort to hyperbole, because its own insistence that all of its tropes have only death as their burden is itself so hyperbolical. With that caution, I shall make the per-haps hyperbolic claim that in "A spirit haunts the year's last hours" Tennyson takes as his topic the decay of the figures by which Western European lyric has signified the immanence in its texts of a presence or a voice. Such a presence literally has no place in this poem, which is instead haunted by a belated and out-of-place spirit.

In the rest of this chapter we will be examining other figures who, like the spirit of this poem, are irremediably in the wrong place. But before moving on, I want to look briefly at the relation of Tennyson's poem to a more specific precursor text, Keats's "To Autumn." The spirit of Tennyson's song who performs the work of time in bending down the stalks of the flowers is a belated version of the spirit of Keats's autumn, who bends the apple branches with fruit and

sets[s] budding more,

And still more, later flowers for the bees,

Until they think warm days will never cease.

(ll. 8–10)

But the hint of irony in Keats's poem, that warm days *will* cease, becomes the full burden of Tennyson's, where the heaviness of the flower stalks is not that of an extravagant fruitfulness, but that of death. In Keats's stanzas there is a continuous ironic suggestion of morbidity in the notion of perfect ripeness; in Tennyson, as the reference to "the moist rich smell of the rotting leaves" implies, there is no distinction between riches and rot (l. 17). The gesture that thus collapses richness into decay is cognate with that which pushes an autumnal landscape into the last hours of the year.

Tennyson's poem, in short, tropes Keats's irony as a hyperbolic belatedness. The specific sign of this belatedness is the apparent absence of the sun in his poem's late evening, an absence whose index is the hanging down of the sunflower. In "To Autumn" the sun appears in the first stanza as autumn's friend and coconspirator. It is under the sun that autumn's

fruits swell and ripen, and it is under the sun that the late flowers prolife-
rate to deceive the bees. Although Keats does not specify autumn's gender, the sun is personified as "him" (l. 3) and is almost imagined as an
agent of both impregnation and dissemination.

I have already argued that the proliferation of fruits and flowers under
the sun in the opening stanza of "To Autumn" figures a rhetorical profusion, born out of nostalgia, that blocks an authentically autumnal or
Western song.[2] The sun conspires with autumn to produce beautiful
fictions—which, however, end with the day and give way to the songs of
the poem's concluding catalog, which describes them all at evening
time—"While barred clouds bloom the soft-dying day" (l. 25). In Keats's
poem, then, the setting of the sun accompanies the naturalizing or chas-
tening of a certain figural extravagance. The law of figurality here is that it
follows the sun; as the sun sets, a kind of truth emerges which may be the
truth that even the voices of autumn are figures that follow the sun, if not
in sinking at evening time, then south for the winter.

In revising "To Autumn," Tennyson's poem claims that what is left
after the songs of autumn and evening are gone is a grieving spirit. In this
respect it follows the account of the Western philosophical discourse of
metaphor given by Derrida in "White Mythology": The "*end* of metaphor
is not interpreted as a death or dislocation, but as an interiorizing anam-
nesis (*Erinnerung*), a recollection of meaning, a *relève* of living meta-
phoricity into a living state of properness" (*Margins*, 269). I have already
argued that in Tennyson's poem the "end" of metaphor cannot be thought
without recourse to metaphor. Metaphor ends by returning to its beginning; here the new year returns and the flowers return to their beds. These
returns are figured as the work of a spirit who is himself, in an etymological return, resolved into a breath. All of these returns imply the idea of
sameness, as in the notion that the flowers begin and end in the same place;
and we have seen that the poem's conception of sameness is itself indebted
to metaphor. I want to finish by suggesting that the insistence of metaphor is figured by a certain insistent tug of the sun.

For the sun does not simply sink without a trace below this text's
horizon. The presence of the sunflower in the catalog of flowers that
makes its refrain invites us to reexamine the metaphorical equation we
saw earlier between the flowers hanging over their graves and the year
suspended in its last hours. The poem represents that metaphor as the
expressive labor of a spirit belonging to a particular hour. But the sunflower hangs down every evening after sunset, by convention not over its
own grave but over the sun's. This fact does not, of course, undo the

metaphor we have already read in the sunflower. But it does make it impossible to see that reading as exhaustive. The same movement that serves as a metaphor for the return of meaning to its proper place also metaphorically represents another movement, the trajectory of the sun, that exists in a place and time absolutely other than those represented in the text. The possibility of such a double reading implies that, at least in this case, there is no end to metaphor. Or that we can situate the end of metaphor in a privileged moment of interiority only by burying or forgetting the reference that it makes to a concept that is in its essence nonsituable, and has no proper place. In this text, and elsewhere in Tennyson, the paradigmatic figure for such a concept is the sun; we shall see in the remainder of this chapter a recurrent tension between his poems' will to bring meaning home and their metaphors' extravagant heliotropism.

II

In reading "A spirit haunts the year's last hours" we saw that metaphor envisions as one of its horizons a return to the ground in which the metaphor would realize its truth in the moment of its decay, like a rotting flower or leaf that dissolves into an odor. We saw further that in such a conception of its trajectory, metaphor can only follow a law, or tend to a truth, whose ground would itself be metaphorical. In this respect the poem points to a recurrent problematic in understandings of metaphor. In the *Rhetoric* Aristotle writes of the "most taking" form of metaphor as the metaphor from proportion (1411a), of which his fullest definition is found elsewhere, in the *Poetics:*

> *A proportional metaphor means that of four things the second is to the first as the fourth is to the third. The fourth can thus be used for the second, or the second for the fourth, and sometimes the term to which the transferred term was related may be added. For example: the cup is to Dionysus what the shield is to Ares; one may then speak of the cup as the shield of Dionysus, or of the shield as the cup of Ares. Or again: old age is*
>
> (*Poetics* 1457b)
>
> *to life as evening is to day; one may then speak of the evening as the day's old age, or of old age as the evening of life. . . . At times there may be no name in use for some of the terms of the analogy, but we can use this kind of metaphor none the less. For example, to cast seed is to sow, but there is no special word for the casting of rays by the sun [i.e., it is nameless— "anonymon"]; yet this is to sunlight as sowing is to seed, and therefore it has been said of the sun that it is "sowing its divine rays."*

In the last of these examples, the meaning Aristotle gives for his metaphor is a phenomenon for which there is no name; that is to say, it has no literal designation but may be referred to only by metaphor. The possibility of such a phenomenon in effect calls into question the whole category of the literal. If we read it back against Aristotle's earlier examples we may ask, for instance, to what extent the term *old age*—especially in English—has in its reference to human life a *literal* sense, from which its *metaphorical* meaning departs. Derrida writes that "marking the moment of the turn or of the detour during which meaning might seem to venture forth alone, unloosed from the very thing it aims at however, from the truth which attunes it to its referent, metaphor also opens the wanderings of the semantic. The sense of a noun, instead of designating the thing which the noun habitually must designate, carries itself elsewhere. If I say that the evening is the old age of the day, or that old age is the evening of life, 'the evening,' although having the same sense, will no longer designate the same things" (*Margins*, 241). If metaphor envisions a return to the literal, it also necessarily brings about within literality a sort of perturbation or decay.

This consideration of metaphor and "A spirit haunts the year's last hours" may seem a peculiar way to begin a reading of "Ulysses." Indeed, we can open by listing the topics of the earlier poem that are absent or refused in the later. These would include the concept of interiority, or of pathos; while the speaker of "A spirit" *grieves,* Ulysses *suffers* or *enjoys.* He seems, moreover, to do both simultaneously, or indiscriminately ("Ulysses," ll. 7–8). Further, while the spirit in the garden speaks only to himself and while the poem in which he appears says nothing of what he speaks about, the text of "Ulysses" insists on the referential capacity of Ulysses' discourse and on its status as an address to a determinate audience: "This is my son, mine own Telemachus" (l. 33), Ulysses says, and later he addresses "My mariners, / Souls that have toiled, and wrought, and thought with me" (ll. 45–46). If, then, "A spirit" may be understood as representing the interior site of an utterance that can resolve itself into affect without reference to an exterior, "Ulysses," on the contrary, represents an utterance that insists on its capacity to refer to multiple places in a world external to its speaker.

Such a list of topics would also include the concept of return, which is built into the form of "A spirit" as well as figured in its representation of the cycles of the seasons and the growth and decay of flowers. No principle of return governs the form of "Ulysses." The poem's representation of time will concern us presently; for now, however, it is worth noting the marked absence of plant life in its landscape, which is described as "barren" (l. 2). Moreover, and more centrally, the whole direction of the poem's argument is determined by the claim that the narrative of return that constitutes the life of Ulysses in the Homeric epics is inadequate or incomplete. If this argument can be paraphrased in a sentence, it asserts that the desire that brings Ulysses back to Ithaca at the end of the *Odyssey* exceeds its supposed object, whose attainment thus does not bring it to an end.[3]

My point in listing this set of contrasts is to underline the conjunction in "A spirit" of the topic of return with a drive to self-enclosure in the lyric subject and the suspension of the semantic or referential function of language in favor of metaphor. In contrast, "Ulysses" represents a subject who can speak to others and who, more importantly, can also be unequivocally named by them. "I am become a name. . . . I am a part of all that I have met," Ulysses says in the parallel main clauses of successive sentences (ll. 11, 18). In so saying, he implicitly claims, among other things, that he is known and referred to by name in many places and that the person thus named is the same as the person who speaks the lines. Ulysses' name thus circulates at large. But it does so without becoming involved, on the one hand, in the topics of decay that often haunt representations of the signifier as circulating at an increasing spatiotemporal distance from their signifieds. When those he has met in other places and times refer to him by name as he was, they also refer to what he has "become," without any decay or slippage in the connection between the name and the man. And, on the other hand, his name circulates without becoming involved in the topic—entirely symmetrical with that of decay—of meaning as held in abeyance, while the signifier awaits some connection or reconnection with the signified. The meaning of Ulysses' name does not await his return to the place where it is uttered, or any other event. In connection with Ulysses' name, then, the poem refuses the topics of displacement, suspense, and decay—so often associated with metaphor—in favor of a thematic of the literal.

The poem's insistence on the inseparability of Ulysses' name from the person it literally designates informs more than the few lines it actually devotes to the topic. As the last example from Aristotle suggests, the topic of insemination, and hence of paternity, has since classical times been closely bound up with that of metaphor. And in the West, with some exceptions, the institution of paternity has also entailed the displacement of the paternal name, a name that thus does not refer exclusively to the father but rather awaits either the fullness or the decay of its meaning in the child it also names. The displacement of the father's name onto the child signals the availability of the child's life as a metaphor for the father's. In Tennyson's poem, then, the resistance of the barren Ithacan crags to seed would be cognate with the poem's resistance to displacements of meaning, as, more centrally, would Ulysses' terse assessment of the differences between himself and his son, Telemachus:

> Most blameless is he, centred in the sphere
> Of common duties, decent not to fail
(ll. 39–43) In offices of tenderness, and pay
> Meet adoration to my household gods,
> When I am gone. He works his work, I mine.

These lines have at times seemed egregious or underdetermined to a criticism seeking a psychological understanding of Tennyson's Ulysses.[4] In their refusal of a metaphorical dimension to paternity, however, and in their insistence that what is proper to Ulysses, his work, is proper to him alone, they seem entirely congruent with what I have so far traced as the poem's argument.

That argument may be summarized in the abstract as claiming that a proper name, more than any other kind of word, is the paradigmatic instance of the literal, and as such, refuses the displacement within the sign that defines the trope of metaphor. The point of such a claim in Tennyson's poem is clarified when we recall that it does not refer to the poem alone. When Ulysses is represented as saying "I am become a name" (l. 11), he speaks in a fictional time coterminous with that represented in the *Iliad* and the *Odyssey*. His claim then certainly refers to the fame he has acquired in that fictional time. But insofar as this claim is also that of Tennyson's text, which exists in a different temporal order, it refers to Ulysses' fame as it is circulated *by* the Homeric epics, as well as *within* them, and also by—to name only the most salient moments in a long history—the *Epistles* of Horace, by Dante's *Inferno,* and by Tennyson's poem itself, which may here be taken as reflecting on its own enterprise. In the implicit claim that the name Ulysses designates the single "I" that speaks in his poem, Tennyson implies that all of these texts, with all of their divergences from one another's narratives, refer to a single fictional person whose life exists in different versions.

Tennyson's poem is, then, among other things, both an argument for a continuity within a certain textual tradition and a meditation on the ground of that continuity. This ground it locates in the power of a name to refer to a single character. The poem is thus set at the center of a contradiction in the received narratives of Ulysses' life. In the *Odyssey,* Ulysses' wanderings end in Ithaca, where he returns as Tiresias had prophesied in book 11, having suffered "the loss of all [his] companions / in someone else's ship" (*Odyssey* 11.114–15). In Ithaca, Tiresias also prophesied, he will eventually die (11.132–37; the Greek in this passage is ambiguous and makes of the place of Ulysses' death a crux within the *Odyssey* itself). In another tradition, canto 26 of Dante's *Inferno* represents Ulysses as having sailed westward with his crew from the island of Circe without ever having returned to Ithaca, until his ship is overwhelmed by a whirlwind five days after having passed the Pillars of Hercules.

Tennyson of course adopts as part of his poem's context the Homeric narrative of Ulysses' return. But the character of Ulysses, whose essence is a "zeal . . . / T'explore the world" (*Inferno* 26.97–98), he takes from Dante, arguing that Ulysses is really himself when he is voyaging. The Ulysses who actually returns to Ithaca and lives there thus becomes one who is not truly himself. Others, seeing him there, do not truly know him ("Ulysses," l. 5); only during his wanderings was he both able to see and know, and to be known, and hence "honoured of . . . all" (l. 15). In voyaging, he performs his "work"; in Ithaca he is an "idle king" (ll. 43, 1), that is, one who is temporarily not performing what is proper to him. He is hence not only "idle," but also an *idol*—a false representation.[5] At the opening of the poem, Ulysses is in this sense false to himself. Only at the close, when he has reaffirmed his "purpose" (l. 59)—a design that is his and that is also the final cause that makes him himself—and when he speaks to the crew who can recognize him for what he is, can he say of himself and them, that they are what they are (l. 67).

To the problem that the divergent traditions about Ulysses' actions pose for an essentializing account of his character, Tennyson's solution is the entirely conventional one of representing certain moments in the tradition as moments when Ulysses is not properly himself. The poem thus represents a character claiming the power once again to become the character he already truly is. In so doing, it claims for itself the power to name that character and to anchor his name in its representation of the preexisting truth of his being. Ulysses' name, in spite of its long journey west, and in spite of its translation from a Greek form to a Latin and an Italian one, and finally into its anglicized version, nonetheless remains the same name inasmuch as it designates the same person. The westward displacement of Ulysses' name, the text implies, is not a metaphorical displacement.

This reading of the poem implies a structural opposition between the designatory function of the name and the referential function of its pronouns and other semantic units. I have argued that the poem mentions the name as an instance of the literal, as a word that continues to designate the same person, regardless of context. I have further argued that in order to preserve the continuity of Ulysses' identity as the bearer of his name, the poem is obliged to represent Ulysses as acting at certain moments in ways that are not proper to him. In this poem, which represents Ulysses' discourse, this means that the ways in which he signifies himself in discourse do not properly refer to him, or do not refer to the self that is named by his name.

We shall pursue some of the broader significance of this opposition of designation and syntactic reference below; first, however, I want to look at some awkwardnesses in Ulysses' references to himself in the poem's opening lines. One of the most marked of these is the way that Ulysses seems constantly about to speak of himself in the third person. Hence the deferral of the "I" in the poem's first sentence until the end of line 3, which makes the appositional phrase "an idle king" seem like the grammatical subject, and indeed delays the reader's awareness that Ulysses himself is speaking. Again, in line 15, the position of the words "Myself not least" at the end of Ulysses' catalog of things he has seen and known in his travels makes it seem for a moment as if he is remembering having seen and known himself.

These moments of hesitation in the poem's syntax may be said to produce a kind of oscillation or disequilibrium in its positioning of the speaking subject. As it unfolds, these effects become more radically ambiguous. When Ulysses asserts in lines 24–26 that his desire is always disproportionately great in relation to his life, he begins by figuring life as a substance of which any amount would be insufficient: "Life piled on life / Were all too little." In the second half of the same sentence, however, life becomes, not a substance of which one might have much or little, but an object to be counted in units of one per person: "and of one to me / Little remains." Life is both what Ulysses desires—"I want more life"—and something that is proper to him as a subject—"I have one and only one life." It is, thus, in one of these figurations conceived as what can only be *expended*—"little remains" of Ulysses' life—and in the other as what desire seeks to *accumulate*. Provisionally, we may say that the difference between these figurations marks a contradiction in the speaking subject's relation to the signifier. This becomes clear in the following clause:

<blockquote>
                    every hour is saved
(ll. 26–28)   From that eternal silence, something more,
                    A bringer of new things.
</blockquote>

The syntactic function of the various phrases in these lines is far from clear. But we may open our reading with the predicate: What would it mean for an hour—or something—to be saved from silence? Presumably the answer has to do with speech; insofar as these lines have to do with what Ulysses refers to above as "experience" (l. 19), they refer to an experience that is in its essential form voiced. What is saved from silence is not just a new thing but a "*bringer* of new things"—the signifier that is in its essence the bearer of signification. Nonetheless, the agency of signification is here radically unclear. The lines could plausibly be paraphrased as meaning that "every hour during which *I* am saved from that eternal silence will be a bringer of new things to me." Ulysses would then be saying that he will go on having new experiences for as long as he keeps on talking—a reading that has the virtue of suggesting a way to read the poem as a whole. But the lines also demand readings in which, not Ulysses, but the hours, the something more, the bringers of new things are saved from silence, readings in which Ulysses' experience would apparently be conceived as the liberation of a discourse addressed to him rather than spoken by him.

How, then, are we to understand Ulysses' relation to the signifier? Is he the speaker of his own experience? Or is experience itself a discourse addressed to him from some place other than the place in which he speaks? We can read this problematic back against the poem's ambiguity about whether Ulysses' life is his own to spend or whether it is something given to him from elsewhere, of which he longs for more. And against his tendency to split off the syntactical location of the subject of his experiences—of being an idle king, of being among those he has met—from that of the grammatical subject who speaks of them.

According to Lacan, that split is inescapable for the subject of any discourse whatsoever.[6] Nonetheless, it is true to say that "Ulysses" insists on it to a remarkable degree. One further instance will suffice, from the final lines of the third verse paragraph, which follow immediately upon those we have just been considering:

<blockquote>
vile it were
For some three suns to hoard and store myself,
(ll. 28–32)   And this gray spirit yearning in desire
To follow knowledge like a sinking star,
Beyond the utmost bound of human thought.
</blockquote>

These lines include the poem's most notorious syntactic crux. It is undecidable whether the phrase "this gray spirit" should be regarded as an accusative, parallel to "myself," or as an absolute, independent of the previous clause.[7] At issue here in essence is the syntactic position of desire. Is it an object, something that the subject could hoard up; or is it identified with the subject's own agency? The indeterminacy of the subject's position with respect to his desire is, finally, only emphasized by the simile of line 31, where the image of a sinking star could refer either to the manner in which the spirit yearns to follow knowledge or to knowledge itself. The effect of the whole passage is to emphasize the extreme instability of the position of the poem's speaking subject, whose references to the dramas of his experience, his desire—indeed, of his life—seem constantly to set him apart from them, as speaking of them from another place.

This feature of the poem's syntax is of a piece with the inconsistency many readers have noticed in the poem's implications about the place in which Ulysses is speaking. If he stands by his hearth at the outset, by line 44 ("There lies the port") he seems to be outdoors, and by line 58, where he tells his mariners to push off and begin to row, we must suppose that he has embarked and speaks from on board ship. Moreover, not only the physical site but the discursive context of Ulysses' utterance shifts in the course of the poem. At the opening, the tone of his references to Penelope and to his subjects has led most commentators to assume that he is alone.[8] By line 33, he can gesture with the demonstrative *this* to Telemachus, implying that Telemachus at least is present. Finally, in line 45, he directly apostrophizes his crew: "my mariners," implying that they form the audience for what he says.

The remarkable thing about these displacements is the fact that they occur, like everything that occurs in the poem, without any apparent act of will recorded in Ulysses' discourse. They are marked in that discourse only by apostrophes or deictics that designate particular objects or persons as present to the speaker. Ulysses' place is thus legible in this text exclusively as an effect of the referents of his discourse, rather than as, say, an effect of predication in that discourse.

Readers of the poem have invariably taken these effects for granted. Nobody doubts that "Ulysses" represents its speaker as speaking in Ithaca and on its shore. The poem's intelligibility depends upon this reading, even though it must take otherwise than literally the passages in which the "I" of the poem is actually the subject of predication. For those passages characteristically stress the subject's existence in a place other than the place in which he speaks. "I am a part of all that I have met" (l. 18), he says; and our question will have to do with the relation between the Ulysses referred to in this line and the Ulysses who refers demonstratively to "my son, mine own Telemachus"—or, for that matter, to himself, as "this gray spirit" (ll. 33, 30).

We saw at the start of this chapter that in "A spirit haunts the year's last hours" the conception of spirit as an interior site at which utterance, affect, and referent would coincide is grounded in metaphors whose hyperbolic extension to their limit we read as the poem's topic. In "Ulysses," on the contrary, we find an insistence on the capacity of names to make literal reference combined with a refusal of the concept of interiority and with a dramatic displacement, indeed dispersal, of the subject. It is possible to see, however, that the opposition between the two texts is structured by a consistent set of ideas—or fantasies—about names, interiority, and metaphor. It is entirely in keeping with the decorum of "A spirit" that it should be a virtually nameless poem about an anonymous spirit. The spirit of the poem is metaphorically identified with its own utterance and with that utterance's time and place. The spirit's anonymity perhaps implies that to give it a name would disrupt those identifications—as if the possibility of naming the spirit would threaten to give it an identity outside the metaphors that constitute its being. This possibility is of course embraced by Ulysses, who *is* a name, and therefore also "a part of all that [he has] met."

Briefly, these poems seem to be governed by a conception of interiority as constituted by a taboo on naming; or, to put it otherwise, by a sense that any utterance may be identified with the interior site in which it originates and which it constitutes *except* the utterer's name, which is supposed to be infinitely citable, and whose citation within a subject's utterance would disrupt the constitutive identification of the subject's interiority with the origin of its utterance. Even more briefly, in these texts subjects cannot speak where they are named. That is why it is so hard in much of "Ulysses" to say where Ulysses speaks—or even to say with assurance that it is he himself who speaks, since at the moment he articulates his demand for more life his very discourse seems suddenly to turn back on him and to be addressed to him from out of an eternal silence—from the dead.

Our discussion of the place from which Ulysses speaks has hitherto been concerned with questions of grammar and semantics; that such questions do not suffice to dismiss the issue will by this time have become abundantly evident. The moment in the text that makes this insufficiency clearest occurs in the course of its most elaborate metaphor:

(ll. 18–21)

> I am a part of all that I have met;
> Yet all experience is an arch wherethrough
> Gleams that untravelled world, whose margin fades
> For ever and for ever when I move.

These lines imply certain assertions about their speaker's place while at the same time leaving it radically unclear whether place is an object of semantic or metaphorical reference. When Ulysses uses the demonstrative *that* in line 20 to refer to an "untravelled world," he implicitly situates that world as part of the context of his utterance—that is to say, as an object outside his discourse to which that discourse can refer. The gleam of this world, however, shines through an arch whose status is quite different; it is explicitly a discursive construct, having no existence except in the metaphor for experience with which Ulysses calls it into being. The untraveled world and the arch in these lines are thus the objects of different kinds of reference. Nonetheless, the gleam of one shines through the other, situating them in the same prospect.

It is, moreover, in relation to this prospect that the lines situate their speaker, since he says that the "margin" of the untraveled world fades when he moves. So do we understand the place in which Ulysses stands in these lines to have a literal existence, as part of the context of his speech? Or do we understand it solely as part of an elaborated metaphor for his relation to his experience? The same questions apply with respect to the movement referred to in line 21; and in this poem, whose central wagers are that it is possible for an utterance to have a literal reference and that it is possible finally, literally, to move from one place to another, they are not questions that can be simply incidental.

We need not be surprised that this figure poses questions of this kind. For its point is paradoxical: Ulysses speaks from one position that is not a part of his experience and looks from it toward another. As its derivation from the Latin "experiri," "to put to the test," implies, the term *experience* necessarily implies a dialectic in which a concept is opposed to, tested by, an event, which also, in another sense, determines it. Such a dialectic depends for its own conceptualization on a distinction between the internal site of thought and the external one of objects and events. This dialectic is one of the meanings of the arch, with its two bases, that Ulysses uses to figure his experience. The other meaning is that the arch graphically represents the narrative of departure and return to the ground that constitutes Ulysses' experience in the Homeric poems, up to the moment at which Tennyson has him speak.

From the highly equivocal place in which he speaks in this figure, then, Ulysses refers to an untraveled world toward which he moves, or could move. It is banal to say that, were he to reach it, the untraveled world wouldn't be untraveled anymore—still, much of what Ulysses says is banal. The untraveled world is always elsewhere. But this is a reductive version of Ulysses' figure. We can also say that were Ulysses to travel to the place that he sees, it would enter his experience and hence become involved in the narrative of sublation and internalization I have proposed as inherent in the concept of experience. Now, my argument so far has consistently implied that in these poems the representation of interiority is dependent upon metaphor, though that claim has so far remained signally untheorized. If this claim is valid, the movement Ulysses refers to in these lines, like the arch to which he compares his experience, would be a metaphor for the extension of metaphor itself.

As such, this movement is not the movement for which Ulysses yearns. The extension of interiority, or the accumulation of experience, is, I suggest, what the poem disparages as hoarding (see lines 5 and 29). The point of the figure I have been discussing is precisely to represent that which cannot be hoarded up, which is not subject to the model of experience as accumulation. The gleam of light from the untraveled world that Ulysses sees is visible only from elsewhere; it is the text's figure for what is always exterior to the place of experience.[9] And the constant fading at the margin of the untraveled world that Ulysses registers as he moves marks the poem's sense that the sublation of events into experience entails a loss, a certain continuous fading at the limit of things.

Such a fading at the limit, which is also a fading *of* limits that nonetheless remain in place, is a recurring figure in the first 32 lines of the poem. It is worth considering other instances in which it appears. Take Ulysses' complaint of lines 22–23: "How dull it is to pause, to make an end, / To rust unburnished, not to shine in use." The second of these lines seems to be a metaphor amplifying the first: "to pause, to make an end" *is* "To rust unburnished, not to shine in use." There is, however, an odd slippage in the move from the literal to the figural. The first line describes the dullness of pausing or making an end in terms that make these willed acts. In the second, however, the word *use* makes it clear that Ulysses does not imagine himself as acting or ceasing to act on his own initiative but as an instrument, longing to be taken up again by some other who has laid him aside.[10] The effect of Ulysses' figuring himself as an instrument, rather than an agent, like that of much of his syntax, is to situate the question of agency in some place other than where he speaks. Another way of making the same point is to say that the term *use* implies a distinction between the place where the profit of a given practice accrues and the site of an expenditure or wearing-down that makes the profit possible.[11]

In saying so much, however, we have ignored the metaphor's main point, which is not to register the expenditures or profits that are entailed by the concept of use. The point is to contrast the shine of an instrument in use with the dullness and rust of an idle one. This metaphor thus dismisses the economic questions of gain and loss that come with the concept of use and concerns itself instead with the contrast of rust and shininess as indexes of idleness and use. It is thus not so much concerned with idleness and use as such as it is with their signification, which it figures as essentially a process of consumption. In spite of the opposition between the rust of idleness and the shine of use, both involve the consumption of the instrument on which they appear—rust by the process of oxidation that produces it, the shine by the very process of use.[12]

Both of the figures I have been discussing in lines 19–23 thus concern a light that shines at an edge that is continually wearing away. Across this homology there is, however, a difference in their topics. One of them is about Ulysses' place, the other about his will. But is it possible to understand Ulysses' will in this poem except as a place he has not found? When Ulysses finally wills an action in this poem, it is impossible to say whether the self-displacement involved is literal or metaphorical—an effect of what I described above as the perturbation of the literal by metaphor. In fact, in "Ulysses" a motif of use, consumption, or fading within metaphor consistently undoes differences in topic like that which appears to divide these two figures. This is evidently the case in the metaphor that ends the poem's first paragraph, in which, as I have noted, it is unclear whether the figure of the sinking star describes Ulysses himself or the knowledge he seeks. But the same can be said of every moment in the poem's first paragraph when Ulysses represents himself as taking any kind of action. Consider for instance the figure in which he announces, conventionally enough, that he "will drink / Life to the lees" (ll. 6–7). Life here is something that is consumed by being lived. But because it is also a cup it is death to drain, we may also say that life is figured as a poison to whoever consumes it. Thus, since Ulysses at once consumes life and is consumed by it, this line at once asserts his will and at the same time announces a destiny to which his will is wholly immaterial.

I have claimed that the place of speech is in this poem represented as riven by a split between designatory and syntactic reference. Ulysses' name, I have said, is imagined as referring literally to the truth of his being—elsewhere. In consequence, when he is represented as speaking, it remains in different ways equivocal who could answer for his speech, or act upon it.[13] The split between designatory and syntactical reference produces in the poem a logic of displacement that might be paraphrased as asserting "not here, but there," or "not this, but that"—thus, "I cannot rest from travel: I will drink / Life to the lees," or "How dull it is . . . / To rust unburnished, not to shine in use" (ll. 6–7, 22–23). Where Ulysses is in these lines, is not resting from travel; what he does is not to shine in use. It is not surprising that what those who see and hear him in Ithaca know is "not me" (l. 5).

Under the name of metaphor, however, I have discussed in the text another logic of displacement, ultimately incompatible with or subversive of the first. In one formulation, this incompatibility could be said to stem from what I have called a perturbation introduced by metaphor into the notion of the literal. That is to say that when they are touched by metaphor, even the places and objects that Ulysses refers to as literally "there" are seen to be shifting, already subject to an ongoing displacement. In another formulation, we could say that the negation that semantically characterizes the "here" in Ulysses' discourse is displaced by metaphor to encompass everything he refers to. The sign of this negation is the fading or wear that is the burden of every metaphor in the poem and that undercuts the negative-positive oppositions we mentioned in the last paragraph. To rust unburnished and to shine in use are both modes of wear. To drink life to the lees is not only to refuse rest from travel but also to sink toward it.

Tennyson's Ulysses seeks to be properly himself, or to become the person to whom his name literally refers. In a language as saturated with metaphor as his, such a desire is necessarily indistinguishable from the desire of death. In the first 33 lines of the poem, it is at no point finally decidable what Ulysses wants—more life or an end to life in death. Indeed, to conceive of life and death as opposites in this way is to misread the text, where to live is in one aspect constantly to yield life up to death, and in another constantly to save life from it. Death is not life's opposite but its limit, the limit at which it is worn away and at which its value appears.

Such a construction of value this text shows to have two determinants. One is Ulysses' identification of what signifies him—his name—as proper to him. And the other is the nonetheless insistent tug westward, toward a limit that it itself constitutes, of the law of metaphor. In another formulation, Derrida's "White Mythology" punningly designates this law as one of *usure,* a term that can be translated both as "wear" and as "usury" and refers to the way metaphor produces meaning as wearing away (*Margins,* 209–19).[14] The double logic of displacement and *usure* that determines Ulysses' self-representation is the effect of his speaking and acting as if his speech or action could be proper to a name that nonetheless remains subject as a signifier to the fading and the displacements of metaphor.

Metaphor forces us to think of the signifier's value as coming into being as a kind of loss; of its place as a displacement to the west; of its life as a kind of death. These figures are metaphors of metaphor, and Tennyson's poem is haunted by them: it is haunted on one hand because it refuses metaphor and assumes that effects of designation and syntax in Ulysses' speech can refer literally to objects, denying the possibility that the terms of the speech will slide metaphorically away from their referents; it is haunted on the other by the reappearance of all of these figures as topics in the literal to which Ulysses' speech is presumed to refer. Consider first the Ulysses who is represented here. We have examined at length the equivocality of his desire and his self-representation as he articulates them in the first part of the poem. It is worth briefly mentioning the possible contexts for his discourse, at least to raise the questions that we beg in assigning these equivocations to a living subject named Ulysses. The Ulysses who speaks here stalks Ithaca like a ghost. If we accept the authority of the *Odyssey,* he is doubly a revenant there, both because he has descended to the underworld and returned and because he has returned to Ithaca after having been given up for dead (as in, for instance, *Odyssey* 1.161–68). Perhaps more importantly, however, much of what he says derives from Dante's account in the *Inferno* of Ulysses' speech to his mariners, which ends

> Call to mind from whence ye sprang:
> (26.118–20)   Ye were not formed to live the life of brutes,
> But virtue to pursue and knowledge high.

When Ulysses speaks these words to Dante, he speaks in Hell, citing the speech he gave when he was alive. The wish of Tennyson's Ulysses "to follow knowledge" (l. 31) is, then, a citation of the dead Ulysses' citation of himself. Is it possible to arrest the effect of this moment of citation? If we were to follow its clue, it would lead to a reading of the whole of Ulysses' monologue as his citation in Hell of his own last words. The effects of reference we have laboriously noted in the poem would become effects of citation, conveying no implication at all about the presence or absence to the speaker of the objects referred to. The effect of such a reading, with its suspension of the referential function, would be, not surprisingly, to find in the poem a metaphor. It would have it say, roughly, that home is Hell.

Tennyson's poem does not enable us at any moment to distinguish between Ulysses' life and his death. The two terms appear as continuous with one another, each constituting the site of the other's meaning and value. The importance of this effect on the reader is underlined by the way it is reproduced within Ulysses' discourse. When Ulysses addresses "My mariners, / Souls that have toiled, and wrought, and thought with me" (ll. 45–46), he remembers the events narrated in the *Odyssey*. But he forgets that in the *Odyssey* all of his mariners die. As Tiresias prophesied in book 11, when Ulysses returns to Ithaca, he does so alone. And now, as he addresses the mariners, he seems to forget their deaths or to be unable to distinguish them dead from the living.

This effect is not only an intertextual one. Ulysses can forget death in the time of a dozen lines of his own discourse. "Death closes all," he says (l. 51); but twelve lines later he imagines that in the course of the voyage he projects, "It may be we shall touch the Happy Isles, / And see the great Achilles, whom we knew" (ll. 63–64). In naming the dead Achilles, he forgets that he has said death closes all, and calls him into being in a sort of half-life, at the end of metaphor, in the uttermost West, in a place to which he might travel. The geography of a metaphorical representation of death determines the literal geography of the poem so that it assumes the form of an allegory. On this map it would finally be impossible for anyone to speak or act literally or to be the literal bearer of a proper name. The resistance of Tennyson's text to this all-encompassing quality of the geography of metaphor that determines its longing for a literal of naming—a longing that leads it to the claim of summoning up dead heroes by name and, in consequence, also to a catastrophic and debilitating inability to distinguish the living and the dead.[15]

There is a long tradition of skepticism in Tennyson criticism about Ulysses' will to leave Ithaca. It dates at least from 1855, when Goldwin Smith wrote that in Tennyson's poem "the Homeric Ulysses, the man of purpose and action, seeking with the most desperate aim to regain his own home and that of his companions, becomes a 'hungry heart,' roving aimlessly . . . merely to relieve his *ennui*. . . . We say he roams aimlessly—we should rather say, he intends to roam, but stands for ever a listless and melancholy figure on the shore." In this century, Robert Langbaum has written that critics who read "Ulysses" as a poem of strenuousness have failed to hear the "enervated cadence" of its music. Our summary of this tradition comes from Christopher Ricks, who draws the following balanced conclusion: "Ulysses yearns to believe that his life is not just a past, that it still has a future. But this is a yearning, and not a confident assurance," a position he supports by noting the poem's reluctance to use the future tense (*Tennyson,* 123). My own claims about the text are similar to these, though I would say that, even in the future that Ulysses yearns for, he remains on the shore, where Goldwin Smith represents him. Ulysses' desire can only construe its object as being at a limit or on a margin, a construction, I have argued, determined by the rhetorical and formal features of his discourse.

Nevertheless, an account of this poem in terms of what I have called Ulysses' debility cannot be considered complete. In trying to understand how this text achieves a kind of closure, albeit one that remains deeply problematized by the structures we have already discussed, I shall be most concerned with two remarkable features of the poem's final paragraph. The first is what I take to be its echo of Exodus 3:14 in Ulysses' closing claims about himself and his crew: "That which we are, we are" (Tucker, *Tennyson and the Doom of Romanticism,* 236, discusses the same echo). And the second is the oddity in the context of the rest of the poem of Ulysses' assertion in the final line of his will "To strive, to seek, to find, and not to yield." The agonism that Ulysses anticipates in this line is unlike anything else he desires or wills in the poem. What does he anticipate *finding?* And, more centrally, against what or whom does he expect to have to defend it? In the context of the rest of the poem, where desire is figured as seeking a constant expenditure, the sudden introduction of a refusal to yield something demands our attention.

The biblical narrative that begins with the book of Exodus (which Jews, incidentally, call by its first words, "These are the names") and extends through the remaining three books of the Pentateuch might be defined by a drastic reduction to three themes. The first would be a problematizing of the representation of God. To each of the Patriarchs, Abraham, Isaac, and Jacob, God had at different times spoken face to face, whilst the only direct sight of God that any of the Jews is allowed during the period of the Exodus is when Moses is permitted to see his hinder parts as he departs from Sinai.[16] Instead of showing himself to sight as hitherto, God now manifests himself in various typical or metaphorical forms—notably those of fire and cloud—whose function is both to reveal

his nature and at the same time to veil him or dazzle those who would see
him.

This occlusion of the sight of God accompanies the narrative of the
institution of the Law, the second of the three themes with which we are
concerned. This institution takes the form of writing, first in the tablets of
the Law and in the Book of the Covenant, and ultimately, by virtue of a
metaphor, in the hearts of the Jews (see Deuteronomy 6:4–9). As a written
text, the Law is portable; it constitutes the Jews as a people subject to the
word of God regardless of their place. There is thus a logical relation
between the theme of the institution of the Law and the third and central
theme of the Exodus narrative, that of the Jews' displacement during the
years of wandering between the flight from Egypt and the return to the
Promised Land. As writing, the Law is materialized at the heart of the
Jewish people, where it travels in the ark of the covenant, and within its
subjects, on whose hearts it is written.

These, then, are three central themes of the Exodus narrative: the
occlusion of the visible presence of God, the institution of the Law as text,
and the Law's consequent availability as a materialized signifier for displacement and introjection. The narrative which we have schematically
traced lies at the center of Freud's and Lacan's understanding of the process
by which the subject introjects the Law. At a critical moment in *Moses and
Monotheism,* the text in which he discusses the Exodus narrative and the
institution of the Law among the Jews, Freud discusses the prohibition on
images and likens it to "other processes of the same character in the
development of human civilization." It is worth following the analogies
by which he develops his argument:

> *[The prohibition on making an image of God] must have a profound
> effect. For it meant that a sensory perception was given second place to
> what may be called an abstract idea—a triumph of intellectuality over
> sensuality or, strictly speaking, an instinctual renunciation, with all its
> necessary psychological consequences.*
>
> *This may not seem obvious at first sight, and before it can carry con-
> viction we must recall other processes of the same character in the develop-
> ment of human civilization. The earliest of these and perhaps the most
> important is merged in the obscurity of primaeval ages. Its astonishing
> effects compel us to assert its occurrence. In our children, in adults who are
> neurotic, as well as in primitive peoples, we meet with the mental phe-
> nomenon which we describe as a belief in the "omnipotence of thoughts".
> In our judgement this lies in an over-estimation of the influence which our*

(*SE* 23:113–14)

mental (in this case, intellectual) acts can exercise in altering the external world. At bottom, all magic, the precursor of our technology, rests on this premiss. All the magic of words, too, has its place here, and the conviction of the power which is bound up with the knowledge and pronouncing of a name. The "omnipotence of thoughts" was, we suppose, an expression of the pride of mankind in the development of speech, which resulted in such an extraordinary advancement of intellectual activities. . . .

We can far more easily grasp another process of a later date. Under the influence of external factors into which we need not enter here and which are also in part insufficiently known, it came about that the matriarchal social order was succeeded by the patriarchal one—which, of course, involved a revolution in the juridical conditions that had so far prevailed. . . . But this turning from the mother to the father points in addition to a victory of intellectuality over sensuality—that is, an advance in civilization, since maternity is proved by the evidence of the senses while paternity is a hypothesis, based on an inference and a premiss. Taking sides in this way with a thought-process in preference to a sense perception has proved to be a momentous step.

At some point between the two events that I have mentioned there was another which shows the most affinity to what we are investigating in the history of religion. Human beings found themselves obliged in general to recognize "intellectual [geistige]" forces—forces, that is, which cannot be grasped by the senses (particularly by the sight) but which none the less produce undoubted and indeed extremely powerful effects. If we may rely upon the evidence of language, it was movement of the air that provided the prototype of intellectuality [Geistigkeit], for intellect [Geist] derives its name from a breath of wind—"animus", "spiritus", and the Hebrew "ruach (breath)". This too led to the discovery of the mind [seele (soul)] as that of the intellectual [geistigen] principle in individual human beings. Observation found the movement of air once again in men's breathing, which ceases when they die. To this day a dying man "breathes out his spirit [seele]."

In each of the moments Freud hypothesizes, "a sensory perception was given second place to what may be called an abstract idea"—or to what, following Lacan, we should call the signifier. For it is in truth with the autonomous movement of the signifier that Freud is here concerned, as his analogy between the phenomenon of "the magic of words" and names and the institution of patriarchy suggests. But the point is clearest in his discussion of the way in which the inner life of the subject is constituted and symbolized by the metaphorical displacement of the signifier. Freud argues that "intellectual forces" such as the soul come into being as introjected signifiers, whose introjection is made possible by the displacement of the signifier from the signified along the axis of metaphor.

In my view, this passage more than any other underwrites Lacan's consistent claim that the Name of the Father as the signifier of the Law is introjected by a metaphor.[17] It is, moreover, Freud's analogy between the institution of paternity and the prohibition of graven images that determines Lacan's understanding of metaphor in general, and of the paternal metaphor in particular, as the occulting of another, prior signifier, which is by its operation excluded from the Symbolic order. (*Occulting* is not the only term Lacan uses for this process—others include *elision* and *replacement*—but I select it here because of its suggestion of an interruption specifically in the visual field, that is, of the loss of an *image*. It appears in "The Agency of the Letter in the Unconscious" [*Ecrits: A Selection*, 157].) This understanding of metaphor is theoretically productive within Lacanian theory, but it must be said that it is impoverished in relation to the concept's broader history. Specifically, it ignores our own topic in this chapter, metaphor's long-standing connection with a thematic of displacement. It is no coincidence that the topic arises in Freud in connection with the institution of a Law whose function is not only to advance the "triumph of intellectuality" but also—and primarily—to constitute a displaced people as a nation of subjects.

Nor, conversely, is it a coincidence that in conjunction with the topic of displacement in "Ulysses" we find a subordinate thematic of the renunciation of idols. I have already suggested that Ulysses conceives of his subjects' relation to him as an idolatrous one; to that suggestion I would add the point that when Ulysses leaves Ithaca, the work he assigns to Telemachus is to "pay / Meet adoration to my household gods" (ll. 41–42). His own work, unspecified, is different. More generally, the tone of Ulysses' initial repudiation of his subjects, who "hoard, and sleep, and feed, and know not me" (l. 5), echoes that of the rebuke to the Jews that the Psalmist ventriloquizes for a God who recalls their fallings-away from the Law during the wanderings after the Exodus: "Forty years long was I grieved with that generation, and said / 'It is a people that do err in their hearts, for they have not known my ways' " (Psalm 95:10).[18] Nor, furthermore, given Freud's alignment of the institution of the Law with the renunciation of the mother, should it seem coincidental that "Ulysses" begins, in its analogy between the "barren crags" of Ithaca and the speaker's "agèd wife" (ll. 2–3), and in its rejection of both, with a gesture of misogyny.

In Exodus, then, the signifier of the Law is subject to displacement and constitutes the Law specifically as demanding displacement. We could at this point conclude that "Ulysses" stages certain of the gestures that institute the Law for the subject. But what I have already said would suggest that this staging is itself motivated by a failure in the Symbolic of the metaphorical function and a consequent crisis in the symbolization of the Law. The point in what I have said so far about Exodus has been to suggest why this crisis should manifest itself around the topic of displacement.

My analysis so far suggests that this crisis remains in the poem essentially unresolved. To understand why this is not wholly the case, I want to examine in more detail the topics of introjection and naming. We may return to the book of Exodus, where the inaugural moment of the narrative is the moment echoed in the last lines of "Ulysses" and the moment when God reveals his name:

> *And Moses said unto God, Behold,* when *I come unto the children of Israel, and shall say unto them, The God of your fathers hath sent me unto you; and they shall say to me, What* is *his name? what shall I say unto them. And God said unto Moses,* I AM THAT I AM *[Ehyeh asher ehyeh]: and he said, Thus shalt thou say unto the children of Israel,* I AM *[Ehyeh] hath sent me unto you. And God said moreover unto Moses, Thus shalt thou say unto the children of Israel, the* LORD *[Yahweh] God of your fathers, the God of Abraham, the God of Isaac, and the God of Jacob, hath sent me unto you: this* is *my name for ever, and this* is *my memorial unto all generations.*

(Exodus
3:13–15)

This passage marks the first moment in Scripture when God explicitly reveals his name, Yahweh (consistently rendered in the King James version as "the LORD"), to one of his people.[19] Before he does so, however, God replies to Moses' question with the conundrum that Tennyson echoes: "I AM THAT I AM . . . say unto the children of Israel, I AM hath sent me unto you." In a double sense, this conundrum amounts to an unnaming, a proleptic occlusion of the revelation that follows. The first sense in which this is the case is etymological. The sense of the Hebrew "ehyeh asher ehyeh," which the King James Bible translates "I AM THAT I AM," remains a vexed issue; it does, however, seem clear that one of the conundrum's functions is to provide an etymology for the name Yahweh, which a long tradition of commentary has derived from the Hebrew "to be" (hayah), of which I AM (ehyeh) is also a form.[20] To show that a name derives from or encodes a semantic unit is precisely to undo its function as a name. It is to show that, rather than uniquely designating a particular person or object, the name signifies a whole class of objects—in this case, the class of objects that exist.[21] In Exodus, then, the moment at which God becomes a person in whose name Moses can give the Law is also the moment when that name ceases in this sense to have a particular reference.

The second sense in which this passage effects an un-naming is not etymological but syntactic. I am not competent to discuss the various possible meanings of the formulation "ehyeh asher ehyeh," but I will take it that at in at least some possible renderings, as in the King James translation that Tennyson knew, it is tautological. For our purposes, tautology may be described as an effect of self-citation. Its force here is both to make the name in which the Law is given infinitely citable, since tautology's truth is independent of any context, and to make it at its origin an effect of citation, whose only reference can be to its own iteration. The fact that the name in which the Law is given can only be thought as a citation closes off its effect as the designation of a particular person; this accounts at the level of the signifier for Lacan's literalizing claim that the father of the Law is always the dead father (e.g., in *Ecrits: A Selection,* 199).

The theoretical consequence of my claim is that the metaphoric introjection of the Name of the Father is also and at once an un-naming of any person who might speak in the name of the Law—a class of person that includes every subject who speaks. In the patrilineal cultures of the West out of which psychoanalysis evolved, the Name of the Father is the name of the subject under the Law. The effect we have here been describing by which the introjection of the Name of the Father both names and un-names is thus under the regime of patrilineality primarily one that bears on the way in which the subject itself is signified. The same principle is apparent under the related but distinct theological regime instituted in Exodus when God commands Moses to speak for him to the Jews in the name of "I AM." In this mythical narrative, the means by which any subject from this moment on asserts his or her being will be a citation of the name of God.

Tennyson's choice in "Ulysses" to take as his subject a figure who could be regarded as the first to bear his name—as having been *the* Ulysses—is an attempt to circumvent the imperative by which the subject's assumption of a name is also an un-naming. But in my view it is an imperative that returns in the poem's closing citation of the line from Exodus, in which I have argued that this imperative is staged in the naming of God. I would claim that this citation in Tennyson's poem marks its recognition of the formal necessity by which Ulysses cannot speak uniquely or properly in his own name.

The equivocality of God's self-naming in Exodus both enforces the taboo on pronouncing God's proper name and calls into question the category of the proper name as such. The text's principal figure for this double gesture is the flame of fire by which God manifests himself to Moses. This flame manifests God, but it also mediates a presence that remains suspended; strictly, it is God's angel (lit. "messenger") that appears in the flame (Exodus 3:2). Indeed, the fire that appears in this passage may be regarded as the type of all the mediations by which the materialized word of God directs the Jews in their wanderings. It is as a moving fire that God leads the Jews out of Egypt (Exodus 13:22) and appears again on Mount Sinai to deliver the Law (20:18).

If God's appearance to Moses in this passage inaugurates a regime of Law as mediation and displacement, it also institutes a taboo that appertains to a particular place. As Moses draws near the burning bush, God calls him and says: "Draw not nigh hither: put off thy shoes from upon thy feet, for the place whereon thou standest is holy ground" (Exodus 3:5). The fire out of which God speaks burns in a bush without consuming it. Does it thus figure that which preserves its origin inviolate or that which has no origin? We may say, rather, that it figures the consumption of the place of the origin as such, which remains nonetheless as a trace, or as taboo. The flame of fire in this passage may, then, be taken as a figure for the double gesture that constituted the proper name and the proper place of God as taboo while at the same time subsuming both concepts in an order of mediation and displacement.

As we have seen throughout, Tennyson's early poetry is obsessively concerned with this gesture, which is indeed its founding allegory of the subject. In 1830 he published a version of this allegory, "The Poet's Mind," which seems specifically to echo Exodus 3, as Christopher Ricks notes (*Poems,* 1:246): "Dark-browed sophist, come not anear; / All the place is holy ground" (ll. 8–9). This text allegorizes the poet's mind as a holy place which the "Dark-browed sophist" to whom it is addressed is forbidden to enter. He is forbidden because at the mind's center voices appear which his presence would silence:

In the heart of the garden the merry bird chants.
It would fall to the ground if you came in.
   In the middle leaps a fountain. . . .
And it sings a song of undying love;
And yet, though its voice be so clear and so full,

(ll. 22–24, 33–37)

You never would hear it; you ears are so dull;
So keep where you are: you are foul with sin;
It would shrink to the earth if you came in.

If the poet's mind is here figured as a place that enfolds voices, these voices are nonetheless radically distinct from the discourse of the poem itself, which apostrophizes the very person whose presence, it claims, would silence the voices to which it refers. The poem thus enfolds a voice but constitutes itself in its difference from it. The spatial metaphor it elaborates includes no point of origin for the poem itself. The figuration of the poet's mind as the site of a taboo is thus instituted in a discourse whose origin is with respect to that site absolutely displaced or mediated.

Insofar as "Ulysses" is a poem about place, it describes a topography from which the taboo has been virtually effaced. In this respect "Ulysses" reveals its affinity with its main Romantic precursor text, Wordsworth's Intimations Ode.[22] It also effectively shatters the spatial metaphors and the particular figures of interiority that organize much of Tennyson's early poetry.[23] What it articulates in their place, I propose, is the regime of a Law that is introjected in a moment of un-naming. The metaphor of interiority implies by the notion of introjection may be unapt, but it is worth retaining if we recall that it names a process that Freud associates with the physical function of eating (for example, in "Negation," *SE* 19:237). In "Ulysses" the subject who speaks under the Law has consumed it and is consumed by it, not according to a logic of inside and outside, but as a fire consumes. What remains as a trace is an insufficiency of naming, an inadequacy of any name to fully govern a discourse that we cannot properly any longer assign to Ulysses.

Without a signature, the imperatives of the poem's last line have no context; without a context, they cannot refer to any particular object. To read them is first and perhaps last to cite them: "To strive, to seek, to find, and not to yield." Our argument virtually disables us from interpreting them further, but we may close with two suggestions. One is that they mark in this poem's rendering of the Law a nostalgic imperative as it were to reconquer place, a territory lost at its inception. And the other is that they articulate in a discourse newly anonymous the desire to find and not yield a name. In this reading, the apt final imperative of this text would be to refuse to reveal an identity.

"Ulysses" was completed, virtually as Tennyson eventually published it in 1842, on October 20, 1833. It was very nearly the first poem he finished after the critical event of his adult life, the death of Arthur Hallam, of which he learned shortly after October 1. This fact of course informs my claim that "Ulysses" stages a crisis in the Symbolic order. It should be emphasized, however, that this staging does not take place from any point of view that could be described as Tennyson's, or, more aptly, in a discourse in which we can at any point read his signature. There is no way to say at what point—if anywhere—in the text Ulysses speaks *on behalf* of Tennyson. There is equally no way to say whether Tennyson at any point speaks *about* Ulysses in a signed discourse framing or supplementing the text of the poem.

One of the ways in which critics have sought to produce an effect of signature in the poem, and to decide whether Tennyson either under-writes Ulysses' discourse or signs the text as it were from outside, in a effect of ironic self-distanciation or judgment, is to set the poem in the context of other texts that Tennyson might be considered to have signed. To illustrate the problems posed by such readings, we may briefly look at two such contexts. The *Memoir* of Tennyson written by his son quotes him as saying late in life that "Ulysses" "was written soon after Arthur Hallam's death, and it gave my feeling about the need of going forward and braving the struggle of life perhaps more simply than anything in *In Memoriam*."[24] Whatever its ambiguities (discussed in Tucker, *Tennyson and the Doom of Romanticism*, 211–12), this comment clearly identifies Ulysses' wish to go somewhere as a need to go *forward*—and hence as not regressive or nostalgic—and his will "to strive" as a will to brave the struggles of life—and hence implicitly not a will to die. More importantly, it identifies these attitudes as "my" feelings, and hence proposes that the feelings that Tennyson takes the poem to express were in fact feelings that appertained to him, that were proper to him, at the moment of his bereavement.

Such a reading of the poem is certainly possible; but it is equally certainly a partial reading, and one that scants the burden that made it necessary for Tennyson to write about Ulysses, and a Ulysses who is not properly himself, in the first place. I have argued that this burden is an apprehension that, at least under some circumstances, utterance can only come into being by virtue of not being proper to any given subject; and that under such circumstances, to attempt to bring discourse home to someone, or to read or write a signature in it, is to identify the subject of the signature with the dead.

This was my argument above, and it is one that can be extended to readings of the poem in its biographical context. For if the comment quoted above describes "Ulysses" as expressing Tennyson's feelings at his bereavement, another possible intertext for the poem will generate a different reading. Within a few months of "Ulysses," Tennyson wrote "Morte d'Arthur," a poem with which it shares a number of points in common. Both poems present an old king who, facing death, leaves his kingdom and departs on an ambiguously characterized journey into the west. The critical tradition in the case of "Morte d'Arthur" identifies Arthur the king with Arthur Hallam, an identification that has some support elsewhere in Tennyson, where it is in at least one poem made explicit (see "Merlin and the Gleam," ll. 77–80). But the analogies between "Morte d'Arthur" and "Ulysses" suggest that in the latter poem also the departing king could be identified as Hallam—a wishful version of Hallam, who is given the chance to arrange his departure from life and to will his own death.

My point is not to propose that we should read "Ulysses" this way. It is rather to say that if we assume that the poem's meaning is determined by Tennyson's signature of it, then we must read it in this way, just as we must also read it as expressing Tennyson's will in 1833 to go on living. To the extent that we assume an effect of signature to operate on the poem, we read it as unable to distinguish representations of the living from the dead and of the will to live from the will to die. Hence my claim that the poem's project is to reinstitute the Symbolic order around an utterance that is in an absolute sense unsigned and that could establish as a founding gesture of subjectivity the possibility of speaking otherwise than as one is named.

Tennyson's mourning of Hallam eventually led to the publication in 1850 of *In Memoriam*. The poem was published anonymously, and, in a departure from elegiac convention, does not make much play of naming the dead. Its full title, *In Memoriam A. H. H.,* is markedly reticent about the name of the person it memorializes, while the whole text mentions the name Arthur only four times.

That Tennyson needed after the death of Hallam to perform a labor of un-naming, and to insist on the citational quality of all effects of signature and designation, is perhaps most clearly demonstrated by the central poetic task of the remainder of his life. For from 1833 to 1874, in what were eventually to become the *Idylls of the King,* Tennyson evolved a vast lament, not for the loss of Arthur Hallam, but for the failure and death of another hero of the same name.

IV

Last Words

I

IT HAS BEEN my consistent practice in this book to assume analogies
between the places that Tennyson's poems represent and formal characteristics of the poems themselves and of the subjectivities that they articulate. My questions about how places are represented, and particularly
about how they are delineated or marked, have formed by analogy the
basis for analyses of the poems' formal characteristics and their relations
with various precursors and intertexts. By a further set of analogies, I
have read these ways of representing place, and the poems' formal co-
herences and incoherences, as configurations of human subjectivity and
self-signification.

The question of analogy itself, or the trope of metaphor, formed the
topic of chapter 3. In a reading of "A spirit haunts the year's last hours," I
argued that the topics of poetic form as the site of a return, and of the
subject as origin and end of its own discourse, were in this text represented
in a series of metaphors, not arbitrarily, but rather because they are in
themselves irreducibly metaphoric—that is to say, inconceivable outside
the logic of metaphor. That logic, we saw from Derrida, has as one of its
ordering principles a narrative of displacement whose double movement
is simultaneously toward the west, in a figure of aging, and along a
trajectory of departure and return. Metaphor, in these regards, follows the
sun, and, in so doing, it regulates itself according to a law that is itself
metaphorical. Hence, Derrida argues, when we understand the displacement of the signifier that constitutes metaphor, we can do so only in
metaphoric terms. The movement of the signifier in a metaphor is itself
metaphorically identified with the sun.

The end or horizon of metaphor is a return to the literal. But that
horizon is the close of the trajectory I have described, and hence the close
of a trajectory that is unthinkable except as metaphor, so that the literal at
which metaphor ends cannot be thought except within metaphor itself.
This is the paradox that framed my reading of "Ulysses." Although
metaphor is a trope, a swerve of the signifier away from the literal, it has

the daunting effect of making the literal inconceivable except as the signifier's consumption or wearing away. Thus, to bring a metaphoric discourse home, let us say, to a subject whose experience it literally represents, is apparently to efface from that discourse a hidden name or word of power. This is the effect that I described as one of un-naming. It is an effect of the phenomenon of the literal's coming into being in a field that is constituted by metaphor.

The effect of un-naming is moreover one that bears as much on the topic of reading as on the broader topics of the formation of subjectivity in Tennyson and elsewhere, if indeed the topics are distinguishable. To move a discourse toward the literal, or to find in it a name that might underwrite what it says, is an effect of reading. What we have said above implies that either of these operations will impose upon a discourse the erasure or forgetting of its master signifier. This argument makes reading as much a process of effacing what is in the text as of revealing it and renders impossible any ideal of a final and complete reading of metaphor.

II

It was still an easy matter at that time for a living substance to die. . . . For a long time, perhaps, living substance was thus being constantly created afresh and easily dying, till decisive external influences altered in such a way as to oblige the still surviving substance to diverge ever more widely from its original course of life and to make ever more complicated détours before reaching its aim of death. These circuitous paths to death . . . present us to-day with the picture of the phenomena of life.

(Freud,
*Beyond the
Pleasure
Principle*)

*Why should a man desire in any shape
To vary from his kind, or beat the roads
Of life, beyond the goal of ordinance
Where all should pause, as is most meet for all?*

("Tithon")

In the last three months of 1833, during or shortly after the composition of "Ulysses," Tennyson also composed "Tithon." When he eventually published the poem in 1860, after revising it and renaming it "Tithonus," he explicitly associated the two poems, describing "Tithonus" in a letter as "a pendent to the 'Ulysses' in my former volumes."[1] I shall not be concerned in this conclusion with the similarities and symmetries of theme between the two poems, although they have provided the point of departure for most of the criticism "Tithonus" has received.[2] My discussion of the poem will be limited to a consideration of the ways the poem amplifies the crisis in metaphor that we identified in "Ulysses." Specifically, in this poem as in "Ulysses," I shall relate this crisis to a problem in the effect of signature and show that in both texts the effect of signature is only possible within the logic of metaphor.

Like Freud in the epigraph quoted above, Tithonus thinks of death as a return. In asking Aurora to let him die, he asks her to "restore [him] to the ground"—that is to say, to "that dark world where [he] was born" (ll. 72, 33). In the first version of the poem, the longed-for return is also figured as a westering: "let me call thy ministers, the hours, / To take me up, to wind me in their arms, / To shoot the sunny interval of day, / And lap me deep within the lonely west" ("Tithon," ll. 24–27), a figuration that remains only slightly less explicit in the final version, where Tithonus implores Aurora that she "hold me not for ever in thine East" ("Tithonus," l. 64). The movement toward death in this poem is thus represented as obeying the heliotropic logic of metaphor. Moreover, in accordance with this logic, the poem represents the moment of death not only as a fading and a return but also as a fading into expression. Its opening lines describe a landscape and a moment that recall us to the figurations of "A spirit haunts the year's last hours":

(ll. 1–4)
> The woods decay, the woods decay and fall,
> The vapours weep their burthen to the ground,
> Man comes and tills the field and lies beneath,
> And after many a summer dies the swan.

The mention of the swan recalls that by tradition it sings only once, at the moment of its death, a moment that is here imagined, like that of the spirit of the year's last hours, as coming after the fruits of summer.[3] The point of this figuration is clearest in the description of the vapors returning to the ground from which they have risen, condensing into a weeping song whose burden is simply the dissolution and return that they enact.

The figuration of death that orders Tithonus' discourse is determined by the logic of metaphor. More specifically, in these figures the living individual—even the personified mist—is constituted as a signifier moving along the trajectory of metaphor, wearing away as it moves, until its truth is produced at the moment of its simultaneous dissolution and return to its origin.

Now, such a construction of the trajectory of life is by no means limited to Tennyson or Freud. But to understand its determination by the logic of metaphor, I want to turn to one of the earliest texts in which Freud took up the topic of the desire for death, an essay that has several suggestive features in common with "Tithonus." In "The Theme of the Three Caskets," first published in 1913, Freud sets out to explicate two scenes from Shakespeare. The first is the scene of the suitors' choice in *The Merchant of Venice,* and the second is that of Lear's division of his kingdom among his three daughters in *King Lear.* Freud proposes that the two scenes are both displaced versions of the same underlying narrative; his first move is to argue by means of a synecdochic reduction that both scenes in fact concern a choice between women: "If what we were concerned with were a dream, it would occur to us at once that caskets are also women, symbols of what is essential in woman, and therefore of a woman herself. . . . If we boldly assume that there are symbolic substitutions of the same kind in myths as well . . . we see that the theme is a human one, *a man's choice between three women*" (*SE* 12:292). But the argument of the essay goes beyond this claim to ask who these women are and why the man's choice ultimately falls on the third of them, as it does in both plays and in a series of legends and tales that Freud lists.

I will abbreviate an elaborate and not uniformly satisfactory argument by summarizing Freud's conclusion. He proposes that in each of these series the third and last woman represents death. This mode of representing death, he says, is a wish fulfillment in that it gratifyingly transforms the necessity of the encounter with death into a scenario of free choice. And he argues that the scenes have an allegorical significance; that they represent "the three inevitable relations a man has with a woman— the woman who bears him, the woman who is his mate and the woman who destroys him; or that they are the three forms taken by the figure of the mother in the course of a man's life—the mother herself, the beloved one who is chosen after her pattern, and lastly the Mother Earth who receives him once more" (*SE* 12:301).

The conception of death as a return clearly functions as an unexamined premise in this text. Because death can be conceived as a return, Freud is able to represent it as a relation to a woman—as a return to the mother. But beyond underwriting this argument, the logic of return seems to exercise a certain compulsion in Freud's text, or to bring compulsion with it at a point where, according to the argument, it should not appear. Freud had initially proposed that the representation of death as a woman was motivated by a wishful substitution of choice for necessity (*SE* 12:299). But in the closing paragraph just quoted, men's relations with women become themselves inexplicably subject to necessity in ways that subvert the essay's larger argument. Whatever wish is gratified by representing the encounter with death as man's "inevitable encounter" with "the woman who destroys him," it is evidently not the wish to substitute choice for compulsion.

Freud's grounds for proposing an analogy between the third casket in *The Merchant of Venice* and the character of Cordelia in *King Lear* include a point that we have yet to consider. There is, he proposes, an analogy between Cordelia's silence and the plainness of the leaden casket that Bassanio chooses after rejecting those of gold and silver: "In Bassanio's short speech while he is choosing the casket, he says of lead (without in any way leading up to the remark): 'Thy paleness moves me more than eloquence.' That is to say: 'Thy plainness moves me more than the blatant nature of the other two.' Gold and silver are 'loud'; lead is dumb—in fact like Cordelia, who 'loves and is silent'" (*SE* 12:294). This analogy is a version of the heliotrope, the metaphoric identification of words with light. Freud argues that the leaden casket by its paleness and Cordelia by her silence announce death to the persons who seek in them love, in spite of the argument of both plays that each in fact figures a love whose literal truth precedes and excludes all representation and rhetoric. It is characteristic of the uncontrolled operation of the logic of metaphor in Freud's text that it can read such a construction of truth only as the site of a return, and hence as figuring death.

Freud's text, then, figures death as a woman because of the operation in it of a logic of return. But, as I have said, we can understand this logic as specifically a logic of metaphor only if we understand the subject as itself coming into being as a signifier. Metaphor is the trope of the displacement and return of the signifier to its proper place. If this trope determines Freud's narrative of human life, it can only be because in that narrative subjectivity is conceived as subjection to a logic that bears upon it as a signifier. Indeed, it seems that subjectivity is so conceived in "The Theme of the Three Caskets," since one of the essay's premises is that silence figures death. In Freud's analysis, the end of the subject's life is announced by a silence in a woman's discourse, or by an occultation of the light that figures her language—or by a cut in the yarn that she spins, as in the myth of the Fates, to which Freud alludes. In this essay, the subject's life is spun out as the discourse of a woman or is coterminous with what signifies for her.

These notes on "The Theme of the Three Caskets" help clarify the logic that is in crisis in "Tithonus." Tithonus' monologue articulates the metaphoric identification of death with the signifier's return to its truth.

But the situation in which the monologue is uttered is so constructed as to expose this identification as a nostalgic illusion. The logic of return in this situation is that by which Aurora daily returns to Tithonus without bringing with her either death or truth. The poem insists precisely on the emptiness for Tithonus of the heliotrope. Aurora brightens every day with the rising of the sun, but her brightening says nothing to him: "Lo! ever thus thou growest beautiful / In silence" (ll. 43–44).

Tithonus' principal grounds of complaint, however, are not that Aurora does not reply to him. Even in his recollection, their relationship has never been that of interlocutors, and Aurora's discourse, such as it has been, has never taken the form of an address. On the only occasion when Tithonus represents her as actually having spoken, he did not know what she was saying—he says she whispered "I knew not what of wild and sweet" (l. 61). Tithonus' readings of Aurora's other ways of expressing herself show the same problem; when she granted him immortality, he says, she did so "with a smile, / Like wealthy men who care not how they give" (ll. 16–17). Even if we assume that Tithonus has properly read this smile, his point is that it is careless, that it conveys only the meaninglessness to Aurora of the gift that she is bestowing upon him. And if we assume, as the poem surely permits us to do, that Tithonus misreads Aurora's smile, then we are all the more clearly led to recognize that its meaning for Tithonus does not derive from any force it might have as a communication addressed to him. Its meaning lies rather in what it performs. Tithonus construes Aurora's smile as the signifier by which she performs the act of granting him eternal life. In fact, Tithonus stands in the same magical relation to the signifier as the Freudian subject. Aurora's smile does not function as an address to Tithonus but as the material cause of his continuance in being.

If this reading of "then didst thou grant mine asking with a smile" seems to take the word *with* in too strong a sense, making the smile the instrumental rather than the accidental accompaniment to the gift of immortality, then it is worth noting other analogous effects of the signifier in the poem. Let us take first the other quasi-discursive act that Tithonus attributes to Aurora, her choice of him as her lover. He refers to this act in the course of his lament for what he used to be:

(ll. 11–14)
> Alas! for this grey shadow, once a man—
> So glorious in his beauty and thy choice,
> Who madest him thy chosen, that he seemed
> To his great heart none other than a God!

Aurora's choice is not read as an expression of her desire but as a property of Tithonus' being, which leads him to see himself as a God. Tithonus' being is constituted in Aurora's signifying act, an act whose expressive or communicative force, like that of her smile, remains throughout the poem profoundly equivocal.

That the poem represents Aurora's discourse as in itself summoning objects and their properties into being is clearest from its figuration of her speech. As I mentioned above, on the one occasion when Tithonus represents Aurora as having spoken, he did not understand what she said. But he does say that her whispers were "Like that strange song I heard Apollo sing, / While Ilion like a mist rose into towers" (ll. 62–63). For Tithonus, Aurora's whisper, like Apollo's song, can magically summon things into being.[4]

The governing fiction of "Tithonus," as of Freud's "Theme of the Three Caskets," is that the signifier gives the subject life. Freud's essay makes clear that this fiction derives from a phase of childhood before the institution of the Oedipus complex, when the child's life appears to it as the unmediated gift of the mother. Within this Freudian text it remains an unresolved question why the subject so conceived must also be conceived as driven to choose its own death, which Freud represents as also the mother's gift. Freud was to return to this question in a series of essays composed over the following seven years, including "Mourning and Melancholia," "The Uncanny," and finally *Beyond the Pleasure Principle,* in which he proposes the existence in all human subjects, and indeed in all organic life, of a drive to death. This drive expresses itself in various forms of repetition-compulsion, which Freud understands as a manifestation of a compulsion to return to a prior—ultimately inorganic—state.

Our project here does not encompass the metapsychological arguments of these essays. But as we turn our attention to specific interpretative problems in Tennyson's "Tithonus," it is worth keeping in mind the connection in Freud between the compulsion to repeat, the death drive, and a certain ambiguity or unreadability in the maternal relation. This is from beginning to end the insistent theme of "The Theme of the Three Caskets," which begins with the scenario of Bassanio and Lear confronting three female figures and attempting to decipher their meanings for them, and ends with Freud's fiction of the male subject's three inevitable relations with the mother, a construction that seems to restage the original scenario rather than explaining it.

In returning to "Tithonus" at this point, I shall postpone for the moment consideration of the poem's representation of the maternal as

such to consider first the sense in which the poem poses the problem of
reading a woman's meaning. I have said that Tithonus' life as the speaker of
the poem is represented as Aurora's gift, that his being is constituted in the
signifier of her desire. In fact, however, Aurora's gift is more ambiguous
than we have so far seen. Tithonus recalls that she granted his demand for
immortality "with a smile, / Like wealthy men who care not how they
give." In these lines Tithonus blames Aurora at least for a certain carelessness in her manner of granting what he asked, a carelessness that led her to
grant him immortality without thinking to grant with it immunity from
age. But the poem figures this carelessness as bearing, not on Tithonus,
but on the gift itself. Tithonus does not complain directly that Aurora was
careless of him in allowing him to grow old forever; rather, in an apparent
displacement, he complains that she did not care about the gift she gave
him, which he figures as having come out of a surplus and hence as having
cost her nothing.

The interest of this figuration is that it puts at the center of the poem a
radical indeterminacy of the signifier's value, which arises independently
of what it signifies. The poem does not put Aurora's desire into question;
Tithonus never asks whether Aurora's apparent carelessness betrays an
insufficiency in her love. But her gift to him, although it answers his
demand, seems to him from the beginning to be insufficient in that it does
not correspond to a loss in her. And because of this insufficiency the gift
eventually institutes in him a need that can only issue in a renewed
demand:

> Can thy love,
> Thy beauty, make amends, though even now,
(ll. 23–27)   Close over us, the silver star, thy guide,
> Shines in those tremulous eyes that fill with tears
> To hear me? Let me go: take back thy gift

Tithonus seeks amends for Aurora's gift, or failing that, asks that she take
it back. The only kind of gift for which it would be necessary or possible
to make amends would be one that was also a loss. The signifier in
"Tithonus" thus circulates in an economy where it functions indeterminately as gain or loss, as a possession or as a lack. This is why Tithonus'
demand that Aurora take back her gift of immortality repeats as well as
countermands his original demand that she grant it; both are demands for a
sign of love. If it were not so, why would Tithonus address his demand for
death to Aurora and not some other god?

That Tithonus' demand for death is structured as a repetition of his demand for immortality accounts for the open-endedness of this poem, which seems on the face of it so much at odds with its demand for closure. In "Ulysses" we saw how a demand for closure is subverted by an incapacity to distinguish life from death, such that each appears as the double of the other. For Tithonus, too, death appears as life's double; his discourse constructs both as gifts that would signify an unchanging desire in the dawn. The dawn would not change if Tithonus were dead:

> Release me, and restore me to the ground;
> Thou seëst all things, thou wilt see my grave:
> Thou wilt renew thy beauty morn by morn;
> I earth in earth forget these empty courts,
> And thee returning on thy silver wheels.

(ll. 72–76)

The last lines of this passage, which are also the last lines of the poem, amplify and clarify the point. In the most straightforward reading, they enact Tithonus' death, and propose that even in death Tithonus projects himself as speaking to Aurora and about her place. These lines, with their paradox, define the continuity Tithonus envisions between his life and his death as a continuous and constitutive identification of himself with what signifies for Aurora. Even to forget Aurora, he must address himself to her and represent himself to her as forgetting.

We have already seen that Tithonus' being is given as signifying for Aurora. We have also seen that the signifier in which it is thus given is defined within an economy where it functions indeterminately as gain or loss, as possession or lack. These facts determine the form of the poem Tennyson writes under Tithonus' name. It is a monologue in which Tithonus' address to Aurora constitutes his being—whose possible existence in other contexts the poem excludes from representation by shrouding it in darkness. Further, it is a monologue that, while in one sense demanding its own closure, in another subverts that demand by representing its close as contained within itself, as the reinscription rather than the end of its own formal logic.

Even though Tithonus speaks a demand that resists closure, the poem Tennyson writes for him nonetheless rounds to a close. It does so because it is structured, not by Tithonus' demand, but by the events that his discourse represents. The moment of this discourse and of the poem's opening is established in its third verse paragraph as that of Aurora's waking; its turn comes with the negative theophany of her silent departure (ll. 44–45); and it closes with her return to her proper place in the last line. This close is, as we have seen, an equivocal one from Tithonus' point of view. From Aurora's, however, to the extent that we may conceive of Aurora as having a point of view, it appears unambiguous. It marks the close of her daily labor and her return to rest.

Tennyson's poem does not, then, simply express Tithonus' demand. It records that demand as it is articulated in the context of a given time and place, which are constituted by Aurora's departure and return. We can say, therefore, that to the extent the poem represents Tithonus' discourse as a speech event with a context that, though iterable, is nonetheless determinate, it does so by a double figuration of place. The place the text represents as constituted for Aurora by her repeated return to it, it represents for Tithonus as constituted by an interdiction of return. However much he roams (l. 8), he remains in a "here" that is defined by the fact that he cannot return from it to the world below. It is thus for Tithonus a place whose essence is displacement, a place defined for him by an interdiction of return that is also, in another sense, an interdiction of departure.

This double figuration of place alerts us to a contradiction in the poem. Its closure is grounded in its apparent representation of a completed event, whose completion is figured by the dawn's return to her place of departure. Tithonus mentions both her departure and her return—but he does not seem to notice them. Even after he asserts that Aurora has left, he continues to address her, demanding that she not "hold [him] for ever," and asking how his "nature" can any longer "mix with" hers (ll. 64–65). Moreover, if the nature of Aurora's absence during one part of the poem is problematic, so too is the nature of her presence in other parts, since at the outset of his discourse Tithonus describes himself at once as withering in her arms and as

roaming like a dream
The ever-silent spaces of the East,
Far-folded mists, and gleaming halls of morn.

(ll. 8–10)

Aurora's embrace is here functionally identified with the physical features of the place in which Tithonus is confined, which are themselves identified both as the mists of the eastern horizon at dawn and as the architectural features of her palace.

These facts suggest a doubleness not only in the poem's conception of place but in its representation of Aurora herself. The poem gives Tithonus a discourse that affirms her departure but nonetheless seems to require her presence as part of its context. And though it seems at some points to identify Aurora's body with the palace in which Tithonus speaks, nonetheless, at its close it represents the two as distinct by referring to the "empty courts" that await her return. These inconsistencies are to some extent the results of revision. The earliest drafts of the poem do not include the final line, with its reference to Aurora's return; it appears for the first time in the version of the poem (under the title "Tithon") that Tennyson apparently completed and laid aside in 1833. And the lines on Aurora's departure were not written in their published form until the final stages of the poem's revision in 1859. The corresponding lines in "Tithon" are somewhat more equivocal, or at any rate more troubled:

(ll. 38–40)
'Tis ever thus: thou growest more beautiful,
Thou partest: when a little warmth returns
Thou partest, and thy tears are on my cheek.

If these lines describe a departure, why the stuttering repetition of "Thou partest"? Moreover, as an intransitive verb, "to part" usually means "to split" rather than "to depart."[5] Finally, these lines emphasize the sense that remains in the final version of the poem, that Aurora's departure coincides with and is inseparable from the notion of return. Their specification of a return of warmth to Aurora's body makes it clear that they are describing not simply the renewal of her beauty but the renewal and return of her life. The implication is preserved in the final text by the assertion that what is daily renewed for Aurora is her heartbeat and the circulation of her blood (ll. 36–37).

Aurora's presence in the poem can thus be understood as that of a figure who, when she comes to life, has always already departed. Her presence is only the repeated reregistration of her absence, or, to put it otherwise, of the split or threshold between absence and presence.

Aurora's gradual illumination begins in the poem's second verse paragraph with the reflection in her eyes of the light of the Morning Star:

(ll. 24–27)
even now,
Close over us, the silver star, thy guide,
Shines in those tremulous eyes that fill with tears
To hear me.

This fact establishes the time of Tithonus' speech, and invites us to read the reddening and brightening of Aurora's body in the succeeding lines as metaphors for the changes in the eastern sky that precede the dawn. This reading suggests that Tennyson's poem follows the representation of Aurora in the Homeric epics, in which, at the moment of sunrise, she departs from her palace to lead the sun out on its journey westwards. She accompanies the sun on this journey until its midpoint, when she halts and returns to her place of origin in the East. But the clarity of the Homeric narrative, organized as it is by Aurora's relation to the sun, only brings out by contrast the difficulty of reading Aurora's departure and return in "Tithonus." It is far from clear that the time of Tithonus' discourse encompasses sunrise. In the earlier version of the poem it is clear that it does not, since in the last paragraph Tithon refers to the "still fields that dream below" him ("Tithon," l. 59)—still and dreaming presumably because the day of work has not yet begun. In the late revision of the poem Tennyson altered the line to the more noncommittal "dim fields" (l. 69); but there is even in this final version of the text no suggestion that the sun has actually risen during Tithonus' discourse. If we understand the mention of the Morning Star in line 25 as a marker of context that sets Tithonus' utterance in the moment before sunrise, then the non-appearance of the sun leaves it undecidable at what point, if any, this marker ceases to operate. The whole of Tithonus' discourse seems to unfold in a moment before sunrise that has been indefinitely protracted, a moment in which Aurora's departure and return effectively coincide. Moreover, if we move from a semantic to a tropological reading of the poem and read in the changes of Aurora's body an elaborated metaphor for the natural phenomena of the dawn, we find that the metaphor cannot be made to extend to Aurora's departure and return. If the sun does not come up while Tithonus is speaking, Aurora's departure and return do not stand in a relation of analogy to anything. The non-appearance of the sun marks the failure of metaphor in this poem—a point to which we shall return later.

I have argued that the form of "Tithonus" depends upon Aurora's daily departure and return. But it turns out that the poem is incapable of representing Aurora either as fully present or as fully absent. Like the visionary poet's encounter with the city of Timbuctoo that we discussed in chapter 1, Tithonus' encounter with Aurora has always already been missed. But in this poem that missed encounter does not enter the Symbolic as a lack in the subject—the splitting-off of the *objet a* that ultimately underwrites the castration complex. Instead, its shadow falls on the subject's ego, which is inextricably bound up with the decomposition of the object staged in his discourse. We have seen how Tithonus' relation with Aurora is mediated by the gift with which she responds to his demand. This gift I have argued constitutes Tithonus' being; it determines his position as a subject and the context of any utterance that is possible to him. I have discussed this gift as the signifier of Aurora's desire; the fact is, however, that for Tithonus it remains unreadable, being absolutely indeterminate both in its value and its meaning. As we have seen, Tithonus cannot tell whether in granting what he calls her gift Aurora has in fact given him something or taken something away from him.

The unreadability for Tithonus of the gift that mediates his relation with Aurora determines the unrepresentability of that relation. We have seen that the poem cannot represent Aurora either as present or as absent to Tithonus; but we have also seen that the place where Tithonus speaks is constituted precisely by the alternation of her presence and absence in her repeated departures and returns. Consequently, Tithonus' place and being can only be understood as sites of contradiction. Tithonus is not where he is, and speaks where he is not. Hence the poem's radically self-annihilating close, in which Tithonus describes the place where he speaks as empty and affirms the condition of its being at the same time he forgets it: "I earth in earth forget these empty courts, / And thee returning on thy silver wheels."

III

The demand for love can only suffer from a desire whose signifier is alien to it. If the desire of the mother is the phallus, then the child wishes to be the phallus so as to satisfy this desire. Thus the division immanent to desire already makes itself felt in the desire of the Other, since it stops the subject from being satisfied with presenting to the Other anything real it might have which corresponds to this phallus—what he has being worth no more than what he does not have as far as his demand for love is concerned, which requires that he be the phallus.

(Lacan, "The Meaning of the Phallus")

Clinical practice demonstrates that this test of the desire of the Other is not decisive in the sense that he learns from it whether or not he has a real phallus, but inasmuch as he learns that the mother does not.

To close with "Tithonus," a poem that was in substantial part not written until 1859, is to run the risk of violating the already rather sketchy chronology that has organized this book. "Tithonus" is, however, a text that in more than one sense itself violates chronology. As we have seen, it exists in an early version that dates from immediately after Hallam's death in 1833. Tennyson did not publish this version; it survives in the Heath commonplace book and in some early drafts in the manuscripts at Trinity College, Cambridge (*Poems* 2:605–6). There are no manuscripts to suggest that Tennyson looked at the poem again until in 1859 Thackeray asked him for something to print in the new *Cornhill Magazine,* of which he was the first editor. Tennyson initially refused Thackeray's request, but ultimately exhumed his old manuscript, revised it extensively, and agreed to its publication.[6] He subsequently republished it himself in the *Enoch Arden* volume of 1864.

To anyone who has ever returned to revise something written even a few years ago and sentimentally felt that it bore the mark of its particular time of composition, there is something uncanny about Tennyson's ability to pick up, apparently quite arbitrarily, a poem he had left off more than twenty-five years before. According to the logic that leads us to assign a time—"earliness" or "lateness"—or date to a text, we feel bound to read this story either as one in which the revisions of 1859 supplement an "early" poem that was essentially already in existence or as one in which the "early" poem serves only as a pretext for the originary creative act of the "late" poet. In fact, the peculiar inadequacy of either of these scenarios to Tennyson's practice as a writer is at the center of a number of cruxes in interpreting his poetry—the question of the "unity" of his longer poems, for instance, most of which, like *In Memoriam, Maud,* and the *Idylls of the King,* were composed over years by a process of continually setting material already written in new contexts. Such a process defeats any notion of a particular moment in which a text's meaning is produced. And even in shorter poems Tennyson would often incorporate lines and passages remembered from rejected drafts of many years before.[7] For Tennyson, the act of composition was characteristically already a revision.

The circumstances of the writing and composition of "Tithonus" were then by no means unusual. But it is nonetheless unusually engaged with questions of earliness and lateness, and of what it means to assign a particular time to an utterance. For Tennyson imagines the speech he gives to Tithonus as already a repetition or revision, a discourse that returns to him every morning with the dawn, which never gives an answer:

> Lo! ever thus thou growest beautiful
> In silence, then before thine answer given
> Departest.

(ll. 43–45)

So in this poem the necessity of returning to what one has already said is determined by the fact that it has not yet received an answer—and indeed by the return of the woman who does not answer.

My argument in much of this book has been that the woman's answer is what makes Tennyson's poems legible—or, to put the point more precisely: it is the lack in the woman that answers to the poet's eye, or the song whose burden is her loss that answers to his ear, that enables these texts to find in certain iterated differences the marks of particular places and particular times—and, indeed, enables my own reading to find in these texts a particular mark of Tennyson's early poetry.

When my argument is reformulated this way, it becomes clear that the fantasy of woman's castration performs something of the function of a signature. Whose signature? To the extent that my argument claims for the body of poems it discusses a certain coherence that derives from their production by a single author, I must claim that it is Tennyson's. But there are other possibilities. Could this signature be my own, the mark in my text of my own fixations, here monotonously reiterated? Or perhaps it should be read as the signature of Freud, the authority of whose name, after all, underwrites a great deal of my analysis.

To raise this question is only to underline the fact that the project of psychoanalytic reading precludes a final answer to it. Any of the answers I have suggested above, given exclusively, would vitiate the force of much of my reading of Tennyson—and it is precisely the project of a signature to refer exclusively to a signator. The reason for this apparent problem in psychoanalytic criticism, I suggest, is that within psychoanalysis the castration complex is itself the support for the theory of signature. That is to say, in psychoanalytic discourse the castration complex functions as the structure within which signature becomes possible and must thus be posited as prior to any signature whatsoever.

As I proposed in chapter 1, the theory of the castration complex is bound up in a thematic of the mark. It describes the process by which the child learns to perceive the female genitals as the mark of a particular event—the woman's castration. In this structure the mark is distinguished from the phallic signifier; it functions as the trace of the signifier's history, inscribing it in a narrative of displacement that is legible because the female genitals remain as the mark of the phallus's original or proper place. This is why the father's possession of the phallus becomes crucial to the evolution of the Oedipus complex in children of both sexes; it is because the phallus is in this phantasmal sense proper to the mother that its possession invests the father with the exclusive privilege of access to the maternal body. Hence the possibility of understanding the castration complex as producing an effect of signature. It relies upon the legibility of a mark as a trace at the site of an event, and it guarantees the existence of a signifier invested with the exclusive right of return to that site.[8]

The irony of the oedipal story is that this right of return does not belong to any actual subject. The story can only be told from the point of view of the child, in relation to whom the father is constituted as possessing the phallus and concomitantly the right of access to the mother. Hence Lacan's coinage of the term *Name of the Father* to designate the figure who occupies a hypothetical position at the origin of the infinite regression into which the Freudian theory of paternity leads. And hence Freud's remark in "The Taboo of Virginity" that the man who enters into the heterosexual relation and hence into the position of the father does so always as an "Ersatzmann"—a substitute or placeholder (*SE* 11:203).

These considerations underlay my reading of "Ulysses," a poem whose theme is the renunciation of the project of return and whose formal trajectory culminates in the articulation of a desire signed by a proxy, who speaks only in the name of the father of the Law. In that reading, I argued on biographical grounds that "Ulysses" stages certain of the elementary moments of the male subject's entry into relation with the father as part of the work of mourning. That argument generated the claim that "Ulysses" shows how the function of paternity, or of signature conceived as analogous to paternity, can in psychoanalytic theory take place only in the context of an infinite regress of citation. In this sense, even as it works to recuperate its speaker's melancholic excess of desire to the service of a patriarchal and indeed theological construction of the Law, "Ulysses" also renders visible the frailty of that construction's hold on Tennyson's poems.

So it is a fortiori with "Tithonus." It should be clear that "Tithonus" refuses the structure of the test of desire that Lacan describes in the passage from "The Meaning of the Phallus" quoted as epigraph to this section. This test of desire at the founding moment of the Lacanian Symbolic order requires that the child construe the mother's failure to answer its demand as the effect of a lack. In my terms, this construal actually *makes* an answer of the mother's nonresponse. Tennyson's poem stages a double refusal of this structure. First, as we have seen, Aurora's desire for Tithonus is initially mediated by a gift in which the terms of possession and lack are collapsed. In "Tithonus" the presence of the signifier of desire is inseparable from a thematic of mutilation and wasting away (see ll. 19–20)—a fact that raises the possibility that the function of the castration complex may not be to constitute the signifier but to contain or fix its effects. The signifier that is at once a possession and a lack can be no less than a scandal to a theory in which the signifier is instituted in the opposition of these terms.

Second, precisely because Aurora's response to Tithonus' demand remains unreadable, so too is her failure to respond. The effects of the unreadability of Aurora's gift cannot be arrested; they structure every representation in the poem. Because the gift that mediates Aurora's relation to Tithonus is unreadable to him, so too is she. She is for him a figure he may still possess, or whom he may never have possessed. And because Aurora's gift constitutes Tithonus' own being, it also determines the poem's contradictory representation of him. It is the unreadability of Aurora's gift that situates him in the double bind articulated in his twin complaints that he has lived too long and that he already speaks in a sense from the dead, because he is no longer properly himself. The consequence of this iterated unreadability is that "Tithonus" indefinitely defers the possibility of a moment of full presence and complete intelligibility in the maternal Other like that which for Freud precipitates the castration complex. The problematics of this moment were my principal topic in chapters 1 and 2; the crucial difference between "Tithonus" and the poems discussed in those chapters is that there can be for Tithonus no moment when he sees Aurora, and recognizes that she does not have what he wants her to have.

It is entirely congruent with this double refusal of the structure of the castration complex that the poem does not resolve the indeterminacy of Tithonus and Aurora's relation by mediating it through a third person. Unlike the demand the child addresses to the mother, the demand that Tithonus makes of Aurora is not refused in the name of a paternal rival. This is not to say that the paternal function is simply absent from "Tithonus." In chapter 3 we discussed the Lacanian claim that paternity is constituted by the figure of metaphor. It is thus apt for our argument that the impossibility of the paternal function in "Tithonus" is marked by a failure in metaphor. In "Tithonus" paternity is the site of a catachresis.

As I have said, Tithonus' relation to Aurora is mediated by the signifier. But it is necessary to recall that the signifier in question is after all a fantasy, a dream turned nightmare of an utterance that could mediate a relation without difference. As we have seen, Tithonus represents Aurora's desire literally as summoning him into being. The point is clearest in the poem's sixth verse paragraph, which represents what we could call its primal fantasy.[9] The passage concludes with an analogy between Aurora's whisper and "that strange song I heard Apollo sing, / While Ilion like a mist rose into towers" (ll. 62–63)—an analogy which establishes that the signifier is here conceived theologically, as the divine Logos that constitutes the being of an object to which it is so primordially joined that it does not even need to name it.[10]

When we broach the fantasy of a word that can summon an object into being without deferral or mediation, we may feel safe in assuming that we have come upon a specifically paternal dream of generation. And it is at just this moment that Aurora's language is compared to that of a man—and not to that of just any man, but to that of Apollo, the sun-god. The signifier of Aurora's desire is here "like" the generative music that flows as light from the fatherly sun. We find the same analogy earlier when Aurora's smile, signifying her desire, confers upon Tithonus the gift of eternal life. Again we are told that she is "like" a man (l. 17)—and in this man too, the wealthy man who cares not how he gives, who scatters his gold abroad without judgment or reserve, we can recognize the outline of the figure of the sun.

At these two moments, then, the topic of the generative power of the signifier in Aurora's relation to Tithonus is linked by analogy to figures of paternity and the sun. In fact, not only in Tennyson's poem but also in the Homeric epics, Aurora's life is wholly ordered by analogy with the sun's trajectory of departure and return. Together with the institution of the solar day as articulated by the opposition of a departure to work and a return to rest, it provides the concepts that structure her daily life.

But we have seen that Tennyson's poem invokes these analogies only to put them in crisis. More specifically, we have shown that, although the poem elaborates a metaphorical identification of the daily changes in Aurora's body with the natural phenomena of the dawn, it does not extend this metaphor to encompass the actual rising of the sun. In Tennyson's sources Aurora departs from her palace to lead the sun out of the East; her departure is the model and metaphor for his. But in our text the place in which Tithonus speaks is one where sunrise never occurs. In that place, Aurora's departure remains unintelligible as a metaphor as well as being, as we have seen, the occasion of a sustained problem of reference in Tithonus' discourse. In short, the sun's nonappearance in the poem puts in crisis both its use of metaphor and its narrative of departure and return.

The representation of Aurora is thus in one aspect determined by a series of analogies. In another, it is determined by a structure of mediation. Aurora's body is the medium through whose portals and over whose thresholds the sun is to pass (ll. 57, 68), and around whose outlines its light shines and from whose surfaces it steals (ll. 53, 34). Aurora's body is, then, in one aspect a medium that transmits the sun's light and in another a figure that embodies its truth. Each of these structures entails the presence of something behind—of a light behind the gleam or of a truth behind the figure; nonetheless, the poem remains fixed in the mediating body. Tithonus' wrinkled feet, perpetually poised on a glimmering threshold they never cross, are its best image for itself as a text whose metronomic regularity takes it nowhere but which by iteration has written itself on a body that it wastes away.

The consequence of this fixation is that the poem's figuration of the dawn is in multiple senses unreadable; properly neither absent nor present, it brings with it at once life and death, possession and loss. The poem's resumptive figure for this multiple unreadability is that of the woman who does not answer. Standing as it were at the horizon of metaphor, she defines the margin across which its substitutions take place while herself remaining irreducible to them. A naturalizing irony that surely hangs over the poem tells us that, after all, the sun really always does come up, swallowing the epiphenomena of the dawn in light. So, similarly, does the romance narrative that structures much of psychoanalytic theory tell us that the father, or at least the paternal metaphor, will always turn up in the end. I have argued that the minimal form of the father's turning-up is the effect of signature, which is necessarily structured as a citation of the Name of the Father. But "Tithonus" is a text in the name of someone whose being is constituted in the unreadable meaning of the figure of the dawn. Who speaks in "Tithonus"? A shadow, who endlessly repeats the demand of the subject he no longer is. The burden of the poem is that there is no way of returning the demand it articulates to its origin, or, perhaps better, no way of reversing the limitless decay that is always already the history of the signifier, even at its dawn.

In "The Theme of the Three Caskets," Freud reads the woman who does not answer as figuring death; in "Tithonus" this reading could only be a consoling reduction. Nevertheless, it seems plausible that "Tithonus" is in some sense addressed to the topic of death because we know that Tennyson began it, like "Ulysses," shortly after learning of the death of Arthur Hallam. I do not want to make too much of this fact. Much of the continuity of my argument depends upon the recurrence in Tennyson of a construction of woman as the site of a problem in reading; in this respect the representation of Aurora in "Tithonus" is continuous with that of other women in the early poetry, such as Mariana and the pale priestess in "Timbuctoo," to name only two. Nonetheless, the continuity between "Tithonus" and these earlier poems is marked by a critical break. I have argued that the earlier poems allegorize their own formal unity and closure by representing themselves as occupying the place of a woman's loss, or of a lost woman. "Tithonus" does not stage such an allegory and in conse-quence articulates a demand that can only endlessly articulate its own difference from itself. It renders visible a formal possibility that the allegory just mentioned is designed to foreclose.

The effect of Hallam's death on Tennyson's early poetry may be most discernible in this critical break that marks the continuity between the texts of before and after October 1833. This conclusion, however, raises more questions than it answers. Why should we suppose that Tennyson's feelings after Hallam's death would find expression in a task of criticism? Even if we accept that "Ulysses" and "Tithonus" return critically to the figural and formal logic of Tennyson's earlier poems, it is by no means obvious how this return might express his feelings in the latter part of 1833. Can we read in this return an effect of signature?

In the context of this book, moreover, a further problem arises. My argument about the poems I have discussed has been a deconstructive one; I have traced in each of them a moment where by a structural necessity their allegorization of their own formal unity lapses into incoherence. It follows from my argument that the critical break I have proposed separates the poems of late 1833 from the earlier poems is in fact already legible in the earlier poems themselves. A deconstructive argument will tend to see the later poems, not as making a critical return to the earlier, but more simply as reiterating a problematic within which they are already situated. Such a reading of the later poems will tend to see what I have called a critical break as an instance of repetition, and hence, one would think, to vitiate the possibility of seeing in it a mark in the texts of "Ulysses" and "Tithonus" that would enable us to return them to a specific context of origin.

A difference that seems to mark "Ulysses" and "Tithonus" as the work of a particular person at a particular moment thus turns out also to be legible as an effect of repetition or citation. We find ourselves again within a problematic that has shaped our readings of the effect of signature in "Ulysses" and of the subject's demand in "Tithonus." I would not wish to scant a general claim that this problematic will always haunt attempts to read a given discourse as proper to a specific subject. But I nonetheless wish to close by suggesting that this problematic may have its greatest visibility in discourses of mourning, which more than others perhaps run the risk of not being proper to the circumstances of their origin.

To make this suggestion, I shall leave Tennyson, and turn to a moment in that text of Freud's where he takes up more fully than elsewhere the question of repetition. I am referring to *Beyond the Pleasure Principle,* and in particular to the analysis of the game of fort-da that occupies most of the book's second section (*SE* 18:14–15). In this section,

without naming any of the persons he mentions or specifying his relationship to them, Freud describes a game invented by his one-and-a-half-year-
old grandson Ernst, the child of his daughter Sophie Halberstadt. This
game consisted in the child's habit "of taking any small objects he could get
hold of and throwing them away from him into a corner, under the bed,
and so on. . . . As he did this he gave vent to a loud, long-drawn-out
'o-o-o-o,' accompanied by an expression of interest and satisfaction."
Freud tells us that he and the child's mother concurred that this exclama-
tion "represented the German word '*fort*' ['gone']." And he asserts that this
view was confirmed when one day he observed the boy playing his game
with a reel attached to a piece of string. On this occasion he would throw
the reel away, as he had his other toys, "at the same time uttering his
expressive 'o-o-o-o'"; then, however, he would follow by pulling on the
string and making the reel reappear, whereupon he would greet it "with a
joyful '*da*' ['there']." Freud proposes that this "was the complete game—
disappearance and return. As a rule one only witnessed its first act, which
was repeated untiringly as a game in itself, though there is no doubt that
the greater pleasure was attached to the second act."

Barring this one habit of throwing his toys away, Freud observes that
Ernst was a remarkably good boy. He stresses above all that he "never
cried when his mother left him for a few hours"—this in spite of the fact
that he was "greatly attached" to her. In interpreting the boy's fort-da
game, Freud proposes that it is an effect of the "instinctual renunciation . . .
which he had made in allowing his mother to go away without protesting.
He compensated himself for this, as it were, by himself staging the
disappearance and return of the objects within his reach."

Freud describes the fort-da game as an instance of the problem that
occupies him throughout the first three sections of *Beyond the Pleasure
Principle*. Briefly, that problem is an apparent human tendency to repeat
traumatic events. What, Freud asks, is the psychic benefit of repeating a
painful experience? Among the answers he tentatively gives in this instance is that, by repeating as a game a painful experience over which he
had initially had no control, the child changed his part in the situation from
a passive to an active one. At issue in this tentative solution is the possibility of theorizing a drive to mastery that would operate independently
of and at times overcome the pleasure principle, so as to impel subjects to
act in ways they experienced as unpleasurable. The status of the drive to
mastery remains vexed in *Beyond the Pleasure Principle* and indeed in
psychoanalytic theory generally—we need not pursue it here.[11] But we
should observe how odd it is to interpret a repetition of a painful experi-

ence as an instance of a drive to mastery—and not just a single repetition, but an apparently open-ended series. Has the subject who stages such a series mastered the original experience or been mastered by it? Is the fort-da game a moment when the child recovers mastery of an object or a moment when he once again loses it? The question seems undecidable— which leads us to the conclusion that where mastery is concerned, the moment of recovery ("da") is identical with the moment of loss ("fort").[12]

My principal concern here is not with the psychic economy of Freud's grandson but with a particular moment in which the circumstances of his book's composition seem peculiarly to have marked it. These circumstances require some explanation. Freud began writing *Beyond the Pleasure Principle* in March 1919; Ernest Jones asserts that he had completed a first draft before the summer (3:49–50). At that time he seems to have put the manuscript aside until the following summer; it was eventually published only in the fall of 1920.

In January of 1920, during the interval between his two periods of work on *Beyond the Pleasure Principle,* Freud's daughter Sophie, the mother of the inventor of the fort-da game, died of influenza complicated by pneumonia. Her death was sudden and unexpected; the Freuds received a telegram from her home in Hamburg on January 22 announcing her illness, and on the twenty-fifth another to say that she had died. Work stoppages in the railway system prevented them from reaching Hamburg before she died, or even to see her cremated.[13] There is no question that Freud was profoundly affected. He wrote to Max Eitingon describing his feelings: "I do not know what more there is to say. It is such a paralyzing event, which can stir no afterthoughts when one is not a believer and so is spared all the conflicts that go with that. Blunt necessity, mute submission." To Sandor Ferenczi he described the death as a "deep narcissistic hurt that is not be healed" (Jones 3:19–20).

Sophie Halberstadt died at a moment when Freud had already done considerable work on *Beyond the Pleasure Principle* but before its final revision or publication. When he completed the book he displayed a marked anxiety that it might be read as the product of his bereavement. On July 18, 1920, he wrote to Eitingon: "The *Beyond* is now finally finished. You will be able to confirm that it was half ready when Sophie lived and flourished" (Gay, 703). And indeed, in 1923 Fritz Wittels suggested the interpretation that Freud had anticipated: "When Freud made this communication [of the theory of the death drive in *Beyond the Pleasure Principle*] to an attentive world, he was under the impress of the death of a blooming daughter" (Gay, 395). Freud wrote to him: "That always seemed interesting to me. I certainly would have stressed the connection between the death of the daughter and the Concepts of the Hereafter in any analytic study on someone else. Yet still it is wrong. The Hereafter [i.e., *Jenseits (des Lustprinzips)*] was written in 1919 when my daughter was young and blooming, she died in 1920. In September of 1919 I left the manuscript of the little book with some friends in Berlin for their perusal, it lacked then only the part on mortality or immortality of the protozoa. *Probability is not always the truth*" (Jones 3:40–41).[14]

While denying its truth, Freud here acknowledges the plausibility of Wittels's view that his text bore the mark of Sophie Halberstadt's death. He had in any case already implicitly recognized the possibility of this reading when he had earlier asked Eitingon to be ready to confirm the facts necessary to refute it. Freud seems in this story curiously invested, not only in proving that *Beyond the Pleasure Principle* was not influenced by his bereavement, but also in the possibility of reading it as if it had been. The letter to Eitingon was not prompted by anyone's suggestion of the reading it sought to forestall; it invites the hypothesis that part of Freud wished to have his book read as a work of mourning. The letter to Wittels strikes an almost congratulatory note, as Freud identifies himself with Wittels's reading even as he disavows it. The letter repeatedly plays at bringing Sophie Halberstadt's death back into the text, each time only to reject it anew: Wittels's interpretation is "*interesting . . . yet still . . . wrong . . . probability*" but not "*truth.*"

Freud in fact did include in *Beyond the Pleasure Principle* one unequivocal footnote reference to his daughter's death. The note reads in full: "When this child [Ernst] was five and three-quarters, his mother died. Now that she was really 'gone' ('o-o-o'), the little boy showed no signs of grief. It is true that in the interval a second child had been born and had roused him to violent jealousy" (*SE* 18:16). This note is a puzzling one. Appended after the fact to the discussion of the fort-da game, it seems to reverse the chronology that ordered it. Whereas in the body of the text, Freud represents the game as a playful repetition in which the child sought to master a prior trauma, he here seems to conceive of both the child's initial separation from his mother and the subsequent game as rehearsals for the moment when she is "*really* 'gone' ('o-o-o')." In this play of deferred action, the moment of "real" loss can be discovered only as a repetition.

To amplify the point, we may ask who could answer for the "o-o-o" that Freud disavows by marking it as a quotation?[15] Not Sophie Halberstadt's now older son Ernst, of whom the note tells us that he "showed no signs of grief" at his mother's death and that he had now reached the age of five and three-quarters and so would presumably no longer mispronounce the word *fort*. The "o-o-o" thus ineluctably returns us to the young Ernst, the one-and-a-half-year-old boy on the threshold of language who sought to master his mother's departure by playing "gone" (*fortsein zu spielern*) with his toys. Of this game Freud writes that it is "of course a matter of indifference from the point of view of judging the effective nature of the game whether the child invented it himself or took it over on some outside suggestion" (*SE* 18:15). When Freud cites the child's game in his note, he thus does so having already remarked that the game's origin is "a matter of indifference." His discussion in fact envisions no moment at which "o-o-o" could certainly have been uttered without already being marked as a quotation.

When Freud describes Sophie Halberstadt as " 'gone' ('o-o-o')" he gives a citation whose origin is itself gone beyond any possibility of return. The signator of his reference to her death lies outside the system of his discourse. And yet in spite of this infinite regress of citation we know that this death was for Freud a profoundly traumatic loss. And I think we must discern in this "o-o-o" that refuses any signature an articulation of grief that, if it does not formally return to Freud, nonetheless speaks for him—just as "Ulysses" and "Tithonus," speaking of deaths that have not yet occurred in discourses that formally resist all signature, nonetheless speak for Tennyson of the death of his friend. Freud's "o-o-o" figures the irruption of lyric into the analytic decorum of his writing; if formally the *o* in "o-o-o" is always a repetition, iconically it graphs the trajectory of a lyric voice whose beginning and end are always simultaneously copresent in an inarticulate "o" of grief.[16]

Freud's work is not rich in lyrical moments; and in spite of our efforts in this book, it is not obvious that it is rich in theoretical insight into lyric. Like the "Freudian" lyric I have been discussing, a "Freudian" theory of lyric may well turn out to depend on quotation out of context. In that spirit, I cite this odd lyrical moment in *Beyond the Pleasure Principle* as at once a necessary founding moment and a point of maximum resistance for any theory of lyric that might be advanced in Freud's name.

Notes

Works Cited

Index

Notes

Introduction

1. This formula is a reduction of that given by de Man in *Allegories of Reading*, 205.

2. The name *Lacan* designates effects whose status is in dispute on a number of fronts. Lacan's often elliptical prose style, to begin with, has made it difficult without reductionism to derive from his writings a series of propositions that it would be possible to give in his name. The difficulty of the written prose, moreover, results in some measure from the fact that Lacan's writings are, virtually without exception, the more or less mediated transcriptions of material first delivered orally, either in lectures or in the seminars he gave in different venues every year from 1953 to 1980. All the available Lacanian texts bear the marks of the specific institutional contexts of these lectures or seminars—sometimes in obvious ways, sometimes in ways that are now probably irrecoverable. These texts continually remind us that "Lacan" is an effect of these contexts. (There are even competing texts of some of the seminars. For an account of these, and of the legal dispute they have occasioned over what can be published in Lacan's name, see Macey, 7–8.) Furthermore, particularly in the writings of the fifties and sixties with which I shall be most concerned, Lacan insists at every turn that his project is a return to Freud and an explication, faithful to the letter, of what Freud wrote. In these texts, where could one identify the authority of "Lacan"? In fact, such effects of the veiling, deferral, or suspension of authority are typical of Lacanian discourse and might be said paradoxically to constitute the effect of signature by which his authority over that discourse is most manifest. In any case, this book most shows its affiliation with Lacan in its attempts to problematize effects of citation and authority in Tennyson.

3. To the extent that Freud anticipates this view, he does so in his account of the development of women. In the late essay "Femininity" he argues that the female subject typically denies her castration, which she is thus doomed repeatedly to rediscover. For Freud this characteristic of women's psychic life produces a certain fixity or resistance to change, which he represents as aberrant with respect to a male norm. In Lacan there is a sense in which the woman—or perhaps more properly the hysteric—provides the normative instance of human subjectivity.

4. See Shell, 32–36, on the relation between money and the *symbolon* (token) in Greek thinking and law.

5. Goux has written at length on the homology between the phallus, as theorized

by Lacan, and the money form of value. Goux's account expands the Marxian analysis of money as a general equivalent, arguing that the phallus functions as the general equivalent for sexual objects just as money does for the products of labor. He argues, moreover, that the homology between these functions has the force of a historical necessity, in accordance with which the phallocentric organization of desire and the money economy arise in the same era. See especially *Symbolic Economies,* 21–34, 126–29, and "The Phallus," 58–73.

My argument here suggests a similar and equally totalizing homology between the material institutions of the phallus and the linguistic signifier. In this respect, it gives an overschematic reduction of the readings that follow. Without claiming to have thought my way beyond phallocentrism, I shall later open to question the opposition of possession and lack in which it locates the elementary form of signifying difference. In performing this critique, I shall appropriate certain of the categories within which Derrida has theorized the dispersal of the effects of materiality throughout the signifying field. Of particular relevance will be the thematics of writing, which Derrida explores above all in *Of Grammatology,* and of iteration, which he pursues with respect to the effect of signature in "Signature Event Context" (*Margins of Philosophy,* 307–30) and *La Carte Postale,* and with respect to the function of the mark or trace in "Freud and the Scene of Writing" (*Writing and Difference,* 196–231) and "My Chances."

6. For a discussion of the importance of phonic play in Tennyson's composition process, see Hair, 72–73.

7. I follow Freud in using the term *penis.* Elsewhere I adopt the standard Lacanian terminology, which uses *penis* as an anatomical term and *phallus* to designate the signifier that is constituted by the castration complex. It is by no means clear that the objects designated by these two terms can be distinguished—one might say that it would be necessary to stand outside the castration complex in order to do so. The question is again that of the relation between the signifier and its material support. For recent discussions of the phallus-penis distinction, see Gallop, *Reading Lacan,* 133–56, and *Thinking Through the Body,* 124–32; the Spring 1992 issue of *Differences* gathers articles on "The Phallus Issue." The contributions of Silverman, Bernheimer, and Butler are especially relevant to these questions. Butler's essay, in particular, reclaims Lacan's early writings on the Imaginary—which I have scanted in this book—in the service of a lesbian deconstruction of the institution of the phallus.

8. For a discussion of Freud's attempts so to specify this moment, see Juliet Mitchell's introduction to the collection of essays by Lacan and members of his school that she and Jaqueline Rose have edited under the title *Feminine Sexuality,* 13–14.

9. Kristeva has also argued that the subject's primary relations with objects are characterized by rhythm, and that this rhythm is most apparent in the rhythms of poetic language. For Kristeva, however, the priority of rhythm is not only structural but also chronological because it is for her founded in the period of the child's preoedipal relations with the mother. This claim leads her to the view that the rhythms of poetry are inherently subversive of the paternal Law that founds the Lacanian Symbolic (*Desire in Language,* 134–37). Tennyson appears to me to pose a strong counterexample to this view.

10. I am grateful to Juliet Fleming for drawing my attention to the Tennyson references in *Wives and Daughters*.

11. "Events such as dreams or jokes only come to be in and through the production of after-effects from which they are distinctively separated and yet on which they necessarily depend: the dream, in the narration that disfigures it; the joke, in the laughter that displaces it. Such after-effects repeat the event they follow, but they also alter it, and it is precisely this process of repetitive alteration that renders the event effective, psychically 'real' " (Weber, 147). For repression and repetition, see Freud's claim that "repression (Verdrängen) proper . . . is actually an after-pressure (Nachdrängen)," in "Repression" (*SE* 14:148). For repetition as constitutive of object relations, see the passage from *Three Essays on the Theory of Sexuality* cited as epigraph above (*SE* 7:222); also Freud's discussion of the genesis of reality testing in "Negation" (*SE* 19:237–38). For Freud's discussion of transference as an instance of repetition, see "Remembering, Repeating and Working-Through" (*SE* 12:147–56). For repetition and the castration complex, see chapter 1.

I: Memory and the Place of the Eye

1. Ricks quotes Sir Charles Tennyson: "*Armageddon* is evidently very early work and this is probably an early draft, seeming from the handwriting to have been written when the poet was not more than fifteen." And, for further evidence, Ricks cites the date of the watermark (from *Harvard Notebook 2*) as 1824 (*Poems* 1:73).

2. "A different version of *Armageddon* in *Trinity Notebook 18* shows that about 120 lines, roughly half of *Timbuctoo,* were taken over almost verbatim from *Armageddon.* The whole central vision of *Timbuctoo* (62–190) was present, with a few trivial variants, in *Armageddon* in this notebook (which is dated 10 Jan. 1828)" (*Poems* 1:73). A photographic reproduction of *Trinity Notebook 18* is now available in vol. 12 of Ricks and Aidan Day's *The Tennyson Archive,* from which I have transcribed the passages from the 1828 "Armageddon" quoted in text.

3. Anatomically, a breath is a contraction of the muscles of the diaphragm.

4. See Lacan's "Of the Gaze as *Objet Petit a*" (*Four Fundamental Concepts,* 67–119).

5. The lower-case *a* in this term distinguishes the object that is split off into the field of the other (autre) as a signifier from any signifier of the Other (Autre) that precedes the institution of the subject in this split. Lacan himself refused to allow the term to be defined or translated, wishing to reserve for it something of the nature of an algebraic symbol.

6. Both the sun and the moon appear as "orbs"—the sun as a "burning orb" (1.35), the moon as a "dilated orb" (1.101); Daniel Albright has commented on the ocular imagery in both passages (15, 17). Among the many recollections of *Paradise Lost* in "Armageddon" should be counted the double sense of the word *orb,* which Milton uses to refer both to the eye and to the heavenly bodies. Tennyson emphasized this play on words when he revised the poem as "Timbuctoo" by altering the angel's "shining eyes" ("Armageddon" [1824] 2.5) to "shining orbs" ("Timbuctoo," l. 66)—a phrase which, as Ricks notes,

appears twice in *Paradise Lost* (3.668, 670.), where, however, it refers to planets. Tennyson uses the word in a double sense again in the "Prologue" to *In Memoriam*—"Thine are these orbs of light and shade" (l. 5).

7. Albright says of this passage that "there is little or no distinction between the landscape of the simile, felt inside the poet's body, and the external landscape, which is a magnified image of his optic nerve" (17).

8. This account of perspective is an enormous oversimplification. The general principle that perspective is constructed by inscribing the place of the eye in the image allows for many variants. In the perspective that characterizes the picturesque, for instance, the place of the eye is usually inscribed in the foreground, so that the picture appears to recede from it into an infinite distance.

9. "Inutterable" appears in the text on one other occasion only, to describe the "shining eyes" of the angel that descends to the speaker ("Armageddon" [1824] 2.5).

10. Another version of this configuration appears in "Mariana," as I will show in chapter 2.

11. The conclusion of the 1824 "Armageddon"—"clear stars / Shone out with keen but fixed intensity, / All-silence, looking steadfast consciousness / Upon the dark and windy waste of Earth" (4.24–27)—also echoes a passage from Coleridge that is concerned with looking: "May all the stars hang bright above her dwelling, / Silent as though they watched the sleeping Earth!" ("Dejection: An Ode," ll. 130–31). Tennyson's stars, less peaceable than Coleridge's, look consciousness rather than sleep upon the earth they watch.

12. See "The Function and Field of Speech and Language in Psychoanalysis," where Lacan cites Mallarmé's remark that "compares the common use of language to the exchange of a coin whose obverse and reverse no longer bear any but effaced figures" (*Ecrits: A Selection,* 43). Such a coin would resemble what in English is called a blank.

13. This passage is drawn from the essay "Some Psychical Consequences of the Anatomical Distinction between the Sexes" (*SE* 19:252), which was first published in 1925. Freud's difficulties with the temporal relation of seeing and knowing may be suggested by the fact that in an essay of the previous year, on "The Dissolution of the Oedipus Complex," he assigns to the threat of castration and the sight of the female genitals the reverse of the temporal order given them in the passage just quoted. In this text, it is the *later* sight of the female genitals that gives the threat of castration its deferred effect (*SE* 19:175–79). What seems important in any Freudian account of the passing of the Oedipus complex, however, is the sense of epistemological leverage that both Freud and his small male protagonist gain from the notion of deferred action, in the possibility of a moment in which one says "Aha! *Now* I know what it was." Most important for my purposes is the way this account thinks of the look itself as always lacking something, as being in need of supplementation.

14. The dream of the first passage quoted is not just a dream but a dream of not having to see in order to know where one is. Freud's dreamer recognizes where he is when he "says to himself, while he is still dreaming: 'this place is familiar to me'" (*SE* 17:245). This is a dream of knowing *without having to wake up to see.*

15. For details about the relation of "Timbuctoo" to the various versions of "Armageddon," see Ricks's headnote (*Poems* 1:187–90) and his article "Tennyson: 'Armageddon' into 'Timbuctoo.' "

16. According to Paden, Murray's book was the standard early nineteenth-century reference work on the exploration of Africa; Paden suggests that Tennyson consulted it in writing his poem (67).

17. It turned out that Adams's real name was Benjamin Rose, that he was not shipwrecked in the year he claimed, and that he could not have known Timbuctoo except by report. See Murray, *Narrative of Discovery and Adventure,* 136. In spite of the similarity in titles, this is a quite different work from the one cited above.

18. Murray, *Narrative of Discovery and Adventure,* 224. For an account of Caillié's expedition, whose success occasioned the setting of "Timbuctoo" as the subject for the 1829 Chancellor's Gold Medal, see Bryant's "The African Genesis of Tennyson's 'Timbuctoo.' "

19. Paden argues in *Tennyson in Egypt* (69, 143–47) that the specific source for lines 158–80 of "Timbuctoo" was the fictitious *Memoirs of Signior Gaudentio di Lucca* (written in English and first published in 1737) and an English translation of Claude Etienne de Savary's *Letters on Egypt* (London: 1799). No compelling evidence exists that Tennyson read the *Memoirs,* though Paden should be consulted; that he read de Savary is unquestionable—a copy of the 1799 translation (not quite identical to the one Paden quotes) was in his father's library; he appears to echo it in a number of other poems besides "Timbuctoo" (e.g., "Recollections of the Arabian Nights"); and one of the *Poems by Two Brothers* ("Egypt"), written at least partly by Alfred, in fact versifies a passage from Savary, who is cited in a note.

20. One of the Miltonic echoes that Ricks sees in this passage is of the description of Imperial Rome in *Paradise Regained* 4.44–54 (*Poems* 1:196). The throne in "Timbuctoo" recalls the throne of another oriental ruler in Tennyson, that of Haroun Alraschid at the end of the "Recollections of the Arabian Nights." The two passages share many details; both conclude by focusing on a piece of hanging fabric: from Haroun Alraschid's throne "Down-drooped, in many a floating fold, / . . . a cloth of gold" (ll. 147–49), while from the throne in "Timbuctoo," "The snowy skirting of a garment hung" (l. 178). These peculiar draperies may be identified as the fascinating veils of the phallus (see Lacan, "The Signification of the Phallus," *Ecrits: A Selection,* 288). The limp male genitals, which they also suggest, may be understood in this context as only one more of these veils.

21. The typical representation of the nabob as grotesquely bloated, like Jos Sedley in *Vanity Fair* or Joey Bagstock in *Dombey and Son,* gave a physical embodiment to the anxiety at work here.

22. That this moment after the fact is the moment of knowledge is further suggested by the way the spirit's interrogative "Seest thou . . . ?" ("Timbuctoo," l. 225) is resolved into the demonstrative "Lo!" (l. 232) that gestures toward the river's disappearance.

23. The topos of the city as a woman reverberates throughout the Bible; in one of her avatars she is Jerusalem, arguably the originary site of homesickness in

Western culture. One thinks, among other passages, of the lamentations that Jeremiah wrote for the exiled Jews: "How doth the city sit solitary, *that was* full of people! *how* is she become as a widow! she *that was* great among the nations, *and* princess among the provinces, *how* is she become tributary! . . . The ways of Zion do mourn, because none come to the solemn feasts: all her gates are desolate: her priests sigh, her virgins are afflicted, and she *is* in bitterness" (Lam. 1:1, 4).

24. My reading of Tennyson here follows closely Lacan's reading of this passage from *The Interpretation of Dreams* in *Four Fundamental Concepts*, 56–58, 68–70.

25. The most suggestive passage in Freud with regard to this poem is to be found in the essay "Repression": "The instinctual representative develops with less interference and more profusely if it is withdrawn by repression from conscious influence. It proliferates in the dark, as it were, and takes on extreme forms of expression, which when they are translated and presented to the neurotic are not only bound to seem alien to him but frighten him by giving him the picture of an extraordinary and dangerous strength of instinct" (*SE* 14:149).

26. There is a curious asymmetry between Freud's metaphors for the processes that constitute what is interior to the mind and what is exterior that may be relevant here. The process of *introjection* (introjektion), according to which the psyche is gradually accreted by a process of internalizing external objects, Freud describes as metaphorically related to eating ("The Ego and the Id," *SE* 19:29.) The term *projection* (projektion), however, which Freud adopts to describe the process that establishes what is exterior to the mind, involves a metaphor which, I have argued about, derives from optics.

II: The Place of Voice

1. Commentators on the poem who follow or elaborate Stange's views include Buckley (47), and, with some reservations, Pitt (59–60). In his response to Stange, Merriman retains the moral categories Stange finds in the poem but reverses his reading, arguing that the poem is a "hard-headed examination of the moral evil, the psychological inadequacy and the pragmatic failure of retreat" (5) and that Tennyson's identification is really with Hercules, the heroic thief who eventually steals the apple. Since then, A. Dwight Culler, reading the Hesperides' apples as representing a privileged poetic knowledge, has acutely argued that the enigmatic response of Hanno to their singing figures the problematic relation of poetic or visionary language to the phenomenal world (49–51). McSweeny's discussion of "The Hesperides" begins by citing Stange, though it goes on to suggest that the poem does not describe the actual conditions of Tennyson's art but a wishful version of them (45–47).

2. All three of these poems were of course written primarily in response to the death of Arthur Hallam in 1833. They also seem colored by the death of Tennyson's father, which had occurred two years earlier. In the case of "Morte d'Arthur," this was first suggested by Paden (86–87); the same suggestion applies at least to *In Memoriam* 103, which is a self-conscious reworking of the earlier poem. None of this biographical material is directly relevant to "The

Hesperides," which was completed by 1830, when both Hallam and Tennyson's father were still alive. However, its affinity with the later texts, if it can be taken as evidence of its similar concerns, suggests all the more strongly that representations of the father's death have in Tennyson's poetry more than a narrowly biographical importance.

3. For discussions of the figure of transumption, see Hollander, *The Figure of Echo*, 133–49, and chap. 3 of Bloom's *The Breaking of the Vessels*. Bloom's most stripped-down formulation may be useful here: "Transumptive or metaleptic literary criticism relies upon a diachronic concept of rhetoric, in which the irony of one age can become the noble synecdoche of another" (74). In what follows, I argue that the golden apples of the Hesperides, which are certainly something like a noble synecdoche carrying the burden of Tennyson's aspirations regarding his own discourse, derive from the ironically belated and figurally overloaded apples of Keats's "To Autumn."

4. See Saville for a more rigorously Lacanian reading than my own of the Lady's web as a defense against castration—an instance of the "dompte-regard," the visual image that "by operating as a veil, mask, or screen may seduce the viewer into the illusion of lack's imminent fulfillment" (75).

5. For other discussions of naming in "The Lady of Shalott," see Colley, 374–75, and Chadwick, 21.

6. The doubling of Lancelot's reflection was first pointed out by Martin (255).

7. "Function and Field of Speech and Language in Psychoanalysis," *Ecrits: A Selection*, 34. Lacan slightly misquotes Browning's *Parleyings*, "With Bernard de Mandeville" ll. 190–91.

8. For discussions of these echoes in Keats's Ode, see Grennan, 276, Brisman, 80–82, and Chase, 217–18.

9. The Greek versions of the Philomela story have Philomela turning into a swallow, and Procne into a nightingale; Ovid does not specify what kinds of bird they become. The version of the story I refer to here, in which Philomela is the nightingale, originated only with later Latin authors. Milton and Keats would nonetheless certainly have known it and have read Ovid through it; Keats would have seen it in Lempriére's *Bibliotheca Classica* and in the notes to Sandys's translation of the *Metamorphoses*, both texts he knew well.

10. For a phenomenological discussion of this question, see Boyd and Williams's "Tennyson's 'Mariana' and 'Lyric Perspective.'" My conclusions about "Mariana" will suggest the problems it poses for a theory of lyric, such as this essay proposes, based on optical metaphors of "perspective" or "point of view."

11. It is worth remarking that this complaint takes a different form at the end of the final stanza: "'He will not come,' she said" (l. 82). This change in the refrain achieves the effect of closure because it speaks the possibility of death as something that forecloses the future in a way that the present tense of the earlier refrains does not.

12. Lorenzo complains, "I am a shadow now, alas! alas!" ("Isabella," l. 305); compare also Tennyson's "a white-haired shadow roaming like a dream" ("Tithon" [1833], l. 8) and "Alas! for this gray shadow, once a man" ("Tithonus" [1860], l. 11).

13. See "From the History of an Infantile Neurosis," *SE* 17:46; "The Medusa's Head," *SE* 18:273–74; "Fetishism," *SE* 21:152–57.

14. It is Lacan who insists that the father of the Law, or the Symbolic father, is always dead. See "The Subversion of the Subject and the Dialectic of Desire in the Freudian Unconscious," *Ecrits: A Selection,* 310.

15. For a straightforward statement of this view, see the passage from "Some Psychical Consequences of the Anatomical Distinctions between the Sexes," *SE* 19:252, which I have discussed above. Freud's fullest, and most anxious, examination of the consequences for analysis of the notion of deferred action is to be found in "From the History of an Infantile Neurosis," the case history of the "Wolf-Man." Here Freud argues that the deferred effects of his subject's observation of his parents' intercourse when he was one and a half years old appear following a dream he has just before his fourth birthday, after he has been threatened with castration by his nurse. Throughout the case history Freud is engaged in a defense of the reality of the "primal scene," which he introduces as the "picture . . . calculated to create a conviction of the reality of the existence of castration" (*SE* 17:36) that the material of the analysis demanded for its explanation. If the primal scene induces in the little boy "conviction" of the reality of castration, however, Freud worries that it will itself carry no conviction to his readers, "I am afraid," he goes on, that this will "be the point at which the reader's belief will abandon me" (*SE* 17:36). There is not space in a note to fully examine the implications of the repeated thematic of *belief* associated with the "picture" of the primal scene. Suffice it to say that within a given language, be it the language of the Law or that of psychoanalysis, the appeal to a picture is a gesture to constitute that language as knowledge. That this gesture is never complete, that the picture always remains a supplement to language rather than a part of a whole called knowledge, is demonstrated by the way it compels repetition.

16. The passage may have been in Tennyson's mind from its association with *Measure for Measure,* for it begins with the verse "Judge not, that ye be not judged. For with what judgment ye judge, ye shall be judged: and with what measure ye mete, it shall be measured to you again" (Matt. 7:1–2).

17. *SE* 4:247; see also Lacan, "Function and Field of Speech and Language in Psychoanalysis," *Ecrits: A Selection,* 106.

18. "The Rhetoric of Temporality" was first published in 1969; the phenomenological tendency it displays largely disappears from de Man's work after that date.

III: Metaphor and Displacement

1. For two articles that reflect illuminatingly on the connection between refrain and death, see Hollander, "Breaking into Song," and Fried.

2. Hartman's essay on "To Autumn" provides a consistently fruitful discussion of the poem's "westerly drift" (*The Fate of Reading,* 124–46).

3. Pucci has shown that the *Odyssey* itself anticipates such an argument, elaborating a counternarrative of endless turning alongside its narrative of return (148–54).

4. Ricks and Mermin, among others, have simply seen these lines as badly written (Ricks, *Tennyson,* 126–27; Mermin, 30–31). Baum found them psychologically inconsistent with the rest of the poem's representation of Ulysses (301). Other critics, notably Chiasson (169–70), have also found the lines inconsistent with the rest of the poem, and have cited this inconsistency as evidence of Ulysses' duplicity rather than as a failing in the poem.

5. The two words are not only homonyms but close etymological cousins whose senses remain closely linked. We shall return to the topic of idolatry.

6. See for instance Lacan's discussion of the *cogito* in "The Agency of the Letter in the Unconscious or Reason since Freud," *Ecrits: A Selection,* 164–66.

7. In an 1888 selection of Tennyson's poems, the editors describe the syntax as "absolute case." Tennyson's copy of the edition bears his handwritten annotation "No. The accusative after *store* etc" (*Poems* 1:617).

8. The presence of soliloquy in the poem was first noted by Brie in 1935. It acquires the status of a minor scandal when Baum (300–301), insists on the inconsistency of the poem's dramatic situation as part of his argument that it is a "muddle." A significant portion of subsequent commentary consists of attempts to explain this inconsistency differently, or to explain it away. We may list some salients in the mostly level waste of this debate. Pettigrew's article of 1963 offers further evidence for a distinction between soliloquy and dramatic monologue in the poem (41), and argues that it is part of a design to reveal an ambivalent Ulysses. Ward in 1974 points again to the shifts in Ulysses' location, which he terms "hallucinatory" (316), as part of an argument that Ulysses is in the poem engaging in fantasy. Here he elaborates the argument of Ryals's "Point of View in Tennyson's 'Ulysses,'" which represents the whole poem as a soliloquy, in which Ulysses only dreams of a journey he will not take. Hughes returns to the debate in 1979, acknowledges the apparent contradictions in the poem's setting and audience, but nonetheless attempts to find in it a Ulysses who is neither hallucinating nor deceiving his audience, and who is unambiguously and heroically committed to leaving Ithaca.

9. It is important to distinguish this gleam from the flash of light we discussed in chapter 2. Our argument there was that a flash of light figured the poet's subjection to the gaze and situated him in a place constituted by a mark. Ulysses is not placed by the gleam. It is figured as visible to him only from a place he has not been to—a place outside his experience. The consequences of this distinction will appear below.

10. The vocabulary of these lines ("dull," "use"), as of others in the poem, seems to echo *Hamlet*—another text where to act and to make an end of action are hard things to distinguish. When Ulysses figures himself as a weapon, we should remember that the eventual destiny of virtually every weapon in *Hamlet* is to be turned against its user. The way in which a logic of instrumentality obscures the concept of agency in *Hamlet* makes it a crucial pre-text for "Ulysses."

11. It is arguable that the distinction between the sites of use and profit in these lines has the eschatological implication of certain New Testament parables concerning use and expenditure. Consider, e.g., the parable of the talents

(Matt. 25) and the command "Lay not up for yourselves treasures upon earth, where moth and rust doth corrupt" (Matt. 6:19).

12. "Use" generally, but not necessarily, involves the consumption of what is used. The assumption that it does so here is supported by the logic of Tennyson's image. A metal object shines in use, not because it is protected against rust, but because rust is continually worn off it as it appears.

13. It is worth nothing that this problematic is virtually constitutive of the dramatic monologue. Moreover, in its exploration of the difficult relation between a speech and the name of the person who might answer for that speech, dramatic monologue only foregrounds or exploits a fault line already present in lyric as such. In dramatic monologue, to name the speaker is necessarily a critical act that makes a break with the discourse which constitutes the text. That necessity is recorded in this poem—as in many other dramatic monologues—by the liminal or supplementary place of the speaker's name in its title. And the name of the speaker already occupies a problematic status even within lyrics that are not strictly dramatic—as can be seen from the sense of a transgression of decorum produced by Renaissance lyrics, like some of Shakespeare's sonnets, that pun on their authors' names.

14. Derrida uses a passage from Hegel to exemplify this construction of metaphor:
   In living languages the difference between actual metaphors (*wirklicher Metaphern*) and words already reduced by usage (*durch die Abnutzung*) to literal expressions (*eigentliche Ausdrücken, expressions propres*) is easily established; whereas in dead languages this is difficult because mere etymology cannot decide this matter in the last resort. The question does not depend on the first origin of a word or on linguistic development generally; on the contrary, the question above all is whether a word which looks entirely pictoral, depictive, and illustrative has not already, in the life of the language, lost its first sensuous meaning, and the memory of it, in the course of its use in a spiritual sense and been *relevé* (AUFGEHOBEN HATTE) into a spiritual meaning. (*Aesthetics*, trans. T. M. Knox, quoted in *Margins,* 225)
   Hegel's narrative of metaphors that become worn down by use into literal or proper names has cognates in much of the writing about language of the English Romantics; Peacock's *The Four Ages of Poetry* and Shelley's "Defence of Poetry" deploy a similar schema. For Hegel, the loss that is implicit in the wearing away of metaphor is recuperated when the language thus constituted, purged of its "sensuous meaning," becomes one in which consciousness, or spirit, is able to describe itself. However, in the less idealistic theories of English Romanticism, the loss remains an absolute one; for Shelley, a language purged of metaphor is dead to all the nobler purposes of human intercourse.

15. Tennyson's critics have worried for many years about the inconsistencies I have noted in these two paragraphs. Hallam Tennyson's note that "perhaps the *Odyssey* has not been strictly adhered to, and some of the old comrades may be still left" (quoted in *Poems* 1:614) is an early registration of the difficulty posed by the mariners' presence in Ithaca. More recent commenta-

tors who raise the issue include Ryals ("Point of View in Tennyson's 'Ulysses,'" 233), Ward (315), and Tucker (*Tennyson and the Doom of Romanticism*, 232). Ward also notes how "Ulysses" contradicts the *Odyssey* by situating Achilles in the Happy Isles.

16. What most scholars read as residue of a contradictory tradition appears in Exodus 33:11—"And the LORD spake unto Moses face to face"—a verse that is directly contradicted in 33:20, "Thou canst not see my face, for there shall no man see me, and live."

17. See *Ecrits: A Selection*, 156–58, 199–200. Thom (185) also argues that Lacan's concept is closely linked to this passage in Freud.

18. I cite the Book of Common Prayer version, because it is the one that would have been most familiar to Tennyson from its appearance in the service of Morning Prayer in the Anglican liturgy.

19. This passage should be contrasted with Genesis 32:29, where God, or his messenger, refuses to reveal a name to Jacob.

20. See Buttrick (1:838) for a discussion of the name Yahweh's derivation.

21. Exodus 3:13–15 has been assigned by biblical critics to that one of the texts making up the Pentateuch which has come to be called the E text, after the word *Elohim*, which it uses to designate God. *Elohim* is simply a plural noun, not a proper name; the passage we have been discussing marks the first moment in the E text where God is given a proper name at all. Its designation of God is one of the most marked features that distinguish E from the other early independent text that was incorporated into the Pentateuch. That text is known as J, from its consistent designation of God by the proper name Yahweh. J and E were composed independently well before they were combined into a single narrative, but internal evidence shows that J is the earlier of the two and was known to the author or authors of E (Buttrick 1:197). We might conclude, in short, that E is influenced by a taboo against giving the proper name of God that, for whatever reason, does not operate in J. However, by including in itself a narrative of the revelation of a name that already appears in the prior text, and by undoing the name's function as such in the way that I have described, the E writer appears to make the taboo effective in J also. After E has written, it seems that J is able to use the name Yahweh only because of the etymological exegesis it receives in E. E's gesture of un-naming Yahweh thus enables it in a gesture of metaleptic reversal to make itself a necessary pre-text to J.

22. See Tucker, *Tennyson and the Doom of Romanticism*, 223–24, for the best available discussion of the relation between the two poems.

23. This is not to say that the historical Tennyson never again wrote a poem having the organization we have been discussing—although it is difficult to think of any of significance. But it is to say that such a poem would be logically incompatible with the corrosive refusal articulated in "Ulysses" to live in any given place whatsoever.

24. Quoted in *Poems* 1:613. The effect of signature in a quoted remark is of course equivocal; moreover, when the same remark is quoted in a note to "Ulysses" in the Eversley Edition of Tennyson's poems, Tennyson's claim to property in the feelings given in the poem is less absolute, since the remark there reads, in

a significant variant, "it gives *the* feeling." As Tennyson's son Hallam was both the author of the *Memoir* and the editor of Eversley, there is no certain way to choose between the two versions.

IV: Last Words

1. Letter to the duke of Argyll, Jan. 27, 1860, quoted in Hallam Tennyson, 1:459.
2. Both poems are dramatic monologues on classical topics; Ulysses is a character who refuses to die, or "pause," as both speakers oddly put it, while Tithonus demands death. Both poems take their occasion from the movement of the sun and might be read as heavily ironized blank verse Pindaric odes to Evening and to Morning, respectively.
3. Tennyson writes explicitly about the swan's death song in "The Dying Swan" and "Morte d'Arthur."
4. Tennyson also describes the walls of Troy rising to music in the fragment "Ilion, Ilion," composed around 1830. Ricks (*Poems* 2:612) compares to this line Milton's description of the building of Pandaemonium, which "Rose like an Exhalation, with the sound / of Dulcet Symphonies and voices sweet" (*Paradise Lost* 1.711–12).
5. The *O.E.D*'s second definition of *part* as a verb is "to suffer division, be divided or severed, to divide, break, cleave, come in two or in pieces." "To take one's leave or departure" is given as the seventh sense and is marked as obscure.
6. See his letter to Thackeray of Nov. 6, 1859, Hallam Tennyson 1:446–47.
7. For discussions of Tennyson's "self-borrowings" (Ricks's term), see Ricks, *Tennyson,* 298–312, and Tucker, "Tennyson and the Measure of Doom," 8.
8. My analysis of the effect of signature, here as elsewhere, derives from Derrida's essay "Signature Event Context" (*Margins,* 307–30, especially 316–18, 328–30). Derrida argues that signature is a specific instance of the general problematic of writing, within which the written signifier is constituted under a displacement that is always potentially irreversible. That is, the written signifier is constituted in the possibility that it may have no proper place to return to. The consequences of this deconstructive analysis of signature for the psychoanalytic theory of castration are central to Derrida's critique of Lacan and of the phallocentrism of Freudian theory, articulated principally in *Positions*—see especially pp. 82–87 and the long note on pp. 107–13—and in *La Carte Postale,* especially the essay "Le Facteur de la Verité," pp. 441–524.
9. It may not be the primal fantasy only of this poem. This scene draws together a series of topics that have recurred throughout our readings of Tennyson. It represents at once a vision of a city in the East (a motif that appears both in the image of the towers of Troy rising to music and in the architectural features of Aurora's palace), a fantasy of complete and unmediated access to the maternal body, and a recollection of a spoken word uttered before the rising of the sun and hence imagined as a moment of the literal prior to the initiation of the westward trajectory of the signifier under the law of metaphor.

10. For Derrida's analysis of a figuration of divine language as inarticulate song, see *Of Grammatology*, 249.

11. See the entry under "Instinct to Master (or for Mastery)" in Laplanche and Pontalis, 217–19.

12. Derrida's "Spéculer—Sur 'Freud,' " in *La Carte Postale*, consists in its entirety of a reading of *Beyond the Pleasure Principle* that pays sustained attention to the topics of signature and mastery. My discussion in this chapter is profoundly indebted to his. His commentary on this passage in Freud's book appears on p. 338: Its mastery "is a mastery that distances itself from itself only to reappropriate itself: tautoteleology which nonetheless either makes or lets the other return as its domestic specter. . . . That which returns . . . will not be, under the name of the death drive or the compulsion to repeat, an other master or a countermaster but something other than mastery—another thing altogether" (my translation).

13. The circumstances here bear comparison to those of Hallam's death as they affected Tennyson. Hallam also died unexpectedly, and at a distance—he was traveling in Vienna when he suffered a cerebral hemorrhage on Sept. 15 1833. It was more than two weeks before word reached Tennyson in England.

14. My attention was drawn to the issue of the relation between Sophie Halberstadt's death and *Beyond the Pleasure Principle,* and in particular to the exchanges with Eitingon and Wittels, by Derrida's *La Carte Postale,* 349–50.

15. Not quite a quotation. As Derrida points out, this is the only point in the text where Freud gives only three *o*'s. *La Carte Postale,* 348.

16. Jonathan Culler's "Apostrophe" also identifies the grapheme *o* as central to the genre of lyric. Culler's *o* is unlike Freud's in that it belongs to the trope of apostrophe—though I would not wish to foreclose the possibility that Freud's *o* is in some way apostrophic. But its effects are similar to those I have examined. For Culler, the *o* of apostrophe situates lyric in a "temporality of writing" (149) in which life and death are collapsed. But Culler implies that this temporality always risks appearing as a repetition, since, as he notes, the apostrophic *o* is necessarily a citation: "The potential addressee of every apostrophe [is] the apostrophic 'O' itself [which] makes every invocation an invocation of invocation" (144). Derrida notes the symmetry of the problematic of address with that of signature in "Signature Event Context" (*Margins of Philosophy*, 316).

     Anyone interested in the topic of signature in relation to psychoanalysis should also consult Fineman's brilliant "The Sound of O in *Othello*." Fineman reads the Shakespearian O as a signature and works out a Lacanian analysis of signature as entailing the evacuation of the signator; I continue to wrestle with and learn from his essay.

Works Cited

Albright, Daniel. *Tennyson: The Muses' Tug-of-War*. Charlottesville: Univ. Press of Virginia, 1986.

Aristotle. *On Poetry and Style*. Trans. G. M. A. Grube. Indianapolis: Library of Liberal Arts, 1958.

———. *Rhetoric*. Trans. W. Rhys Roberts. Vol. 11 of *The Works of Aristotle*. Oxford: Oxford Univ. Press, 1924.

Armstrong, Isobel. "Tennyson's 'The Lady of Shalott': Victorian Mythography and the Politics of Narcissism." In *The Sun Is God: Painting, Literature and Mythology in the Nineteenth Century*. Ed. J. B. Bullen. Oxford: Clarendon Press, 1989.

Baker, Arthur E. *A Concordance to the Poetical and Dramatic Works of Alfred, Lord Tennyson*. London: Routledge and Kegan Paul, 1914.

Baum, Paull F. *Tennyson Sixty Years After*. Chapel Hill: Univ. of North Carolina Press, 1948.

Benjamin, Walter. "The Storyteller." *Illuminations*. Ed. Hannah Arendt. Trans. Harry Zohn. New York: Schoken, 1969.

———. *The Origin of German Tragic Drama*. Trans. John Osborne. London: NLB, 1977.

Bernheimer, Charles. "Penile Reference in Phallic Theory." *Differences: A Journal of Feminist Cultural Studies* 4 (1992): 116–32.

Bloom, Harold. *Poetry and Repression: Revisionism from Blake to Stevens*. New Haven: Yale Univ. Press, 1976.

———. *The Breaking of the Vessels*. Chicago: Univ. of Chicago Press, 1982.

Boyd, John D., and Anne Williams. "Tennyson's 'Mariana' and 'Lyric Perspective.'" *Studies in English Literature 1500–1900* 23 (1983): 579–93.

Brie, Friedrich. "Tennyson's 'Ulysses.'" *Anglia* 59 (1935): 441–47.

Brisman, Leslie. *Romantic Origins*. Ithaca: Cornell Univ. Press, 1978.

Bryant, Hallman B. "The African Genesis of Tennyson's 'Timbuctoo.'" *Tennyson Research Bulletin* 3 (1981): 196–201.

Buckley, Jerome Hamilton. *Tennyson: The Growth of a Poet*. Cambridge: Harvard Univ. Press, 1960.

Butler, Judith. "The Lesbian Phallus and the Morphological Imaginary." *Differences: A Journal of Feminist Cultural Studies* 4 (1992): 133–71.

Buttrick, George Arthur, et al., eds. *The Interpreter's Bible*. 12 vols. New York: Abingdon Cokesbury, 1952.

Chadwick, Joseph. "A Blessing and a Curse: The Poetics of Privacy in Tennyson's 'The Lady of Shalott.' " *Victorian Poetry* 24 (1986): 13–30.

Chapple, J. A. V., and Arthur Pollard, eds. *The Letters of Mrs. Gaskell.* Cambridge: Harvard Univ. Press, 1967.

Chase, Cynthia. " 'Viewless Wings': Intertextual Interpretation of Keats's 'Ode to a Nightingale.' " In *Lyric Poetry: Beyond New Criticism.* Ed. Chaviva Hosek and Patricia Parker. Ithaca: Cornell Univ. Press, 1985.

Chiasson, E. J. "Tennyson's 'Ulysses'—A Reinterpretation." Rpt. in *Critical Essays on the Poems of Tennyson.* Ed. John Killham. London: Routledge and Kegan Paul, 1960.

Coleridge, Samuel Taylor. *The Complete Poetical Works of Samuel Taylor Coleridge.* Ed. Ernest Harley Coleridge. 2 vols. Oxford: Oxford Univ. Press, 1912.

Colley, Ann C. "The Quest for the 'Nameless' in Tennyson's 'The Lady of Shalott.' " *Victorian Poetry* 23 (1985): 374–75.

Culler, A. Dwight. *The Poetry of Tennyson.* New Haven: Yale Univ. Press, 1977.

Culler, Jonathan. "Apostrophe." *The Pursuit of Signs.* Ithaca: Cornell Univ. Press, 1981.

Dante. *The Vision; or, Hell, Purgatory, and Paradise, of Dante Alighieri.* Trans. H. F. Cary. London: Frederick Warne, n.d.

de Man, Paul. *Allegories of Reading: Figural Language in Rousseau, Nietzsche, Rilke, and Proust.* New Haven: Yale Univ. Press, 1979.

———. "The Rhetoric of Temporality." *Blindness and Insight.* 2d ed. Minneapolis: Univ. of Minnesota Press, 1983.

Derrida, Jacques. *Of Grammatology.* Trans. Gayatri C. Spivak. Baltimore: Johns Hopkins Univ. Press, 1976.

———. *Writing and Difference.* Trans. Alan Bass. Chicago: Univ. of Chicago Press, 1978.

———. *La Carte Postale: De Socrate a Freud et au-delà.* Paris: Flammarion, 1980.

———. *Positions.* Chicago: Univ. of Chicago Press, 1981.

———. *Margins of Philosophy.* Trans. Alan Bass. Chicago: Univ. of Chicago Press, 1982.

———. "My Chances/*Mes Chances:* A Rendezvous with Some Epicurean Stereophonies." Trans. Irene Harvey and Avital Ronell. In *Taking Chances: Derrida, Psychoanalysis and Literature.* Ed. Joseph H. Smith and William Kerrigan. Baltimore: Johns Hopkins Univ. Press, 1984.

Fergusson, Rosalind. *The Penguin Rhyming Dictionary.* New York: Viking Penguin, 1985.

Fineman, Joel. "The Sound of O in *Othello:* The Real of the Tragedy of Desire." In *Psychoanalysis and . . . .* Ed. Richard Feldstein and Herbert Sussman. New York: Routledge, 1990.

Fish, Stanley. *Is There a Text in This Class? The Authority of Interpretive Communities.* Cambridge: Harvard Univ. Press, 1980.

Fried, Debra. "Repetition, Refrain, and Epitaph." *ELH* 53 (1986): 615–32.

Freud, Sigmund. *The Standard Edition of the Complete Psychological Works of Sigmund Freud*. Ed. and trans. James Strachey. 24 vols. London: Hogarth Press, 1953–74.

Gallop, Jane. *Reading Lacan*. Ithaca: Cornell Univ. Press, 1985.

———. *Thinking Through the Body*. New York: Columbia Univ. Press, 1988.

Gaskell, Elizabeth. *Wives and Daughters*. 1866. Ed. Frank Glover Smith. Harmondsworth: Penguin, 1969.

Gay, Peter. *Freud: A Life for Our Time*. New York: Norton, 1988.

Goux, Jean-Joseph. *Symbolic Economies: After Marx and Freud*. Trans. Jennifer Curtiss Gage. Ithaca: Cornell Univ. Press, 1990.

———. "The Phallus: Masculine Identity and the 'Exchange of Women.'" Trans. Maria Amuchastegui, Caroline Benforado, Amy Hendrix, and Eleanor Kaufman. *Differences: A Journal of Feminist Cultural Studies* 4 (1992): 40–75.

Grennan, Eamon. "Keats's 'Contemptus Mundi': A Shakespearian Influence on the 'Ode to a Nightingale.'" *Modern Language Quarterly* 36 (1975): 272–92.

Griffiths, Eric. *The Printed Voice of Victorian Poetry*. Oxford: Oxford Univ. Press, 1989.

Gunter, G. O. "Life and Death Symbols in Tennyson's 'Mariana.'" *South Atlantic Bulletin* 36, no. 3 (1971): 64–67.

Hair, Donald S. *Tennyson's Language*. Toronto: Univ. of Toronto Press, 1991.

Hartman, Geoffrey. *Wordsworth's Poetry 1787–1814*. New Haven: Yale Univ. Press, 1964.

———. "Poem and Ideology: A Study of Keats's 'To Autumn.'" *The Fate of Reading*. Chicago: Univ. of Chicago Press, 1975.

———. *Saying the Text: Literature/Derrida/Philosophy*. Baltimore: Johns Hopkins Univ. Press, 1981.

Hollander, John. "Tennyson's Melody." *Georgia Review* 29 (1979): 676–703.

———. *The Figure of Echo: A Mode of Allusion in Milton and After*. Berkeley and Los Angeles: Univ. of California Press, 1982.

———. "Breaking into Song: Some Notes on Refrain." In *Lyric Poetry: Beyond New Criticism*. Ed. Chaviva Hosek and Patricia Parker. Ithaca: Cornell Univ. Press, 1985.

Homer. *The Odyssey*. Trans. Richmond Lattimore. New York: Harper, 1965.

Hughes, Linda K. "Dramatis and Private Personae: 'Ulysses' Revisited." *Victorian Poetry* 17 (1979): 192–203.

Jones, Ernest. *The Life and Work of Sigmund Freud*. 3 vols. New York: Basic Books, 1953–57.

Joseph, Gerhard. "Victorian Weaving: The Alienation of Work into Text in 'The Lady of Shalott.'" *Victorian Newsletter* 71 (1987): 7–10.

Jump, John D., ed. *Tennyson: The Critical Heritage*. London: Routledge and Kegan Paul, 1967.

Keats, John. *The Poems of John Keats*. Ed. Jack Stillinger. Cambridge: Harvard Univ. Press, 1978.

Kristeva, Julia. *Desire in Language: A Semiotic Approach to Literature and Art*. Ed. Leon S. Roudiez. Trans. Thomas Gorz, Alice Jardine, and Leon S. Roudiez. New York: Columbia Univ. Press, 1980.

Lacan, Jacques. *Ecrits*. Paris: Editions du Seuil, 1966.

————. *Ecrits: A Selection*. Trans. Alan Sheridan. New York: Norton, 1977.

————. *The Four Fundamental Concepts of Psycho-Analysis*. Trans. Alan Sheridan. New York: Norton, 1978.

Lacan, Jacques, et al. *Feminine Sexuality*. Ed. Juliet Mitchell and Jaqueline Rose. Trans. Jaqueline Rose. New York: Norton, 1982.

Laplanche, J., and J.-B. Pontalis. *The Language of Psychoanalysis*. Trans. Donald Nicholson-Smith. New York: Norton, 1973.

Lourie, Margaret A. "Below the Thunders of the Upper Deep: Tennyson as Romantic Revisionist." *Studies in Romanticism* 18 (1979): 3–27.

Macey, David. *Lacan in Contexts*. London: Verso, 1988.

McGann, Jerome J. *The Beauty of Inflections: Literary Investigations in Historical Method and Theory*. Oxford: Oxford University Press, 1985.

McSweeny, Kerry. *Tennyson and Swinburne as Romantic Naturalists*. Toronto: Univ. of Toronto Press, 1981.

Marcus, Stephen. *The Other Victorians*. 1964. Reprint. New York: Basic Books, 1974.

Martin, David M. "Romantic Perspectivism in Tennyson's 'The Lady of Shalott.'" *Victorian Poetry* 11 (1973): 255–56.

Mermin, Dorothy. *The Audience in the Poem*. New Brunswick, N.J.: Rutgers Univ. Press, 1983.

Merriman, James D. "The Poet as Heroic Thief: Tennyson's 'The Hesperides' Reexamined." *Victorian Newsletter* 35 (1969): 1–5.

Milton, John. *John Milton: Complete Poems and Major Prose*. Ed. Merritt Y. Hughes. Indianapolis: Odyssey, 1957.

Murray, Hugh. *An Historical Account of Discoveries and Travels in Africa, from the Earliest Times to the Present Day*. 2 vols. Edinburgh, 1812.

————. *Narrative of Discovery and Adventure in Africa from the Earliest Ages to the Present Time*. 3d ed. Edinburgh, 1840.

Ovid. *Metamorphoses*. Trans. Frank Justus Miller. Rev. G. P. Goold. 3d ed. Cambridge: Harvard Univ. Press, 1977.

Paden, W. D. *Tennyson in Egypt: A Study of the Imagery in His Earliest Work*. Lawrence: Univ. of Kansas Publications, 1942.

Park, Mungo. *Travels in the Interior Districts of Africa*. London, 1799.

Pettigrew, John. "Tennyson's 'Ulysses': A Reconciliation of Differences." *Victorian Poetry* 1 (1963): 27–45.

Pitt, Valerie. *Tennyson Laureate*. London: Barrie and Rockliff, 1962.

Plato. *Phaedrus*. Trans. R. Hackforth. *Plato: The Collected Dialogues*. Ed. Edith Hamilton and Huntington Cairns. Princeton: Princeton Univ. Press, 1961.

Pucci, Pietro. *Odysseus Polutropos: Intertextual Readings in the Odyssey and the Iliad*. Ithaca: Cornell Univ. Press, 1987.

Ricks, Christopher. "Tennyson: 'Armageddon' into 'Timbuctoo.' " *Modern Language Review* 61 (1966): 23–24.

———. "The Tennyson Manuscripts." *Times Literary Supplement* 3, no. 521 (1969): 918–22.

———. *Tennyson*. New York: Macmillan, 1972.

Ricks, Christopher, and Aidan Day, eds. *The Tennyson Archive*. 30 vols. New York: Garland, 1986–.

Roscoe, Thomas, ed. and trans. *The Italian Novelists*. 1825. 2d ed. 4 vols. London, 1836.

Ryals, Clyde de L. "Point of View in Tennyson's 'Ulysses.' " *Archiv für das Studium der neueren Sprachen und Literaturen* 199 (1962): 232–34.

———. *Theme and Symbol in Tennyson's Poems to 1850*. Philadelphia: Univ. of Pennsylvania Press, 1964.

Saussure, Ferdinand de. *Course in General Linguistics*. Ed. Charles Bally and Albert Sechehaye. Trans. Wade Baskin. New York: Philosophical Library, 1959.

Saville, Julia. " 'The Lady of Shalott': a Lacanian Romance." *Word and Image* 8 (1992): 71–87.

Scott, Walter. *Sir Walter Scott's Minstrelsy of the Scottish Border*. Ed. T. F. Henderson. 4 vols. Edinburgh and London: William Blackwood, 1902.

Shakespeare, William. *The Riverside Shakespeare*. Ed. G. Blakemore Evans. Boston: Houghton Mifflin, 1974.

Shell, Marc. *The Economy of Literature*. Baltimore: Johns Hopkins Univ. Press, 1978.

Silverman, Kaja. "The Lacanian Phallus." *Differences: A Journal of Feminist Cultural Studies* 4 (1992): 84–115.

Spenser, Edmund. *The Faerie Queene*. Ed. Thomas P. Roche, Jr. Middlesex: Penguin, 1978.

Stange, G. Robert. "Tennyson's Garden of Art: A Study of 'The Hesperides.' " *PMLA* 67 (1952): 732–45. Rpt. in *Critical Essays on the Poetry of Tennyson*. Ed. John Killham. London: Routledge and Kegan Paul, 1960.

Stewart, Garrett. *Reading Voices: Literature and the Phonotext*. Berkeley and Los Angeles: Univ. of California Press, 1990.

Tennyson, Alfred. *The Poems of Tennyson*. Ed. Christopher Ricks. 2d ed. 3 vols. Berkeley and Los Angeles: Univ. of California Press, 1987.

Tennyson, Hallam. *Alfred Lord Tennyson: A Memoir by His Son*. 2 vols. London: Macmillan, 1897.

Thom, Martin. "Verneinung, Verwerfung, Ausstossung: A Problem in the Interpretation of Freud." In *The Talking Cure: Essays in Psychoanalysis and Language*. Ed. Colin MacCabe. New York: St. Martin's, 1986.

Trilling, Lionel. *The Liberal Imagination*. New York: Viking, 1950.

Tucker, Herbert F. "Strange Comfort: A Reading of Tennyson's Unpublished Juvenilia." *Victorian Poetry* 21 (1983): 1–25.

———. "Tennyson and the Measure of Doom." *PMLA* 98 (1983): 8–20.

————. *Tennyson and the Doom of Romanticism*. Cambridge: Harvard Univ. Press, 1988.

Vendler, Helen. "The Experiential Beginnings of Keats's Odes." *Studies in Romanticism* 12 (1973): 591–606.

Walker, John. *A Rhyming Dictionary: Answering, at the same time, the purposes of spelling and pronouncing the English Language*. London, 1806.

Ward, Arthur D. "'Ulysses' and 'Tithonus': Tunnel Vision and Idle Tears." *Victorian Poetry* 12 (1974): 311–19.

Weber, Samuel. *The Legend of Freud*. Minneapolis: Univ. of Minnesota Press, 1982.

Wordsworth, William. *William Wordsworth: Selected Poems and Prefaces*. Ed. Jack Stillinger. Boston: Houghton Mifflin, 1965.

Index